D0519453

SECRET FORCES OF WORLD WAR II

ABOUT THE AUTHOR

Philip Warner (1914-2000) enlisted in the Royal Corps of Signals after graduating from St Catharine's, Cambridge in 1939. He fought in Malaya and spent 1,100 days as 'a guest of the Emperor' in Changi, on the Railway of Death and in the mines of Japan, an experience he never discussed. A legendary figure to generations of cadets during his thirty years as a Senior Lecturer at the Royal Military Academy, Sandhurst, he will also be long remembered for his contribution of more than 2,000 obituaries of prominent army figures to *The Daily Telegraph.*

In addition he wrote fifty-four books on all aspects of military history, ranging from castles and battlefields in Britain, to biographies of prominent military figures (such as *Kitchener: The Man Behind The Legend, Field Marshal Earl Haig, Horrocks: The General Who Led From The Front* and *Auchinleck: The Lonely Soldier*) to major histories of the SAS, the Special Boat Services and the Royal Corps of Signals.

The D-Day Landings was republished by Pen & Sword Books to mark the 60th Anniversary of this historic event and was adopted by *The Daily Telegraph* as its offical commemorative book.

Phantom is to be shortly reprinted by Pen & Sword Books

* * *

By the same author:

Alamein
Army Life in the 1890s
Auchinleck: The Lonely Soldier
Battle of France
Battle of Loos
Best of British Pluck
Best of Chums
British Battlefields 1: The North
British Battlefields 2: The South
British Battlefields 3: The Midlands
British Battlefields 4: Scotland
Daily Telegraph Book of British Battlefields
British Cavalry
Castles in Britain *(illustrated edition)*
Civil Service
Crimean War
D-Day Landings
(republished by Pen & Sword, 2004)
Dervish
Disputed Territories
Distant Battle
Famous Scottish Battles
Famous Welsh Battles
Field Marshal Earl Haig
Fields of War: Letters Home from the Crimea
Firepower
The Great British Soldier
Growing Up in the First World War
A Guide to the Castles in the British Isles
The History of the Harlequins
Horrocks: The General Who Led from the Front
Invasion Road
The Japanese Army of World War II
Kitchener: The Man Behind the Legend
Making Model Forts & Castles
The Medieval Castle in Peace & War
Panzer
Passchendaele
Phantom *(to be republished by Pen & Sword, 2005)*
Political Parties
Roman Roads
Sieges of the Middle Ages
Soldier: His Life in Peace and War
Special Air Service (Official History)
Special Boat Service
Stories of Famous Regiments
Vital Link: Official History of the Royal Corps of Signals
World War I: A Narrative
World War II: The Untold Story
Zeebrugge Raid

SECRET FORCES OF WORLD WAR II

PHILIP WARNER

Pen & Sword
MILITARY

First published in 1985 by Granada
Published in paperback in 1987 by Harper Collins and
republished in 2004 by
PEN & SWORD MILITARY
an imprint of
Pen & Sword Books Limited
47 Church Street
Barnsley
S. Yorkshire
S70 2AS

Copyright © Philip Warner, 1985, 1987
Copyright © Philip Warner Estate, 2004

ISBN 1 84415 114 X

The right of Philip Warner to be
identified as Author of this Work has
been asserted by him in accordance with
the Copyright, Designs and Patents Act 1988.

A CIP catalogue record for this book
is available from the British Library.

*All rights reserved. No part of this book may be reproduced or
transmitted in any form or by any means, electronic or mechanical
including photocopying, recording or by any information storage
and retrieval system, without permission from the Publisher in writing.*

Printed and bound in Great Britain by
CPI UK

Pen & Sword Books Ltd incorporates the imprints of
Pen & Sword Aviation, Pen & Sword Maritime, Pen & Sword Military,
Wharncliffe Local History, Pen & Sword Select,
Pen & Sword Military Classics and Leo Cooper.

For a complete list of Pen & Sword titles please contact:
PEN & SWORD BOOKS LIMITED
47 Church Street, Barnsley, South Yorkshire, S70 2AS, England.
E-mail: enquiries@pen-and-sword.co.uk
Website: www.pen-and-sword.co.uk

Contents

Preface

During the decades since the end of World War II, many surprising revelations have been made, but many secrets have remained firmly kept and the secret information that has emerged has been released piecemeal. The result has been that World War II in hindsight seems a jumble of unlinked operations.

This book is the first to make a general survey of secret forces, to show how they were interrelated, and what effect they had on the war as a whole. It is an astonishing story.

The vast range of the subject has meant that nothing could be treated as fully as I would have wished. However, sample incidents have been described in detail.

Some readers may be astonished to find how much rivalry there was between different departments and even between different arms. Most of the 'inner' departments, SOE, SIS, MI5, etc., were keenly competitive (to put it in its best light); the regular forces were always slightly suspicious of 'wartime only' enlistments; and orthodox thinkers nurtured a deep resentment of the 'funnies' – specialist groups like the SAS, LRDG, Paras and Commandos. Politicians, apart from Churchill, were collectively and individually thought to be a 'blight', although in those days the politickings of Beaverbrook, Crossman and Dalton were unknown except to their close colleagues. Civilians, with the exception of one's own family and friends, were a race apart; most of them had well-paid jobs in factories and, even if their lives were by no means comfortable or safe, they were much more so than the life of a sailor on a destroyer, a soldier in jungle or desert, or a member of an aircrew. The unifying bond was that everyone hated the enemy more than they resented the actions or privileges of their fellows or Allies.

After the war had dragged to an end in 1945, most people wished to forget the loneliness, the frustrations, the fears, the triumphs and disasters, the good news and the bad. But as the scars healed the war began to be seen in perspective. It soon became clear that much more had gone on during those six years than most of the participants realized. Vastly interesting it was, too, even though difficult to understand. This book aims to make one part of it a little easier to grasp.

Acknowledgements

In researching for this book I have received help and encouragement from many sources. I am particularly indebted to the librarians and their staffs who have taken enormous trouble to track down obscure books and documents. In particular I must mention Mr John Hunt and Mr M. H. Wright of the Royal Military Academy, Sandhurst, and Mr John Andrews of the Ministry of Defence. Anyone who writes a book of this type will owe a great debt to the ever-helpful staff at the Public Record Office, at the Staff College, at the National Army Museum, at the Imperial War Museum, and to a surprisingly large number of military historical museums at home and abroad.

Among those who have been exceptionally helpful are: Mr F. W. E. Appleyard, Lieutenant-Colonel M. H. Broadway, Major-General R. L. T. Burges, CBE, DSO, Captain R. Folkes, Mr C. D'O. Gowan, Mr G. H. Haddow, Mr R. J. Holmes, MBE, Mr R. E. M. Hughes, MC, Mr W. G. Jenkins, DSO, Major-General D. L. Lloyd-Owen, CB, DSO, OBE, MC, Miss H. March-Phillips, Mr M. Muggeridge, Mr J. A. Nasmyth, Major C. L. D. Newell, OBE, Mr C. Nicholson, Lieutenant-Colonel R. P. D. F. Painter, Major R. C. Pringle, Mr G. F. N. Reddaway, CBE, Professor J. Scott, Lieutenant-Colonel G. A. Shepperd, OBE, Dr G. Screech, Dr J. S. Sweetman, Lieutenant-Colonel P. Worrall, OBE, and Brigadier P. Young, DSO, MC.

For assistance with obtaining the illustrations and permission to use them I wish to express my gratitude to Mr Brian Johnson, Mrs F. Spencer-Chapman, Mrs Jasper Maskelyne, Mr Leo Cooper, Mr Peter Calvocoressi, the United States Army, the United States Navy, the Imperial War Museum, Jonathan Cape Ltd, and William Kimber Ltd. Every attempt has been made to trace the holders of existing copyrights; if any has inadvertently been overlooked perhaps the owner would be kind enough to get in touch with the author.

Principal Events 1939–1945 and their relation to secret forces

1939 Soviet–German Pact (August)
Poland invaded and defeated by Germany (September). Britain and France declare war on Germany but can take no action to help Poland. No action in the west except at sea.
Russia and Germany partition Poland.
Russia invades and defeats Finland.

1940 April–June. Germany overruns Norway, Denmark, Belgium, Luxembourg, Holland. Defeat of Allies in France leads to Dunkirk. France surrenders. Britain fights on alone. Churchill orders: 'Set Europe Ablaze.'
Beginning of Parachute regiments, Commandos, and SOE.
USA takes first steps to formation of OSS, for secret operations abroad, though still remaining neutral.
First Commando raids over the English Channel.
Italians invade Egypt.

1941 Germany invades Russia (June).
Japan attacks Pearl Harbor (December), Malaya, East Indies, Burma.
USA declares war on Rome/Berlin/Tokyo Axis.
Italy heavily defeated in Middle East but then reinforced by Rommel.
Germany occupies Greece, Yugoslavia, Crete.
Lofoten Islands and Vaagso raids by Commandos.

1942 Rommel checked in Middle East at Alamein and retreats.
1st Army lands in North Africa (Torch). US Rangers in action. SAS now founded and works in conjunction with LRDG. PPA operates. OSS in North Africa. SOE continue operations. Dieppe raid.

1943 Russians defeat Germans at Stalingrad.
Final defeat of Italians and Germans in North Africa.
SAS in Italy, LRDG and SBS in Greek islands and Yugoslavia.

1944 Americans begin conquest of Japan by advancing through Pacific islands.
Allies land in France, cross Europe. Battle of Arnhem. Japanese begin retreat in Burma, harassed by SOE and OSS.
Activity by OSS, SOE, and BAAG in China.
Battle of the Ardennes.

1945 Americans closing in on Japan. President Roosevelt dies in April. British defeat Japanese in Burma.
Final Russian offensive begins. Russians reach Berlin.
Germany and Italy surrender.
War with Japan continues until 15 August.

1: *Introduction*

A unique feature of World War II was the astonishing number of unorthodox military formations which it brought into existence. In previous wars the majority of the fighting had been between armies and navies which were large in numbers and predictable in their movements. There was, of course, plenty of action between such units in World War II – vast armies locked together in the snows of Russia, a huge expeditionary force landing on D-Day, enormous naval battles in the Pacific and air armadas cruising to their targets in thousand-bomber raids. Huge numbers were involved also in the desert, in the jungle, in Italy and in France. Without those massive forces the war could not have been won.

However, it may fairly be claimed that if unorthodox units had not existed, those large forces might have fared differently and less successfully. Only now, forty-plus years after the end of World War II, can the whole process of the war be properly assessed. Nearly all the histories, official and otherwise, were written before the existence of 'Ultra' - the system by which the Allies read all the German military codes – was revealed to the public. Now we also know something of 'Magic', the means by which Japanese codes in the Pacific were broken. Even so, it seems likely that there will always be some dark corners which will not be illuminated. Much documentary evidence has been destroyed on the basis that it was 'not in the public interest' to disclose it – whatever that may mean. Officially, a report was required on every military activity, but some were never written because the participants were either killed or immediately sent to another assignment without having time to give more than a verbal summary. Nevertheless, much interesting information is now available through people's memories and personal diaries. Official papers are still released from time to time while others, it is officially stated, will not be open to the public for some years. However, while gaps still exist, and may always do so, it is now possible to obtain a fair picture of the interlocking activities of orthodox and unorthodox forces during World War II.

The reason for the creation of large numbers of special and secret forces is to be found in the dark days of 1940. World War II began when Hitler's German armies invaded Poland on 1 September 1939 and Britain and France promptly declared war, but there was a feeling in the West that Hitler was bluffing and that his outwardly impressive show of force masked great internal weaknesses. Once Britain and France had shown, by mobilizing, what they thought of Hitler, he would soon realize his mistake and make an inglorious retreat. Some of those in the West who had seen Hitler's troops did not necessarily share that view, but the newly created Ministry of Economic Warfare was so convinced of Germany's shortage of essential raw materials that a duration of ten months was suggested as being the outside limit of time for which Hitler could continue his bluff.

The fact that the Ministry's estimate was vastly wide of the truth made little difference, for Hitler speeded up the tempo of the war a mere eight months later, first by invading Norway and Denmark, then by overwhelming Belgium, Holland and France. In all these countries Allied armies were decisively defeated, and either made prisoner or ignominiously chased out. By July 1940 Hitler and his armies were masters of the whole of Europe from northern Norway to southern France. His ally Mussolini controlled Italy. Within the next year (by June 1941) the German armies had overrun Romania, Bulgaria, Yugoslavia, Greece and Crete. Furthermore, there were German troops in North Africa to assist the Italians against the British. Europe, in fact, was lost. Soon the Far East would be lost too, but the principal shock which led to the creation of special and secret forces was the string of defeats in the spring of 1940.

It was sadly obvious in mid 1940 that now the British army had been destroyed, it would take a very long time to build up another one and to assemble sufficient assault craft to put it back on the continent of Europe. The essence of the problem was to create a force large enough to defeat the apparently invincible German armies which, by that time, would have constructed fortifications, if they did not actually disdain to do so.

But there were other plans which could be put into operation at fairly short notice. One was to form small groups which could infiltrate, collect information and engage in sabotage; the other was to train larger units which could assault and harass the enemy from the sea or air. The former became Special Operations Executive (SOE) and its allied groups, the second became the Parachutists and the Commandos.

Initially, considerable secrecy surrounded all 'special' units. In wartime, of course, there is secrecy about everything, although some secrets appear to have been widely shared. But now there were secrets within secrets. Even units like Phantom, which had had no special need to be secret, soon became quite mysterious, whether it wished to be so or not. To the rest of the world Britain's plight must have seemed pathetic. The Germans merely needed a little more time before their aircraft and armies crossed the Channel and hammered the obstinate British into submission. That was how the scene looked to America, at this time keeping well clear of European entanglements in accordance with the Neutrality Acts which Congress had recently renewed. It looked much the same to the Germans. It looked positively dazzling to Mussolini, who was hoping that from all these victories there would be rich pickings for him, possibly in North Africa.

There were already small examples of special forces in existence, some of which introduced entirely new equipment, and some of which merely made novel use of existing material. Thus, parachutes were a comparatively new means of reaching a target, but sabotage units merely represented a new application of the well-known fact that small groups of determined men can often infiltrate enemy lines and by the use of camouflage and cunning reach a vital target. Such practices had been recorded as far back as biblical times. Attacking and defending castles in the middle ages had also produced astonishing examples of enterprising tactics. One Scottish castle was captured because the leading assault troops clung to the bellies of sheep being driven into the castle in a flock. There was clearly much to be learned from combining the daring and ingenuity of the past with the inventions of the present.

The principal hope of all the countries which adopted new methods was that they would be able to exploit them to produce surprise. Surprise is valued very highly in warfare, and the desire for surprise accounted for the secrecy surrounding many early ventures. Military parachuting could not be kept a secret, for if men or women descend from aeroplanes high in the sky a large number of people will be witnesses. But the type of weapons and tactics to be used when the parachutists arrive can and will be a very closely guarded secret.

The originator of parachute warfare was not a German or a Russian as is usually surmised: it was an American, Col. Billy Mitchell. In 1918, when the Germans and the Allies were confronting each other over seemingly unbreakable trench lines, Mitchell had the bright idea of dropping a small force of American parachutists into the German rear area. Plans were formulated, but the project was postponed by General Pershing, the American commander-in-chief, as being impracticable at that particular time. One cannot fault the decision, for parachute warfare would have meant allocating scant resources for a project which nobody had had time to ponder properly, and which could well have been an expensive disaster. The war ended before the project could be tried at a later and more convenient date.

However, an interesting new military idea had been produced and would inevitably be tried out by someone, sooner or later. The country which led the way was Italy. It was clear from the outset that this new form of warfare could be fought by light aircraft or gliders as well as by parachutists, but several factors made parachuting the most favoured method. It did not need special aircraft, it could be done at night when aircraft would not have been able to land, it required no special landing ground and it was highly secret. A parachutist can land, bury his parachute and disappear without trace: a glider or a light aircraft pose more problems.

The Italians made their first military parachute drop in 1927, close to Milan. The proceedings were marred by the death of General Guidoni whose parachute failed to open. Nevertheless, the Italians continued their experiments and within the next ten years had complete battalions of parachutists trained and available. None was ever employed in this primary function during World War II, although all saw action as ground troops.

In the earlier stages of military parachuting, participating countries were proud of their initiative and invited witnesses. General Wavell was an observer at an exercise in Russia in 1936. Germany was in no position to train parachutists, for until 1935 it was prohibited by the Versailles Treaty from possessing military aircraft. But even before Hitler repudiated the treaty the Germans were well aware of the possibilities of the new means of warfare. Furthermore, they had some 500 civilian aircraft which could easily be adapted for military purposes. These were the famous Junkers 52.

In April 1937 the Germans were known to possess a parachute regiment, and it was soon known too that the organizer and trainer was one General Student. Student had been a fighter pilot in World War I and when he rejoined the Luftwaffe he was given every opportunity to develop his ideas about airborne warfare. Within months of taking over the task of training an airborne army, Student had at his disposal a division of paratroops, a glider regiment and an airborne army unit. Other countries were now well aware of the expertise which the Germans were developing, but the Germans were not naïve enough to tell others how this new force was destined to be used. That particular lesson came later when parachutists and gliders seized strategic points in their attack on the Low Countries in 1940. To protect the vital bridges of the Meuse and the Albert canal, the Belgians had built an apparently impregnable fortress at Eben Emael. Unknown to the Allies, German parachutists had been practising the capture of an identical full-scale model, and in consequence the 'impregnable' fortress lasted a mere thirty-six hours. Nor was the element of airborne surprise limited to this one valuable target. The potential of parachutists to win battles on their own was demonstrated convincingly on Crete in May 1942 when the island was captured by airborne troops. This was not in accordance with the original German plan, but the seaborne assault force with which they had planned to support the airborne attack was sunk by British naval forces. The German airborne units therefore had to fight the battle of Crete unaided. They won, but the cost in casualties was so high that the Germans, though gratified by the results, were unwilling to repeat such tactics. Nor, after the battle of Arnhem in 1944, were the Allies.

Britain and its allies had no excuse for being taken by surprise by the German use of parachutists, for they had had ample warning. The concept that parachutes were merely a means of escaping from aircraft which had run into trouble seemed so firmly rooted in the British military mind that nothing the Russians or the Germans did in the way of military experiments seemed to be able to dislodge it. Even the progressive thinker Wavell was unable to raise interest in this new arm, although he had been profoundly impressed by that Russian drop of 1,500 men with light supporting arms in 1936. Parachutists in warfare, it was widely believed by the British High Command, would be far too vulnerable to be an effective arm. What could be an easier target than a parachutist slowly floating down from the sky in full view?

Soon after the start of the blitzkrieg in 1940 this view was replaced by one which seemed to hold that a descending parachutist was almost invincible. He would see you from his advantageous position and pick you off with his automatic. For good measure he might destroy your remains with a hand-grenade. The parachute myths of 1940 left nothing to the imagination. Parachutists were said to have been dressed as nuns, to have landed in huge numbers (somewhere else), and even to have scattered poisoned chocolates for children to pick up and eat. The most likely time for the arrival of these airborne invaders was at dusk or dawn. In consequence, in late 1940 all the armed forces, regular or irregular, were required to 'stand-to' at dawn and dusk. Most of them stood in slit strenches peering at the sky and waiting for orders to open fire, but members of the Home Guard, many of whom were armed with weapons roughly similar to, and sometimes even identical with, those carried by Harold's fyrd when confronting the Normans at Hastings in 1066, were convinced that nothing would be more disconcerting to a German parachutist than a pitchfork up his backside. Unfortunately – or perhaps fortunately – these military theories were never tested, for the Junkers 52s never dropped their cargoes on British soil.

However, once the Germans had demonstrated the effectiveness of this new arm, there was no holding back in Britain. Instead of being dismissed as an impracticable means of warfare the parachutist suddenly became the hero of the hour. Numerous ways of deploying parachutists were immediately devised, many of them wildly impracticable. But two in particular prevailed. One was to deposit an airborne regiment or division on the battlefield, the second was to deliver small secret parties of saboteurs.

The snag with the first idea was obvious. A modern army cannot fight with infantry alone and even if it could those infantrymen need an alarmingly large supply of ammunition. But the aircraft of 1940 were not capable of taking large loads, and there were problems even for smaller loads. Adequate aircraft of greater carrying capacity and more portable field artillery were not available until several years after the beginning of the war. Some idea of the initial problem may be gained from the fact that the Blenheim bomber, the maid-of-all-work in 1939–40, had a load-carrying capacity of under half a ton. The 25-pdrs, the standard field artillery gun, weighed 1.75 tons.

The British, urged by Churchill, set about military parachuting with alacrity. The first training school was opened at the Central Landing School at Ringway, near Manchester, on 21 June 1940. Ringway was a civil airport, owned by Manchester Corporation. The initial structure of the school was hybrid. The Royal Air Force was in charge of the actual training, but the military applications were worked out by the army. To complete this joint service ensemble, the first unit to undergo parachute training came from the Commandos.

The men who appeared with No. 2 Commando for parachute training had originally volunteered for the new commando units under the impression that they would raid the enemy-held coast in small fast boats and to do maximum damage before making a hasty departure. These were described as 'butcher and bolt' raids, but the concept was too crude and soon developed a more sophisticated intention. The creation of commando units was one of the many war-winning ideas of Lt-Col. Dudley Clarke, who was Military Assistant to Sir John Dill, Chief of the Imperial General Staff. The initial plan was to raise ten units of 500 volunteers from the Royal Marines and army. Many units were far from enthusiastic about losing some of their most enterprising members to these new and untried formations, but they eventually gave their support.

There were, of course, many teething troubles at Ringway. The RAF had its hands full with the task of defending Britain against aircraft which now arrived in increasing numbers from the nearby French coast. Furthermore, even when the Air Commandos were trained there would be insufficient aircraft to transport them, given the attendant risks of losing valuable machines and crews. The best that could be provided for the initial training was six obsolete Whitley bombers. These needed to be converted for the purpose and there was some uncertainty at first as to the best way for the parachutist to leave the plane – by a door, or through a hole in the floor. Both methods had disadvantages: if the parachutist exited through the door, his parachute might be snagged on the tail fins of the aircraft; if he disappeared through a hole in the floor he was liable to suffer a violent blow on the nose as it caught the edge of the hole in passing. This latter experience became known jocularly as 'ringing the bell' or 'getting a Whitley kiss'. The school was lucky in that it had as its first commander a former army lieutenant-colonel with experience as a successful airman in World War I. He had re-enlisted as Pilot Officer L. Strange, DSO, MC. His advance to wing-commander's rank was, not surprisingly, rapid. The overall commander at Ringway was Group Captain L. G. Harvey. There was a feeling of urgency about the training of British parachutists because much of the Germans' success in the previous months was attributed to their parachutists.

Undoubtedly they had played a useful part, but the contribution of the panzers had been even more decisive.

Alarmed by the success of German parachutists and gliders, the British government adopted a policy to deny them any suitable ground on which they might land and form up into fighting units. In 1940, open spaces all over Britain were to be protected against *Fallschirmjäger* (parachutists). 'Open spaces' meant virtually every park and playing field. Thus in Aldershot, which hardly seems to have been a place in which German parachutists would choose to land, all playing fields were put out of action by placing long spiked poles or concrete blocks at regular intervals. Whether this had a significant effect on German military planning seems debatable, but it certainly prevented any of the thousands of servicemen undergoing training in Aldershot from obtaining any recreation through football, cricket or hockey. Later in the war fixed obstacles were either replaced by movable ones or abandoned altogether.

Training at Ringway went as well as could be expected with converted obsolete aircraft, instructors still lacking experience in training large numbers, and the enthusiastic attention of members of the Army School of Physical Training. But then one man's parachute failed to open and he was killed outright. The fault was traced to the static lines which were used to open the parachute automatically; these removed the need for each parachutist to release his own parachute by what was known as a 'rip-cord'. Within weeks there were two more accidents, one fatal. Parachuting required strong nerves, without the additional strain of wondering whether the parachute would open or not. The volunteers were men of courage and resolution but until the teething problems were overcome they needed all they possessed. Unfortunately, when Ringway had overcome the problems, their findings were not as widely disseminated as they should have been.

While the parachute training was taking place, extensive research was going into finding the most suitable equipment for parachute warfare. This aspect was in the care of Lt-Col. John Rock, a shrewd assessor if ever there was one – sadly, he was killed in a glider crash in 1942. The range of potential equipment was enormous and to some extent influenced by what could be learnt of previous Russian, German and Italian parachuting. It extended well beyond the obvious essentials such as helmets, tunics, boots, gloves, weapons and kit bags. Some of the items adopted at this stage were found later to be unsuitable or inessential and were therefore dispensed with. Respirators were among the items later discarded, as were certain types of body armour, but a surprising amount of the material tried out in the early stages went into permanent use. The Denison smock, a camouflaged lightweight tunic, stood the test of time. Guns were at first on the bulky and heavy side (notably the 'Tommy' gun – Thompson sub-machine gun) and were replaced later with lighter, more lethal, weapons.

In November 1940 the new parachute and glider squadrons ceased to be called Commandos and were renamed 11 Special Air Service Battalion. The use of this name led to much confusion later, for when Lt David Stirling initiated the Special Air Service in July 1941, he named it 'L' Detachment, Special Air Service Brigade. At the time there was no Special Air Service Brigade; in fact, one was not created until January 1944, and for the next three years the SAS, although using the term 'regiment', was hardly above squadron strength.

Ironically, the first of the raids in which Stirling's SAS was later to specialize, was by the 11 Special Air Service Battalion, a fact which causes much confusion among those not fully aware of the origins of the present-day SAS. The objective was the Tragino aqueduct in the southern Apennines. The aqueduct supplied water to 2 million people in the surrounding district which encompassed the important military and naval bases of Taranto, Brindisi and Bari. If this difficult target could be reached and destroyed, it would take some time to repair and this would have a damaging effect on the Italian war effort. It was not, because of the mountainous area in which it lay, a suitable target for an ordinary bombing raid.

In the event the raid was less successful than had been hoped, but it undoubtedly provided useful experience. On 10 February 1941, thirty-five British parachutists, all Commando-trained in addition to their parachuting skills, set off from RAF Mildenhall, in Suffolk, in six Whitley bombers. Dropping a squadron of raiders on or near a target is by no means easy, and in Apulia many were dropped well clear of the target, some in the next valley. However, enough got through to blow a sizeable hole in the aqueduct with 800lb of explosive. The plan was that, when the mission had been accomplished, the parachutists should make their way to the coast, evading detection and capture. If they arrived there within five days they would be picked up by a submarine which would be at the mouth of the river Sele. In the event they never reached the coast; all were captured. Some escaped subsequently.

Among the raiding party was Major T. A. G. Pritchard, inevitably referred to by his nickname of 'Tag', a heavyweight boxer who always wore a monocle with a long black ribbon. As he was a member of the Royal Welch Fusiliers he also wore another distinguishing mark, a black flash at the back of his collar (commemorating an episode in the regiment's history). Another member of the party was Lt Anthony Deane-Drummond, a regular officer from the Royal Signals. Deane-Drummond featured in many daring adventures and escapes later in the war. Not least of his feats was to stand in a cupboard for thirteen days when the Germans occupied the house he had taken refuge in at Arnhem. The most unlucky and perhaps the bravest member of the party was Fortunato Picchi, forty-two-year-old banqueting manager of the Savoy Hotel. Picchi had been added to the party at the last minute as an interpreter and had not had time to make more than one previous parachute jump. After his capture the Italians penetrated his disguised identity and shot him as a traitor. The fact that he had lived in Britain for twenty years and was a naturalized British subject counted for nothing with his captors who insisted he was a traitorous Italian. In the light of later revelations of the activities of British traitors in high places in 1941, one cannot but wonder whether the composition and destination of the party had been leaked to the Italians beforehand. The Soviets at that time were cooperating with Germany and Italy, and Philby, Blunt and Maclean were passing on any information to the Russians which they thought might help them.

The Whitleys which had originally come into service as the only available aircraft were now enjoying something of an apotheosis, being deemed the most suitable machines for the purpose. But the British Airborne arm was far from being universally approved. Regimental commanders strongly disapproved of the way in which their most adventurous officers, NCOs and soldiers were tempted to volunteer for this training which they thought was of dubious value. Their doubts found ready ears among certain members of the higher command who tended to be sceptical of new methods with which they were not familiar. Fortunately for the Airborne forces, Churchill overruled opposition, which usually took the form of delaying action rather than confrontation. Ironically, it was that German pyrrhic victory at Crete which created the necessary climate of enthusiasm for the expansion of British Airborne forces. The price of ultimate victory was some 6,000 Germans dead, and many more wounded, and the loss of 170 troop-carrying aircraft. The strategic value of Crete could hardly justify such a wastage. Hitler himself decreed that the German Airborne forces must not be used in this manner again, and they were not. Doubtless Student's horror at the casualties among his élite troops had been communicated to the Führer. Student attributed many of the losses which the Germans had suffered on Crete to the capture of a German Airborne operational document by the Allies in Holland in 1940. This had set out the pattern of German tactics and had been an invaluable guide for the British defenders of Crete a year later. However, Student had his revenge when commanding the German parachute army which formed a substantial part of the German opposition to the Allies at Arnhem. He had the good fortune to capture the Allied Airborne plan for Arnhem. It had been in a glider which had been forced down in German-controlled territory. On neither occasion should a vital document have been carried anywhere near where it might fall into enemy hands.

But to return to Crete. While the Germans thought that this type of operation was a disaster which should not be repeated, the British High Command interpreted it as a vital feature of future warfare – as, in fact, it turned out to be on D-Day. Churchill sent a letter to the chiefs of staff as soon as the loss of Crete had sunk in, and, in consequence, approval was given to the formation of two parachute brigades and a glider force. For the latter, two glider 'work horses' were given approval. They were the Horsa, which would carry twenty-five men or three tons, and the Hamilcar, which would carry forty men or seven tons. The latter usually carried heavy equipment.

2: *An Established Concept*

1st Parachute Brigade was formed at Hardwick, Derbyshire, by Brigadier R. N. Gale, a veteran of World War I. Gale believed fervently that a good soldier is also a smart soldier; his own turnout was always immaculate. Somewhat individually he wore riding breeches of impeccable cut and high polished boots below his Denison smock. Gale, not surprisingly, was known by the nickname of 'Windy', but was so indifferent to danger that he made his toughest companions apprehensive. One of his officers commented subsequently: 'Windy Gale always used to hold his "O" [orders] groups on crossroads or in other highly dangerous spots. When the shells exploded uncomfortably close, the members of the group used to look wistfully at the nearest ditch but Windy appeared not to notice that the entire group was in imminent danger of being blown to bits at any moment. He never hurried over his instructions either.'

In October of the same year Brigadier F. A. M. Browning, a Grenadier Guardsman, was appointed Commander Paratroops and Airborne Troops, and promoted to major-general. As a Guardsman, 'Boy' Browning (as he was known) would never tolerate anything but the highest standards of turnout and performance. Browning was a superb leader with great presence; it was said that if he had wished he could have become a film star on looks alone, but whether he was the most suitable commander for the Arnhem Airborne force was later questioned. Browning was married to Daphne du Maurier, the novelist.

The Glider Brigade was formed from four infantry battalions and additional units, and put under the command of Brigadier G. F. Hopkinson. Hopkinson, or 'Hoppy', was the co-founder of 'Phantom' (GHQ Liaison Regiment). He was yet another of the spectacular characters whom the war threw into prominence. Unfortunately his military career was short for he was killed by a sniper soon after the

Taranto landing in 1943. In 1940 Hopkinson had quickly realized that if a unit was labelled 'secret' it would be able to acquire much valuable equipment without too many awkward questions being asked. At a time when secrecy was becoming a national preoccupation, Hoppy made full use of its possibilities.

By the end of 1941 Ringway was handling large and assorted numbers of parachutists. Refugees from Poland, Norway, France, Holland, among others had volunteered for training. The Poles appeared in the largest numbers and eventually formed the independent Polish Parachute Brigade. In addition to those who were going to jump in orthodox military formations, there was a large number of people with a very different future. These were the recruits to SOE (Special Operations Executive). They were the loners, the men and women who would parachute down at night into occupied territory, perhaps to link up with local resistance forces, or perhaps to work entirely on their own. They attracted curious glances and even some questions, to which they made no attempt to give a satisfactory answer.

Secrecy had become very important during this war. World War I had stressed secrecy over the timings of shipping but of little else, although the Germans operated a sophisticated spy system. But suddenly in 1940 everyone in Britain was made to be security conscious. The Ministry of Information issued a stream of warnings that 'Careless talk costs lives' and provided amusing posters of Hitler and Goering listening behind doors (to illustrate the fact that 'Walls have ears'). Sailors no longer carried the names of their ships on their hats; soldiers were simply members of a regiment or corps. People were less inclined to discuss the fact that they worked in a factory making tanks now that there seemed to be a chance that careless talk might lead the Luftwaffe to drop a bomb through its roof one night. It is one thing to be careless and boastful about other people's secrets, but a very different matter if you feel you are putting your own life in jeopardy. During the second half of 1940 strangers tended to be met with hostility and suspicion. There was an uneasy feeling that the Germans might have dropped some parachutists during the night who could well be these strangers who, with no trace of the expected German accent, were asking you what the name of the town was, the station, and the best way to get to London. As an anti-parachutist measure, signposts had been removed, the names of railway stations concealed, and all references to the names of towns on shop signs, etc., had to be obliterated. There was a very strong compulsion to mind one's own business and not ask questions. Those who got lost because of the absence of name boards and direction indicators had some alarming experiences. When American troops came to Britain in 1942 they found the absence of signposts totally bewildering. They were not the only people to find their removal maddeningly inconvenient. However, in fairness, it must be said that the biggest problem of a parachutist who descends in a foreign country is to know where he is. Once that fact is established he may join his contacts. Possession of a compass and a map is of little use unless he can first of all find out where he is on that map.

The Germans were able to play on natural fears by using the broadcasting skills of William Joyce, whose strident, sardonic but well-modulated voice earned him the title of 'Lord Haw-Haw'. Although many people claimed that listening to Lord Haw-Haw announcing that the clock on Sheffield town hall was five minutes slow, or that Plymouth or Norwich would be bombed later that night merely amused them, there were undoubtedly others who believed that he was linked to a super-efficient German spy service. In general the German propaganda service was ineffective because it was based on lies, particularly those concerning Allied shipping losses; in contrast the BBC broadcasts were effective because they told the truth – or most of it – even when that truth was unpalatable. 'Scare' stories can be militarily valuable, for they may cause the enemy to disperse his troops in unnecessary and wasteful enterprises. The only lasting effect of the Tragino aqueduct raid was not on the aqueduct itself – which was soon repaired – but on Italian military morale: thenceforward army units guarded all sorts of improbable targets against attacks which never came, and would never have been contemplated.

As the war progressed, parachute training became more and more sophisticated. From a very early date it was realized that 'dropping zones', as landing areas were described, would often be far from ideal, and might involve obstacles. Therefore, techniques had to be devised to steer the parachute in mid-air to avoid such hazards.

While the parachute brigades were being created and assembled in Britain a considerably less orthodox unit was being created in the Middle East. The basis for this was a Commando unit which had been sent out to the Middle East in early 1941 with the object of capturing Rhodes and denying it to the Germans. However, German successes in Yugoslavia, Greece and Crete put an end to these hopes and the unit, 'Layforce', the command of Brig. Robert Laycock, was to be disbanded. 'Layforce', which had originally been about 2,000 strong, contained a number of highly enterprising soldiers: Jock Lewes, Lord Jellicoe, David Sutherland, Tom Langton and, in particular, David Stirling.

David Stirling was a very tall (6ft 5 inches) subaltern from the Scots Guards. His family had been involved in adventurous fighting throughout Scottish history and he himself had already shown a certain impatience with orthodox and standardized approaches to problems. Above all he was a thinker, and at this time he had noted that the German line of communication in North Africa extended back hundreds of miles across the desert. In that extensive rear area were ammunition dumps, vehicle stores and, above all, aircraft and aircraft spares. On those airfields were machines which could fly faster than any of the aircraft which the RAF could put up to confront them. It seemed sensible to Stirling that as these aircraft could not be shot down once they had taken off, they should be destroyed while they were still on the ground. The idea was not as fanciful as it might appear. Airfields were, in fact, flat patches of desert surrounded by a few huts, tents and workshops. They were considered to be too isolated to need more protection than was afforded by their own aircraft and a few anti-aircraft guns.

Furthermore, in the desert, neither soldiers nor airmen wore a standard uniform while working. A pair of shorts and a hat sufficed. Until you got very close – or heard them talking – there was no apparent distinction between a German, an Italian, a Briton, an Australian, a New Zealander, a Pole or a Frenchman. Stirling considered that this anonymous appearance which was common to both sides would serve his purposes well. If he could get close enough it would not be difficult to merge into the general anonymity, particularly at night. Thus he hoped to reach the airfields, and the aircraft, put bombs on the latter, and disappear quickly. The original arrival, he believed, should be by parachute; the return journey would be on foot until a rendezvous could be made with a vehicle capable of crossing the desert. The Special Air Service thus began as a form of military terrorism; ironically, at the present day, one of its principal missions is to thwart urban terrorism.

Having made up his mind that he had a practical and very useful military idea, Stirling had to obtain permission to implement it. The

High Command at the time was not quite sure what to do with the now unemployed Layforce. A suggestion was made that it should be used to make commando raids along the North African coast. However, such landings would require shipping and the cooperation of the Royal Navy, and the navy was far too heavily engaged at the time to contemplate such a possibility. Having discussed the feasibility of an air commando-type of operation with some of his companions, Stirling set about acquiring an aircraft and some parachutes. The aircraft was a Vickers Valentia, a troop-carrying aircraft of a type which had been in service since 1934 and was now obsolete. Valentias were unsuitable for parachuting for there was no provision for static lines and the construction of the aircraft meant that there was a considerable chance of the parachute being snagged on the tail fin. In fact, that very accident happened to Stirling on an early jump. The injuries he sustained caused him to spend two months in hospital, but the enforced rest only sharpened his brain and determination. When he emerged he succeeded in obtaining official permission from the commander-in-chief, then General Sir Claude Auchinleck, to recruit a force of sixty-six (of which seven would be officers) from the remnants of Layforce, and to begin training it for the purpose he had in mind. The first assignment, it was hoped, would knock out several important German airfields the night before Auchinleck's offensive, which was scheduled for 18 November 1941.

Training began in secrecy at Kabrit, in the Canal Zone, but was harder than anything the Commandos had previously experienced. Parachutes had been acquired by the simple process of commandeering a consignment of fifty which had been unloaded by mistake from a cargo destined for India. The fact that no one knew anything about the problems of parachuting did not deter them. It seemed simple enough. All you needed to do was to jump out of a plane, count five and pull the rip-cord which released the parachute. Alternatively, you could attach a static line to something inside the plane – the legs of the aircraft seats seemed adequate – and it would open the parachute when it was a suitable distance from the aircraft. After all, the RAF had been using parachutes to bale out for years without any special preparations . . .

It was not, of course, as easy as that. The static line principle was employed, and a more suitable aircraft, a Bombay, was acquired and brought into service. Even so, its first use produced a disaster in which two men were killed because the clips twisted themselves off the securing rail before the parachutes had opened. A similar accident had occurred at Ringway, but Stirling did not learn about this until much later. Stirling and his fellow officers experimented for a whole day with other clips – on the ground – and then, attached to a new clip, Stirling led with the first jump at dawn the next day. It was a daunting experience, but successful.

But parachuting was only one part of SAS training. Others included self-reliance and the handling of explosives. Self-reliance meant the development of the ability to work alone or in very small – probably four-man – groups. Exceptional powers of endurance were expected, and produced. Men had to be prepared to walk over a hundred miles or more of desert which would be baking hot by day and freezing cold by night. They had to learn to move around in this inhospitable environment without being seen and without much food or water. From the outset some extraordinary feats of endurance were recorded. Conditions in which previously men had got lost, gone mad, or despaired and died, had to be regarded as routine.

Once on an airfield it would not be sufficient to blow up just one aircraft. The men were required to approach stealthily by night, kill any sentries quietly in the commando way, and put charges on all the parked aircraft, so that when one went off, the rest would also blow up. This last technique required the correct type of charge and a sophisticated timing device. Explosives were the province of Jock Lewes, who experimented until he found the right formula: a mixture of oil, plastic explosive and thermite which not only exploded but also set the surrounding material alight. Lewes, sad to say, was killed when returning after an early SAS raid on an airfield at Nufilia.

The first SAS raid, which took place on the night of 17/18 November, was a disaster, for high winds blew up a sandstorm and all the parachutists were blown off their course. Of the sixty SAS men who had set out only twenty-two survived. The rest were killed.

A disaster of this magnitude might have deterred anyone else, but not David Stirling. He now linked up with the Long Range Desert Group (LRDG), with which the SAS has often been confused.

The LRDG was the heir to a long tradition of treating the desert as if it was the open sea (50,000 years earlier the Sahara had been a vast inland lake). During World War I, British Yeomanry units had operated in the desert against enemy forces made up of Germans, Turks and Senussi Arabs, who threatened Egypt. At first the Yeomanry used horses for their patrolling, but later transferred to T

Model Ford cars. With these they protected caravans and vital oases. In the course of their duties they invented the sun compass by which navigation is made possible in the desert, and the water condenser which prevents radiators boiling dry. The desert exploration of the Yeomanry was greatly extended in the inter-war years by amateur explorers who penetrated the impenetrable at their own very considerable expense. They included R. A. Bagnold, W. B. Kennedy-Shaw, G. Prendergast, P. Clayton and E. Mitford. In September 1940 the LRDG was afforded recognition, equipment and arms. Its task was reconnaissance and signalling. For mobility it had eleven 30cwt trucks; for protection it had machine-guns, anti-tank rifles and even a Bofors 37mm anti-tank gun. It was realized that the LRDG could easily run into trouble and would need adequate means to defend itself.

The LRDG was very well established by November 1941 but, because its primary function was unobtrusive reconnaissance, it was something of a contrast to the SAS, which could hardly fail to draw attention to itself. Nevertheless, after the disaster of 17/18 November, the LRDG had been at hand to collect up and carry away all that remained of the SAS force, and when asked if it would be prepared to do the same in future raids readily agreed. Even more to the point, the LRDG agreed to make its resources available for Stirling's men to reach their targets. So, a fruitful cooperation between the SAS and the LRDG was born. LRDG trucks, incidentally, were camouflaged by being painted pink, a colour which made them almost invisible from the air. The properties of pink as a camouflage colour had been discovered by accident: a lone aircraft some years before had been coloured pink, under the impression that this would make it easily visible. However, when it came down in the desert it was not found for several years, and then only by chance.

The existence of the SAS and LRDG in the Middle East was known in Cairo, but the success of both depended on very tight operational security. Not every raid was a success but many were. When the Germans became aware of the continuing nature of the threat, they took more precautions over guarding their airfields. However, they soon found that a sentry sleeping under the wing of an aeroplane was more likely to be killed than to protect the aircraft; wiring and guarding the perimeters was more effective. At an early date Stirling had recruited a man with a genius for SAS-type work, R. B. Mayne, an Irish Rugby football international of immense physical strength, powers of endurance, and leadership. When the raiders ran into trouble, as they occasionally did, Mayne's rapid thinking and simultaneous action often saved them from disaster.

In order to understand the sort of war which was being fought, and the part which the LRDG, SAS and many other units took in it, it is necessary to take a look at the overall strategy. In 1940, when Britain appeared to be on the point of being overwhelmed, Italy had invaded Somaliland and also advanced into Egypt. However, the invasion forces were soon counter-attacked and heavily defeated by British forces under Wavell. In January 1941 the Australians captured Tobruk, a useful North African port, and with it 25,000 Italian prisoners.

Hitler, observing with dissatisfaction the military incompetence of his ally Mussolini, decided to bolster the Italian desert force with a Light Armoured Division commanded by Erwin Rommel, which arrived on 12 February 1941. As Rommel prepared an offensive, Wavell was persuaded to send some 56,000 troops to assist Greece which was being hard-pressed. Although 43,000 were evacuated before Greece surrendered, 15,000 were subsequently taken prisoner in Crete. With his army drained of many of his best troops, there was little that Wavell could do to stop Rommel. Rommel could not recapture Tobruk, but he could and did put it under siege. Wavell (prodded by Churchill) made an unsuccessful attempt to relieve Tobruk, but was driven back to the Egyptian frontier again. He was then replaced by Auchinleck who, as we saw earlier, gave Stirling permission to begin training the SAS in June 1941.

From this point onwards there began what the troops in the desert described as the Benghazi Stakes, in which first one side would take the offensive and gain territory and then the other would attack and the territory would be lost again. The further the line of communication was extended, the easier it was for the SAS and LRDG to operate without detection. The term 'desert' is misleading, for it suggests shifting, dry sand. The desert varies in composition: the northern half is mainly limestone, the southern half mainly sandstone. There are vast sand seas, one of them about the size of Ireland. The whole area is approximately the size of India.

The prize which the Germans wanted was Alexandria, followed by Cairo; the principal wish of the Allies was to clear the Germans and Italians out of North Africa, which in fact was accomplished in May 1943. But until that last objective was reached neither side could be sure what cunning device the opposition would employ next. Rommel was an expert at 'hook' tactics in which a long encircling move would be made round an enemy column. Rommel was likely to begin his offensive a few days before the carefully planned British effort was designed to function. Intelligence about the intentions or capacity or movements or morale or supplies of the other side was therefore of the utmost importance. As we now know, the Ultra intercepts provided invaluable information about German military strategy. They did not, however, prove nearly as useful as had been hoped in the desert. This was because Rommel often said one thing to his superiors and did another, and in the desert the situation was liable to change so quickly that even intercepted messages between senior commanders were out of date by the time they became available to the enemy. For the men on the spot, reconnaissance aircraft and the assiduous work of the LRDG were the most valuable sources of information. One irony was that Rommel constantly sent misleading reports to his higher command complaining about lack of supplies and the poor quality of the material he possessed. Those who opposed him in the desert would have known that he was lying about the quality of his equipment, but unfortunately when his messages were intercepted and made available to Churchill and the War Cabinet they believed every word and could not understand why Auchinleck was not more successful. In fact, up until August 1942 Rommel's equipment was far superior. Auchinleck knew this only too well, but could not possibly explain it to Churchill who believed what Rommel had said, not what Auchinleck had learnt from his own fighting troops and intelligence-gatherers.

But while the LRDG and SAS were probing for German secrets they learnt some chilling lessons about the need for absolute secrecy over their own activities. Following an immensely successful attack on Sidi-Enich airfield by an SAS force of eighteen jeeps – each with four Vickers K machine-guns – which had destroyed every German plane in sight, the SAS paid the penalty for its own success. Planners at GHQ in Cairo decided that the best way to cripple Rommel's next offensive was to launch a large combined raid on Benghazi and Tobruk. There were 4,000 British prisoners at Tobruk and these could be very useful if released. SAS troops were to be launched from the land side while naval commandos came in from the sea. The objectives were 1,500 miles from the starting point. There were many things wrong with this raid, one being that the LRDG was required to lead an attack on an airfield at Barce, another that there would be a preliminary bombardment from the sea, another that the SAS was asked to include 120 men who could not be trained adequately in the time available; but the most damaging feature as far as the SAS was concerned was that it was being asked to operate in a role for which it was not designed. Its ideal use was in small groups, preferably fours; it was not suitable for use as a commando or assault unit. Perhaps the worst aspect of the raid was that because of 'careless talk' it was common knowledge in Cairo ten days before it began. This last fact had undoubtedly helped the Germans to prepare a reception. They may not have known the exact timing of the raid, but they certainly knew what to do when it arrived. Two destroyers were lost, and many casualties were sustained by the land forces.

After Benghazi the SAS and LRDG reverted to their normal role. There was only one coastal road, and the LRDG, assisted by the SAS, maintained a twenty-four-hour watch on it week after week and month after month, noting every German vehicle and enemy tank, and passing the information back to GHQ intelligence. Periodically the SAS blew up targets that clearly required such attention. However, in January 1943 Stirling himself had the misfortune to be captured. He was sent to Colditz and that was the end of his war in spite of several attempts to escape.

From a disastrous beginning the Special Air Service Regiment had become a great success story. Three hundred of the best German aircraft had been destroyed, as had hangars and workshops. Railway lines and telegraph communications had been blown up. Not least of its achievements was that the Germans had diverted hundreds of men from other military tasks and set them to guarding remote airfields, often without success. The SAS would continue its achievements in Sicily, in Italy and particularly in occupied Europe: in 1944 there were many SAS men operating in France, blowing up railway lines and often the trains on them.

The SAS was lucky in that it was not disbanded and dispersed after the end of the North African campaign. The fact that it was successful was no guarantee of its continuance. As manpower grew shorter, orthodox units turned hungry eyes towards special forces to see if they could fill their own vacancies from them. But, fortunately for the SAS, approval was given for the formation of HQ, SAS Troops, under F. A. M. Browning, who was now a lieutenant-general. The SAS became a brigade made up of 1 and 2 SAS Regiments which were British, 3 and 4 which were French, and a Belgian Independent Parachute

Squadron which later became the Belgian SAS Regiment. F Squadron Phantom was attached as the brigade signals section.

The tasks facing the SAS in Europe were very different from the ones which they had undertaken in the desert. For one thing the operational area was much smaller, for another it was more populated. A third factor was that resistance groups and Special Operations Executives (SOE – spies and saboteurs) were already on the scene. It would be all too easy for any one of these to interfere with, obstruct or draw unnecessary attention to the activities of the others. In war national forces and their allies are all supposed to be on the same side, but in practice this is not always apparent. It is well known that some of the resistance groups in France hated each other almost as much as they hated their German occupiers. At times in World War II jealousy and dislike between units and allies often seemed more bitter than feelings towards the common enemy.

Nevertheless, the SAS adapted itself to its new role with success. In France and Italy there was no secure base as there had been in the Middle East. Temporary camps were set up in deep woods and sometimes had to be changed at very short notice. There was no question of being mistaken for enemy troops. The SAS wore uniform and expected, if captured, to be treated according to the conventions of war. However, Hitler had given orders that any SAS men captured were to be executed. And as the war drove into Germany, with a shorter and shorter line of communication, there was no employment for the SAS except unsubtle infantry attacks. In the closing stages of a war the high command makes little or no effort to preserve highly trained specialists. Instead, it is assumed that the purpose for which they were trained is past history and they have become as expendable as anyone else.

The SAS was disbanded in November 1945 but was re-created first as a Territorial regiment, then after considerable success in Malaya, as a regular army regiment. It fought in Borneo, Oman and Aden, but only really came to the public notice when it brought the siege of the Iranian Embassy in London to an end in May 1980. There it was observed in action on live television. Since then it has been considered an anti-terrorist superman unit, a reputation which gives the regiment no pleasure at all. Although not underrating its value in anti-terrorist operations, and the consequent uplift in public morale, the SAS prefers to emphasize that it is a regular regiment in the British army which has in addition developed certain specialist skills.

David Stirling, from the outset, had emphasized that the SAS men should never act or look 'tough' except in action. He had no time for 'canteen cowboys', and insisted on a rigid code of self-discipline. On the occasions when self-discipline has proved inadequate the offender has been dismissed from the unit with a speed which has surprised him. The units deny that secret and special forces require exceptional people, saying that anyone with determination and the right attitude can be successful. To a large measure this is true. However, during World War II special forces were able to draw on a reservoir of exceptional talent. Stirling himself had not given signs of any special qualities in his pre-war days. He was a keen mountaineer, and was interested in strenuous individual games; he was also a creative thinker. He had begun to read architecture at Cambridge University; he had also studied painting, at which he had talent. Jock Lewes was a perfectionist. In his Oxford days, against all the odds he had so trained the rowing team that they won the boat race, thus breaking Cambridge's sequence of thirteen successive wins. But having trained his team he dropped himself from the race, saying he was not good enough to row in it.

Among the other pioneers of the SAS were R. B. Mayne, a quick-tempered man who had considerable literary interests, John Verney, an Oxford graduate who was a writer and a designer, Earl Jellicoe, son of the World War I admiral, who was also a Cambridge graduate and future Minister of the Crown, and Tom Langton, Cambridge graduate and rowing blue. Langton walked 400 miles across the desert after the failure of the Tobruk raid. There were, of course, thousands of graduates in the armed forces, and many of them doubtless possessed considerable determination. Other things being equal, it was probably a help to be a graduate and to have had the opportunity to develop creative thinking, but it was by no means essential. What was essential was the dedication to reach a difficult objective and survive.

The SAS and LRDG were by no means the only special forces operating in the Middle East at this time. Another notable formation was the Special Boat Service. This, like several of its companions, had a variety of titles: today its successor is known as the Special Boat Squadron, a designation it possessed for a short time in 1943. The origins of the SBS may be traced back to the early training of Commandos in Scotland. Among their equipment were folboats. Folboats were collapsible canoes of German origin which had been designed for sporting occasions (the original name was *Folbot*). The driving force behind the folboat sections which came to be attached to each Commando was Roger Courtney, an experienced big-game hunter and explorer. Courtney had come back to England at the outbreak of the war with the conviction that a flimsy canoe had considerable military uses in that it could penetrate shallow waters silently and yet still be navigable in rougher, deeper seas. His suggestions for military uses were originally greeted with amused disbelief by senior officers of navy and army but Courtney soon proved his point by a practical demonstration.

When Layforce was earmarked for the capture of Rhodes, Courtney and fifteen of the canoeists he had trained went with it. When the Rhodes project was abandoned Courtney's men were instructed on how to raid enemy harbours around the Mediterranean. They had now become Z Group and managed a series of successful, though small, raids. The possibilities of canoes in the general pattern of raiding the enemy were soon noted by David Stirling, who was always alert to adding another lethal component to his SAS activities. When Courtney was invalided home, command of the SBS went to Tom Langton. The SBS was soon setting records of its own, one in particular being the 150-mile journey through enemy-infested waters between Ras-el-Tin and Gazala, made by Captain K. Allot and Lieutenant D. Ritchie.

As Crete was now firmly in German hands it seemed appropriate to make the Germans feel less secure about their position there. The Special Boat Service was maintaining a precarious existence which seemed likely to be ended at any moment by some directive from the higher command. It was therefore trying to justify its continuance by raids on Italian shipping, and in addition had already cooperated with the SAS. While the SBS engaged itself raiding a harbour, the SAS would be dealing with a nearby airfield. Sometimes they cooperated on the same task as when three airfields (Heraklion, Kastelli and Timbaki) were visited on Crete. But not every raid was successful; an attempt on Sicily led to the capture of a whole group, which included the writer Eric Newby. The SBS had losses in other engagements and became so depleted in numbers that its survival was possible only by a formal alliance with the SAS from whom they received reinforcements. The SAS had by now also joined itself to the Greek Sacred Squadron, an élite organization which provided a fund of Greek speakers of the highest military calibre.

The SBS turned its attention to Rhodes, as German aircraft from that island were harassing British shipping in the Mediterranean. An SBS party was delivered to the vicinity of the island by submarine and landed by boat. The raid on the airfields at Calato and Marizza was very successful and put both out of action for several weeks. The SBS had split up into two small parties, and one was captured. The other, consisting of Marine Duggan and Captain Sutherland, had to take refuge in the hills from which point they saw their escape boat being towed away by an Italian motor torpedo boat. After lying up for five days without food, for two of those without water, they made their way to the coast and swam out to where they hoped the submarine might be waiting. There were Italian boats in the vicinity but at the end of a mile and a half swim they were spotted by the submarine and picked up. The rescue was just in time. In addition to the problems of hunger, exposure and exhaustion, David Sutherland had now developed a virus infection. He survived.

By 1 April 1943 the SBS had established a firm base at Athlit, just south of Haifa, British Palestine. The unit commander was Major the Earl Jellicoe and originally it had three detachments, L under Langton, S under Sutherland, and M under Maclean. Maclean was Fitzroy Maclean who later wrote of his experience in a book entitled *Eastern Approaches*. As a member of the Diplomatic Service at the outset of the war he had been forbidden to join the army but he applied himself with some ingenuity to getting round the prohibition. He had resigned from the Diplomatic Service in order to stand for Parliament – which he did after the war – but in the meantime joined the Cameron Highlanders and then the SAS. Maclean was a brilliant linguist and when challenged on the Benghazi raid had rebuked the sentry in his own language and insisted on reporting his alleged slackness to the German guard commander. Both were so abashed that Maclean's identity was not questioned. Maclean's detachment of the SBS was subsequently earmarked for a highly promising assignment. At this delicate stage in the war it was thought that the Germans might suddenly launch a thrust through Persia (Iran) and Iraq. A substantial British force known as Paiforce (Persia and Iraq Force) was assembled to counter this potential thrust and M detachment was briefed to harass the German lines of communication if and when the clash came. Although still the Special Boat Service, they would have little to do with boats but operate as parachutists or on foot. They brought off a bloodless coup in capturing General Zahidi, who was planning a German-backed *coup d'état* in Persia. When the threat to Persia was removed by German defeats at Alamein and Stalingrad, Maclean was sent to Yugoslavia.

Soon after its formal establishment, the SBS was joined by two remarkable characters: Anders Lassen and Philip Pinckney. Both came from 62 Commando, which had had a brief existence under the inspired leadership of Capt Gustavus March-Phillips and Capt Geoffrey Appleyard. 62 Commando had specialized in small-scale cross-Channel raiding and in the delivery and collection of SOE agents. March-Phillips was killed in a raid on Port-en-Bessin, Normandy, in November 1942. Appleyard took over but shortly afterwards, when the Commandos were reorganized, 62 was disbanded, and Appleyard went to 2 SAS. He was killed in an aircraft crash in Sicily.

Lassen's ability had been noted when 62 Commando had moved from its normal haunts and raided the West African coast near Dakar. This area was controlled by the Vichy (puppet German) government. The Commando had sunk two German merchantmen and sailed away with a third. Lassen was an unusual person in every way. He was a Dane of aristocratic birth but very democratic habits. At the start of the war he had come to England as a merchant seaman and joined the British army. In 62 Commando he was a lance-corporal, but after the West African raid he was given a commission. Lassen eventually won a Victoria Cross. (Only two foreigners have been awarded VCs in the British army and both have been Danes.) Lassen was destined to show many remarkable qualities of courage and coolness in the SBS. He had a knack of knowing just where to go, and just how long to stay. His usual technique was to arrive at a German headquarters at the head of a small team which, before sentries could give an alarm, would create havoc in the building. Lassen's speciality was moving like lightning and tossing hand-grenades into one room after another. It was said by those near him that 'he moved so quickly and quietly that he did not seem to touch the ground'. During commando training in Scotland he had shown that he, like David Stirling, could stalk a stag and kill it with his knife.

The other notable recruit was Philip Pinckney. Pinckney, although giving little signs of it sartorially, was also of what might be described as 'gentle' birth. He was afraid of nothing but inclined to be a little casual. His great interest in life was survival foods, and he tried out everything personally. He ate twigs, leaves, insects, slugs ... The orderly sergeant used to dread occasions when Pinckney was orderly officer, for he was constantly saying, 'That looks an interesting insect, sergeant, I wonder what it tastes like. Let's try it!' Pinckney's scientific curiosity about what can be used when survival is the only consideration eventually made an enormous contribution to the SAS knowledge of this subject. In fact, Pinckney's pioneering zeal laid the foundation of the SAS survival diet, which has undoubtedly saved many lives. Later Pinckney was captured and shot by the Carabinieri when he had parachuted into Italy to blow up railways near the Brenner Pass. Service in special and secret forces was, of course, more interesting, free and flexible than service in an orthodox unit but one's fate, if captured, was likely to be torture and death. The Gestapo and their kin were no respecters of international convention.

By the end of August 1943 it was clear that Italy, having lost Sicily and knowing that the invasion of the mainland was the next step, would be pleased to break away from the Germans and make a separate peace with the Allies. The Germans, of course, were not unaware of this possibility. At the time the Italians retained control of the islands between Greece and the Turkish mainland. The most important island was Rhodes, which, as we saw, possessed good airfields and was a thorn in the flesh of Allied shipping. If Italy made a separate peace Rhodes must not be allowed to fall into German hands but, as there was an unspecified number of German troops on the island already, this seemed a distinct possibility. The only way in which Rhodes could be acquired by the Allies was through a major bluff, for they had insufficient troops to take the island if the Italians and their allies resisted. There was, however, a chance that if Italy made a separate peace Rhodes would also try to shake off its German allegiance.

The Governor of Rhodes was an Admiral Campioni, and Jellicoe now undertook the task of persuading him to join the Allies. To this end he took a signaller and a forty-two-year-old interpreter who had never parachuted before. Jellicoe carried with him a letter from General Wilson, the area commander, to deliver to the admiral. The three dropped at night, but in the process the interpreter broke a leg. Jellicoe, believing he was about to be captured by Germans, promptly – but not rapidly – ate the letter. It was on thick paper, designed to impress, and took him an hour to dispose of. It then gave him a twenty-four-hour thirst. Nevertheless, hope was not lost and, after they were discovered by Italians, all three were taken to the admiral – the interpreter being carried on a stretcher. Jellicoe gave a confident forecast of the assistance about to supplement his three-man team, but the admiral, well aware of the presence of 10,000 Germans on the island who had just threatened him with dire penalties if he tried to desert them, decided Jellicoe's 'assistance' was too nebulous and capitulated to the Germans instead.

Disappointed but undeterred, Jellicoe decided that if Rhodes had eluded him the rest of the islands should not. Thereupon he began a rapid drive with the SBS to capture the islands in the Dodecanese group and if possible the rest of the Greek islands too. Cos, Leros, Simi, Samos were acquired rapidly, mainly because the Germans were surprised at the sheer audacity of SBS actions with what they suspected could only be a very small force. However, when they recovered from their surprise they made a tremendous counter-attack, which had been ordered by Hitler personally. By the time that was mounted (October 1943) certain islands had been garrisoned by British troops, though not in very large numbers. The Germans delivered a full-scale attack on the lost islands, using Messerschmidts for bombing and ground strafing, parachutists and well-trained soldiers. They were made to pay heavily for their success, losing 1,000 troops, but, having recovered the islands, they established formidable garrisons. In all they spread a total of six divisions – nearly 100,000 men – over the islands, the heaviest concentration being on Rhodes. Undoubtedly, Hitler thought there was a genuine threat of Allied invasion through this area, which Churchill described as 'the soft underbelly of Europe'. Hitler was wrong, for Churchill's efforts to persuade the American chiefs of staff that an invasion in this area would be cheaper and vastly more effective than one elsewhere fell on very deaf ears.

But there was certainly an advantage to the Allies in having six German divisions tied up in the Greek islands. Those six divisions could have played a decisive part in the Italian campaign, been useful on the Russian front or proved a decided asset to German forces in France. As long as they were in the Greek islands they could not be used anywhere else and it therefore became Allied policy to keep them there. The SBS, though little more than two hundred in number, applied itself enthusiastically to making the Germans feel their hold on the islands was under constant threat. Their efforts were supplemented by the RAF operating from bases in Cyprus and by the Royal Navy harassing the shorelines. The Germans could not accept these attentions without demur, for they had aircraft and a good quantity of shipping spread among the islands. The favourite SBS ploy was to lure the Germans to remote islands by staged diversions and then make their return journey exceptionally hazardous. The master-mind behind many of these activities was J. N. Lapraik. Lapraik was an interesting example of how determination can overcome handicaps, and was thus a leader unlikely to be deterred by man-made obstacles. At the age of eight he had contracted a knee infection, which had led to his being handicapped for five years. For two of those five years his knee had been encased in plaster. Once the infection was cured he had embarked on a steady process of building up his general health. He did this so well that by the time he reached the age of twenty he was a middle-distance runner of international standard. However, when he was at Glasgow University he was advised not to play rough or dangerous games. After joining the army he was soon in the Commandos and shortly after that became an expert on handling canoes. On one occasion he paddled a canoe from Malta to Sicily, a distance of some seventy miles. He also proved that it is possible to handle a canoe in near gale-force winds.

The SBS spent much of its time in caiques, small Greek schooners which are used extensively for fishing in those waters and which normally do not attract much attention. The Germans could scarcely stop and search them all, even if they wanted to. Needless to say the SBS caiques were disguised to look like fishing boats of the most innocent variety. And, as the SBS proved its undoubted worth, it was also supplied with fast motor launches to make it even more of a thorn in the flesh of the enemy.

Towards the end of 1944 the SBS decided that a heavy raid on the island of Simi was necessary to wash away the memories it had of being driven out of the island the previous year. Unfortunately there was a good harbour (Portolago) on Leros nearby, and in this lay two Axis destroyers which could emerge at short notice and have a devastating effect on the SBS return journey from Simi, even if they did not actually take part in the defence of the island. Much as Lapraik's team would have liked to go in and cripple these destroyers, they were prevented from doing so by the boom defence of the port.

In consequence, assistance of specialist nature was requested from Britain. It was forthcoming in the shape of Royal Marine Boom Commando (RMBC) troops who, with their highly developed expertise in penetrating harbour defences, went in and crippled the destroyers with limpet bombs. The SBS was pleased with the result but slightly resentful that 'outsiders' should have been brought in. What nobody seemed to realize at the time was that the men of the RMBC team were their blood-brothers in that they had developed from the same origins as the SBS.

Not least of the SBS's accomplishments was the establishment of a signal station on every important Greek island to monitor constantly all movements of enemy shipping and troops. One of these signal stations was on the top of the German commandant's house on Santorini. It was manned for fifteen months and never detected, although transmitting daily. A sample of the accuracy and closeness to sources of intelligence was revealed when the signallers mentioned that two German commandants, one at Kalimnos, the other at Simi, had had the misfortune to lose their testicles. One's had been the victim of a rifle bullet, the other's had been caught by a fragment of a grenade.

The SBS's adventures in the Mediterranean were an unexpected development in the war. Nobody in 1939 had been able to make an accurate prediction of how the war would continue. Assessment of enemy intentions and capabilities depends upon the collection of an adequate quantity of intelligence and astute calculation. Thus, in 1939 Germany was known to have the makings of armoured divisions, but few people in higher British (or American) military circles believed that they could alter the pattern of war as radically as they did in 1940. Equally, it was known that the Germans had a gun, the 88mm, which could be used either as an anti-aircraft gun or as an anti-tank gun. But it was simply not believed that a gun could fulfil two such roles effectively. The lesson was learnt in the Western Desert but never seemed to influence Allied tactical thinkers to use the 3.7-inch anti-aircraft gun in a dual role, although it could probably have performed as well as, if not better than, the 88mm. But the mistaken assessments were not all on one side. The Axis powers (Germany, Italy, Japan – so-called because they began as the Berlin-Rome Axis and widened to include Tokyo) never visualized that when they had made their extensive conquests, overrunning vast tracts of territory, that they would be so harassed by special forces. The forages of the SAS and LRDG in the desert came as an unexpected and unwelcome shock to the Axis, and the SBS was no less of an unwanted opponent round the Greek islands. In areas where special forces had a mainly military role they often used captured weapons, choosing ones most suited to their purpose. Lugers, Walther P.38 automatics and Schmeisser machine pistols proved especially popular. On a larger scale the principle of airborne and armoured warfare may be said to have been copied from the enemy.

Before leaving the Mediterranean we should take a look at one interesting, though not entirely successful, raid which occurred in mid 1943. It falls outside the main areas under discussion and so has been omitted until now. This was on Sardinia, where there were known to be airfields from which aircraft could help in the defence of Sicily. A raid led by John Verney set off by submarine, but the submarine developed engine trouble and had to return. Before it did so, most of the raiders were feeling distinctly unwell. If you have been training arduously in the open air, confinement in close, smelly quarters can upset your general health. Those accustomed to the atmosphere seem to suffer no ill effects but as soon as they emerge for a period into fresh air may succumb to the first cold or other respiratory ailment which is prevalent at the time.

After the abortive attempt by submarine, Verney decided they should go in by parachute. This they did but, having blown up the required airfields, they found themselves unable to reach the coast to escape. They were taken prisoner after delaying their capture as long as possible. Verney was sent to Italy but escaped and later joined the SAS in Europe.

By the autumn of 1944 the Greek Sacred Squadron was sufficiently trained to take over the SBS raiding responsibilities in the Greek islands and the SBS itself moved north west to the Adriatic and Yugoslavia. It would be a more frustrating role but the keynote of the SBS was adaptability and flexibility.

On their way to the Adriatic the SBS were required to play a part in the recapture of Greece. Here their role became less of a special force and more of an infantry unit. Lassen enjoyed himself by moving from place to place so quickly that the SBS were thought to be in greater strength than they actually were. Jellicoe had the satisfaction of reoccupying Athens when the Germans were evacuating it. He landed at Scaramanga from a caique and the only transport available was two bicycles, one of which he appropriated for himself, the other went to his second-in-command. Followed by fifty-five other members of the SBS, they rode into the city. It made a change from 'conquering heroes' riding on elephants, war chariots or prancing horses, but Jellicoe was not given to ostentation and would have declined them if they had been available.

In the Adriatic, as may be expected, opportunities for the employment of the SBS were somewhat limited. The Germans in the northern Adriatic were experienced veterans and were not easily outwitted or outfought. The SBS concentrated on guerrilla warfare, but was hampered by the Yugoslavs who wished to be seen to be liberating areas such as Istria themselves. But there was one advantage in the SBS presence which should not be underrated. On several occasions towards the end of World War II the defeated (particularly the Japanese in the Far East) were inclined to hand over their arms to those most likely to cause trouble to the elected government in the future. The presence of special forces, whose mobility made their numbers appear to be greater than they were, undoubtedly helped to prevent arms falling into the hands of potential terrorists.

The LRDG completed its career among the Greek islands and the Adriatic. When the desert campaign was over, the future of the LRDG came under urgent review. The skills which had enabled the regiment to cover 2,000 miles of featureless desert would no longer be required; future movement would be in tighter limits full of man-made perils. The experience and ability of the regiment's members were too valuable to be wasted but to make proper use of them it was necessary to adapt to short-range work.

The LRDG training for European warfare was in many ways similar to that of the SAS. It involved parachuting, skiing, walking and operating in small units carrying enough food for ten days. The ability to know exactly where one was and what was happening in the district was as important as it had been in the desert days. In addition they were taught German and modern Greek.

But their first employment was disappointing and frustrating. They were transported to the Aegean just at the moment when the Germans were making an all-out bid to recover the islands after the Italian surrender. The LRDG was assigned to the task of keeping watch on the coast, but it was all too clear to them and to others that the Germans had complete air superiority and there was no hope of retaining a foothold unless large reinforcements could be brought in, supported by adequate air cover. GHQ Cairo stubbornly believed that the troops on Leros were adequate to defend it, a view which was not shared by anyone on the island. The key to the situation was the preponderance of Stuka and JU88 attacks. The RAF fought with great skill and courage but their numbers were far too few for the purpose. The battle continued pointlessly until it became impossible to evacuate more than a few men. In retrospect, with the judgement of hindsight, it is obvious that intelligence reports were not being correctly assessed and acted upon.

This was an unpromising start for the LRDG's employment in its new role but although depleted in numbers the regiment had by no means lost heart. However, the next blow was the withdrawal of the invaluable New Zealand Squadron which was required by the New Zealand Division itself. Fortunately for the LRDG, the New Zealanders were replaced by a Rhodesian squadron which soon proved itself ideally suited to the task.

The whole of the LRDG began a period of extensive retraining at the beginning of 1944. The men had to be expert at parachuting, at mountain warfare, at handling small boats, and well-versed in signalling, in handling explosives, in map-reading and in the driving and maintenance of a variety of transport ranging from jeeps to mules. They went up into the mountains of Syria to learn how to move and to fight in the snow. It was a thorough, well-balanced course. But at the end of it, when they were considered trained to everyone's satisfaction, there appeared to be no employment for them. A few interesting operations were at last earmarked for them; they involved dropping by parachute and destroying railway lines in northern Italy. However, after the plans had been worked out the assignment was cancelled because of insufficient aircraft.

David Lloyd-Owen, who was now commanding the regiment, decided that there was nothing to be gained by patience and went to GHQ (now at Caserta) to enquire whether or not there was any serious intention of ever employing the LRDG again. Nobody knew. He therefore suggested that one squadron should be sent to assist Force 266, an organization supporting and coordinating support for the partisans in the Balkan countries. Operational headquarters was set up in Bari in Italy and from then on life became more exciting again. Their first assignment was to spy out the land for an attack on a German radar station on Corfu, then garrisoned by some 2,500 troops. It was followed by a similar mission in Albania. The unit was then briefed to obtain information on German military traffic north of Rome, and despatched patrols by parachute for that purpose. On this occasion men were lost on the drop and others captured. But the information-gathering was a success and the reports sent in were said to be of considerable value to Allied planning for the next phase of the war in that area.

The next assignment took the LRDG to the Dalmatian islands, to obtain reports on all enemy shipping movements. The information was required by both the Royal Navy and the RAF; they would thus know the strength of forces ranged against them and also which targets to attack. The Dalmatians were garrisoned by Germans and the small detachments of the LRDG which established themselves there had to keep on the move, a factor which made their supply by air no slight problem.

The LRDG's first major assignment was against an enemy coast-watching station at Orso Bay in Albania. This was reporting on the movement of Allied shipping in precisely the way the LRDG was reporting on German and Italian sea traffic. Before setting out, the LRDG contacted an officer from Force 266 which had recently been in Albania. He turned out to be Antony Quayle, the future actor-producer, and he provided them with much useful information. The LRDG then conducted a thorough recce. The post was well defended and guarded. After suitable arrangements had been made, the LRDG signalled in three British destroyers which briskly pounded the post to fragments. After this successful venture it seemed that the LRDG would now be fully employed again, for those not required in the Adriatic expected to be helping partisans in northern Italy. This project, too, was cancelled.

But the Adriatic, particularly Yugoslavia, gave plenty of compensation. The regiment was now principally concerned with intelligence-gathering, not because it preferred this to harassing the enemy but because the partisans had been ordered by Tito to ensure that foreign troops did not take part in military action. Yugoslavia must be liberated by the partisans on their own. At first the partisans were friendly to the LRDG, who were proving of great use to them as a source of information and materials. Through the LRDG's wireless link with Italy the partisans were supplied with guns, ammunition and other supplies. But by October 1944 relations had soured. The partisans still wanted the supplies and the help, even to the extent of Allied aircraft supporting their attacks, but they were withholding information from the LRDG and were also restricting its movements. The fact that the Germans were extremely anxious to eliminate the LRDG as being a useful aid to the partisans did little to make life easier for the regiment. Movement had to be almost continuous. One party was captured by German E-boats but, after some unpleasant interrogation, managed to escape.

David Lloyd-Owen was commanding the regiment at this time; he was twenty-six. At various times in his career with the LRDG it seemed unlikely that he would survive to become any older, but he did and completed his army career as a major-general with a CB, DSO, OBE, and MC. In September 1944 he found himself organizing and controlling as many as eighteen different parties spread between Italy and Yugoslavia, Albania and Greece. This was a coverage of 850 miles. Although the Yugoslavs became progressively more obstructive, other nationalities were more helpful: the Greeks were delighted to have assistance in killing Germans. The amount of signals traffic was enormous and Lloyd-Owen paid tribute to his signallers who performed feats which might have seemed impossible.

One of the problems which Lloyd-Owen noted was that the best patrols were usually those readiest to volunteer. Sometimes they had to be ordered to take a rest. Even the hardiest began to show signs of strain after periods of hunger, exhaustion, cold and the frustration of never knowing when the people they were trying to help would respond with active hostility.

Albania was even more frustrating than Yugoslavia. The LRDG found the Albanian partisans unreliable. They seemed interested in the LRDG only as a source of supplies, and members of the regiment were well aware that the 'partisans' would not stop at robbery and murder if the mood took them. They seemed more concerned to adopt Russian-style communism than in helping their allies and suppliers against the Germans and Italians. However, on the few occasions when the latter were brought to battle, the Albanians showed considerable courage. For while the LRDG was trying to enlist them to the task of cutting through the German lines of communication, as the latter tried to retreat through Albania from Greece (in the direction of Yugoslavia), the partisans preferred to take no action. This was principally because they felt that fighting on Yugoslav soil was infinitely preferable to fighting in Albania. The partisan leader Enver Hoxha remained unmoved by the numerous opportunities for ambush as the retreating troops passed through his own country. When 10,000 Germans were in Albania (September 1944), Lloyd-Owen set off from Bari, where he had been planning and coordinating the work of the patrols, and embarked on a heavily-laden Dakota with the intention of parachuting near Hoxha's headquarters and persuading him to take action. His first attempt failed because the pilot lost his way among the enemy searchlights and had to turn back. On the second trip

Lloyd-Owen landed perfectly, discarded his parachute, and set off briskly to his objective. In the dark, almost immediately he fell into a deep ravine. When he was discovered he learnt that his spine was badly damaged. Badly damaged spines do not recover quickly, if at all, and Lloyd-Owen was virtually immobilized for nearly three months. But neither the pain nor the handicap of immobility stopped him directing operations. When he left the area he was told by surgeons that he should spend six months in a plaster jacket, but that an immediate operation might be successful and straighten out the deformity which the injury had caused to his spine. It was, but he still had to wear the plaster jacket, though not for six months. After all this and against all advice, he found his way back to operations, instead of proceeding to home duties as had been prescribed.

Lloyd-Owen spoke highly of a number of his LRDG companions in Albania who caused much inconvenience to the Germans although receiving little help from the partisans. Among them were Stan Eastwood and Andy Bennet. Lloyd-Owen emphasized that the partisans were not lacking in courage when they did decide to fight but were so unpredictable that waiting for their next move was a constant nervous strain.

In northern Albania and Greece the LRDG were concerned less with intelligence-gathering than with straight military action. Captain Stormonth-Darling took two patrols into Florina (Macedonia). This was a high-risk enterprise, for it involved parachuting into enemy-held territory with no certainty that the patrols would be met by friends rather than enemies when they arrived. But arrive safely they did and proceeded to mine roads, lay ambushes and report targets to the Royal Air Force. Other LRDG patrols worked closely with the Special Boat Squadron in Greece. By this time frustrations were mounting rapidly; with the end of the war in sight – in that area at least – rival factions concentrated more on their own internal political struggle than on finishing off the Germans. It was particularly galling to realize that Allied supplies were being used to further local political ambitions rather than for their international purpose.

Intelligence-gathering and secret operations are often seen as a 'glamorous' and exciting form of warfare. In reality the glamour is non-existent, and boredom and discomfort are encountered more frequently than excitement. Discomfort is the prevailing note. In the desert the sand and the flies were an incessant nuisance: in the Adriatic the extremes of heat and cold, the sores, the lice and the fleas, never became tolerable in the way that some forms of discomfort can. Of all the pests which make men almost scratch their skin to shreds, fleas are probably the worst. Bugs can be found and squashed, lice can be picked out, but fleas are never where you are looking for them; they are waiting to torment you again when you have given up the hunt. But, as the LRDG knew, in some respects it was very lucky. Its men had freedom of action and movement (except when the enemy made it too dangerous), they never suffered from gruelling artillery bombardment, and very rarely met the close attention of hostile aircraft. And they were members of a team which had volunteered and been carefully selected and trained.

To their surprise their worst moments came when they were in sight of victory. In Yugoslavia they were not only frustrated by those they were trying to help, they were sometimes imprisoned under vile conditions. The best of their time in 1945 was when they were at Zara (Yugoslavia), a part of what was known as Land Forces Northern Adriatic, which also included some SBS and members of the RAF Regiment. (The principal function of the RAF Regiment was the defence of airfields against attack by airborne or ground-based forces.) The northern Adriatic was being used extensively by German forces which moved at night. The LRDG concerned itself with finding the harbours in which the German ships lay during daylight hours. Everything depended on efficient signals communication under the most adverse conditions, but the success rate was very high. Somewhat disconcertingly for the patrols, the Germans guessed why this was happening and spared no effort to try to track them down. The LRDG, though disgusted by the growing partisan hostility towards them, were astonished at the kindness with which they were now treated by the peasantry, who often sheltered them for the night. Although language barriers usually made communication impossible, the peasants were well aware of the sort of reprisals the Germans would take if they were caught. But it was never safe to relax one's guard. Lloyd-Owen quotes one example on the island of Ist. A small detachment had set up a post on the island and was sharing a house with a local family. Partisans had provided sentries. But the sentry cannot have been awake one night when a German party reached the house and put a bomb on the windowsill. As they moved round the building the alarm was raised and shots were fired. The wireless operator, Signalman Kenneth Smith, woke up and saw the bomb on the window; it was ticking ominously. As he knew there were women and children in the house, he picked it up and began to run away with it. Before he had gone more than a few yards – but far enough to save the others – the bomb exploded and blew him to bits. He was awarded a posthumous George Cross.

After the end of the war in Europe the LRDG heard that there was a distinct prospect it might go to the Far East to operate against the Japanese. On 16 June 1945 the men were told they would be going: on the 21st they were told that, instead, they would be disbanded. By 1 August 1945 the LRDG was no more.

If ever justification is needed for the existence of special forces, it is certainly to be found in the achievements of the LRDG. Their reports in the Western Desert were invaluable to Allied intelligence, their assistance in rescuing, then transporting and cooperating with the SAS ensured the future of that unit, and their work in the Adriatic was of enormous value to both the Royal Navy and the Royal Air Force. And perhaps one should add that the pioneering spirit which the unit had displayed when travelling vast distances (which a generation earlier would have been thought impossible) did much to assist subsequent scientific exploration and discovery.

Just as the SAS and LRDG are frequently confused, so are the LRDG and LRPG (Long Range Penetration Group). The latter was designed to operate behind the Japanese lines in Burma and was a concept of Orde Wingate. He proposed to the Allied Joint Planning Staff in July 1944 that there should be eight groups which would live off their own resources and whatever air supply could provide. Wingate saw this as a means of slashing the Japanese communications to ribbons; others saw it as a way of wasting hundreds of lives and much time and equipment on a doomed enterprise. Auchinleck, Commander-in-Chief India at that time, was not informed until mid August that the project had been approved by his seniors. He promptly pointed out that unless the areas devastated by the activities of the LRPG could be occupied and held, this venture would lead to the most hideous Japanese reprisals on the Burmese villagers in those areas. Auchinleck did not disapprove of the idea of small-scale raids (he had approved the founding of the SAS) but he did question the grandiose nature of the LRPG scheme. Wingate was not one to be concerned with details, but the 'details' of the LRPG would involve several thousand men in the field and several thousand more to supply the back-up service. Behind the lines work is difficult at any time and in any place, but in Burma where the difficulties of survival in the jungle would be supplemented by those of locating suitable dropping zones, it seemed to be verging on the impossible. The LRPG had limited success and came to its end with the death of its inventor, Orde Wingate, in an aeroplane crash. However, although the LRPG's existence was brief, Wingate's other contribution to irregular warfare had a more lasting effect. I shall return to them in the next chapter.

3: *The Airborne Achievement*

Although the Tragino operation had achieved less than had been hoped for, and had been costly as well, much had been learnt from the experience. In February 1942, some of those lessons were applied in the much more important raid on the German radar installation at Bruneval, near Le Havre.

Early in 1942 the Allies had reached the unpleasant conclusion that radar, which earlier had been thought of as virtually a British monopoly, was now being used with great skill by the Germans. In fact, the Germans had developed their own radar, unaware of British progress in the same field and both sides began the war with this 'secret weapon'. By 1942 each side was aware that the other also possessed it. The Germans were using it extensively and the effects of this were largely felt by Bomber Command, whose losses were mounting rapidly. The main instrument was thought to be a new type of radar unit, and by skilful and venturesome air reconnaissance the presence of one of the new installations had been located near Le Havre. The site itself was near a small village. Clearly, at the earliest possible moment the Allies had to discover what this radar unit contained: with that knowledge there would be a good chance of thwarting its companion units.

The site was on the cliffs, close to a ravine, and was of course adequately guarded. The Germans probably thought it secure. Admiral Lord Mountbatten, at that time Chief of Combined Operations, felt that an airborne raid was a feasible project. It took place on 27 February 1942. A force numbering 120 was chosen from the Parachute Regiment and Royal Engineers. It was to be accompanied by two expert radar mechanics (but one was injured in training, only one went). It would be delivered by Whitleys and after the raid would be evacuated by a naval group supplemented by soldiers from the Royal Fusiliers and South Wales Borderers. The attacking force, commanded by Maj. John Frost, later to have the gruelling experience of Arnhem, was split into three sections and, in spite of encountering brisk opposition, succeeded in obtaining the required radar equipment as well as two prisoners who proved very helpful in explaining some of the technical details. An interesting feature of this raid was that two of the leading figures, Major J. D. Frost and Sergeant C. W. H. Cox, the RAF radar expert, were new to parachuting. Cox had come into the RAF two years earlier and had never been in a ship or an aircraft in his life. He had the bewildering experience of suddenly being summoned to the Air Ministry from Devon, and arrived wondering what fearful error he must have committed. He was then asked to volunteer for a secret mission, to which he agreed, and promptly found himself posted to Ringway (which he had never heard of) and being given a concentrated fortnight of parachuting. Even then he was still mystified about the purpose of it all. Fortunately he landed successfully at Bruneval, knew exactly what to take out of the German radar, and was subsequently awarded a Military Medal.

The casualty figures for the Bruneval raid were three killed, seven wounded and six missing. The gain was enormous and undoubtedly saved many RAF lives subsequently. The details of the raid were given in a book by George Millar entitled *The Bruneval Raid.* It includes much information about the radar battle – a battle of brains rather than bodies – for which, unfortunately, there is no space here.

Encouraged by the success of this raid, plans were soon made for another. The next one was to be more complicated, and more distant. In the event it turned out to be a complete and appalling disaster.

The raid, code-named 'Freshman', was to find out what the Germans were up to where something even more vital than radar was concerned. It was known that they were working on an atomic bomb. All through World War II Hitler made threatening reference to a new 'secret weapon' the Nazis were about to bring into use which would win the war effortlessly for them. Every time the Germans produced a new device, it was hailed as 'Hitler's secret weapon' and everyone hoped it was really his last desperate effort. The first of these was the magnetic mine, which in fact had been invented by the British in the closing stages of World War I but then neglected and finally abandoned. Research began again briskly when the Germans started employing magnetic mines in 1939. Thereafter 88mm guns, dive-bombers, Tiger tanks, flying bombs and V2s were among the many developments which the Allies optimistically hoped were what Hitler had been talking about. Unfortunately for the Allies, the Germans did not invent a weapon and then try to prove its value, good or bad, before passing on to its successor. Indeed they were constantly working on a whole range of new weapons and new ideas for improving existing ones. But the one potential weapon which worried the Allies most in 1942 was undoubtedly the atomic bomb. One of the essential components in its manufacture was known as 'heavy water'. This mysterious-sounding liquid consisted of two atoms of deuterium combined with one atom of oxygen. It was a very rare substance but was produced in Norway in the chemical plants which manufactured nitrates.

A raid to demolish the Norsk hydro plant at Vemork, a factory sixty miles west of Oslo and eighty miles inland, was therefore planned and carried out on 19 November 1942. Vemork was two miles fom the small town of Rjukan and looked to be completely inaccessible to raiders. Rjukan was at the bottom of a deep valley, from which the steep sides rose 3,000 feet; the factory itself was on a shelf some 1,000 feet above the river bed. It was clearly a hopeless target for parachutists and would be almost impossible to hit with bombs. There did, however, seem to be a possibility that a glider-borne raid, signalled in by the Norwegian resistance and subsequently guided by them, might reach and destroy it. The difficulties of the task were all too obvious. Flying over Norwegian mountains and through valleys must inevitably be dangerous, locating the dropping zone exceptionally difficult and subsequent escape extremely arduous, if possible at all. These problems in no way deterred those who volunteered for the raid, but because of the uncertainty of success the raiding party went in two identical halves of sixteen men each. The expedition was a Royal Engineers' project, for they alone would have the necessary expertise to demolish the plant if and when they arrived; by this time there were plenty of Sappers (Royal Engineers) trained in airborne warfare. They were to be delivered by Horsa gliders towed by Halifax bombers.

The first party set off at 5.50 on the evening of the 19th; the second party left twenty minutes later. Nothing was heard of them till just before midnight. One aircraft announced that its glider had been released; the other requested a direction bearing for the homeward flight. Only one of the Halifaxes returned; the other, and the two gliders, disappeared and nothing was known of their fate until the war ended in 1945.

The cause of the disaster was the failure of the landing device (known as Rebecca-Eureka). The ground component of this (Eureka) had been delivered to the Norwegian underground before the operation and was one of the cleverest and best-kept secret schemes of the war. Unfortunately, Eureka failed at the critical moment and the Halifaxes with their cumbersome companions had to find a way through the mountains by normal map-reading. However, the first Halifax passed over the top of the destined dropping zone without at first realizing it, and then turned in order to release the glider on the second run. At that moment the Halifax ran into a snow cloud. It was too extensive and thick for them to climb away from it. Ice formed on the wings and on the tow rope which broke: the glider then crashed on to the mountainside below. Eight men, the lucky ones, were killed at once; five were captured and shot by the Gestapo two months later; four were injured but were then poisoned in hospital by doctors acting under Gestapo orders.

The second glider party managed to crash-land successfully but the towing aircraft then failed to clear the mountains ahead of it. All the crew were killed. Of the glider party, three were killed on impact and the others were captured and shot.

Although a disaster, the raid at least demonstrated that such raids at a 400-mile range could work if they had anything like normal good luck. The cause of the failure of 'Freshman' was clearly traceable to Eureka. The raid seems to have lulled the Germans into a sense of false security that the plant was invulnerable to successful enemy attack. Their mistake was shown when a party of nine Norwegian saboteurs destroyed much of it on the night of 28 February 1943. The Germans then spent the next five months repairing it and getting it ready for use. Hardly had they done so when an American daylight bomber raid put its hydro-electric plant out of action. Unfortunately the heavy-water plant was now too heavily protected by concrete to be damaged, although the loss of electric power was a set-back.

The sabotage and the later raids convinced the Germans that the vital but apparently vulnerable heavy water should be transported to Germany as soon as possible. That information came to the knowledge of the Norwegian resistance through some of the plant's engineers and as the heavy water was being ferried across Lake Tinnsjoe the ferry was sunk by saboteurs. The loss of this vital material effectively checked German attempts to experiment further in making the bomb.

For those who have subsequently claimed that the efforts of resistance groups had little effect on the eventual outcome of the war, the Lake Tinnsjoe operation is sufficient answer. Undoubtedly, all the raids contributed to the German loss of confidence in the safety of the Vemork plant and caused them to undertake such a risky operation as transporting heavy water from one country to another.

While these raids were being planned and executed, the main airborne forces were developing steadily and speedily. Although their operations were, of course, shrouded in secrecy, parachutists now had a distinctive emblem: Bellerophon mounted on the winged horse Pegasus. This had been designed for them by Edward Seago, at that time a camouflage officer in Southern Command, but later a famous painter. He was a friend of Field Marshal Sir Claude Auchinleck, who was a painter well above the average.

Towards the end of 1942 the British 8th Army was steadily pushing the German Afrika Korps back towards Tunisia. Nevertheless, the war in Africa was by no means over, and unless it was finished off within a few months could prevent a drive into Europe through Sicily and Italy. In order to hurry the conclusion of hostilities in Africa, and also to give some practice in landing on unfriendly coasts, the 1st Army landed some 500 miles to the east of Bizerta and Tunis. The landing took the Germans by surprise and they were unable to concentrate their counter-attack effectively because the 3rd Parachute Battalion seized the airfield at Bone (between Algiers and Tunis). The Germans, who had planned to capture the airfield themselves from the Vichy French, were on the point of doing so when they discovered they had been forestalled.

Meanwhile the 1st Battalion of the Parachute Regiment occupied the road junction at Beja, ninety miles from Tunis. The 2nd Battalion was allotted Depienne, with instructions to move to the nearby airfield at Oudna and to destroy any German aircraft they found on it. In the event they found none, for the Germans had already abandoned the airfield. 2 Para should then have been relieved by the 1st Army's ground troops, but the 1st Army had been checked and 2 Para found themselves fifty miles behind the German lines and surrounded by Germans who had every intention of making their life uncomfortable. The battalion was commanded by Lt-Col. John Frost. An airborne force such as this is not equipped for sustained ground fighting, but with determination they managed to fight back to their own lines. They lost sixteen officers and 250 parachutists before linking up. As the Allies were heavily outnumbered, the Paras had to abandon their airborne role and take part in normal infantry operations. However, they acquitted themselves extremely well. It was here that the Germans started to refer to the Paras as the 'Red Devils' (*Rote Teufel*) from the colour of their berets and the ferocity of their fighting. The Paras have been happy to keep the title. It will be recalled that in World War I the kilted Seaforth Highlanders were christened by the Germans the 'Ladies from Hell' and were equally proud of the nickname.

The next battlefield was Sicily. Looking at a map today, the sequence seems so predictable that it is hard to believe it could have been a secret. But the landing in Sicily was by no means the only option open to the Allies, and an elaborate deception plan was mounted in order to persuade the Germans to think that it was unlikely. World War II was a war of brains, deception, cunning and subterfuge. Combined with secrecy over the operations themselves there was usually a skilful plan aimed at misleading the enemy about the attackers' intentions. Several years before the war began, the Germans had made a careful study of the countries which they planned to conquer. In Norway, for example, healthy-looking young men had taken adventurous holidays, exploring rivers, climbing mountains, sailing boats in harbours, noting people who might be friendly and assessing the places where resistance to German penetration would be most likely. In 1940 this reconnaissance paid handsome dividends. Likewise in France, Holland and Belgium, all the military key points had been carefully studied. The whole of the 1940 invasion was a huge Abwehr deception plan: an attack came where it was least expected – through the Ardennes – and the methods were a surprise to the Allies because they combined close air support with deep tank probes. Fifth columnists (usually German saboteurs posing as nationals of the countries under attack) did much damage, although it was claimed later they did much less than was supposed at the time. And even though the Allies were able to read many German orders and instructions through code-breaking, by the time they learnt German intentions it was too late for the British and French armies to take preventive action against the next onslaught.

Not surprisingly, the Allies, having learnt a lesson in a very hard way did not forget it. Moves which before the war might scarcely have seemed worth dissimulation now became cloaked in secrecy and were usually linked to other deception plans. There was a small, highly secret committee in London, of which Dennis Wheatley, the thriller-writer, was a member, which specialized in concocting ingenious and plausible schemes to mislead the enemy. Their work varied between inventing suitable code-words to arranging for sizeable expeditionary forces to be assembled for projects which would never be implemented. The committee did not always get its own way over the code-words. 'Torch' was the code name for the North African landings and 'Husky' for the invasion of Sicily, and it would have been a remarkable Abwehr officer who could have made much of those. On the other hand, the adoption of 'Neptune' for the sea-crossing on D-Day, and 'Overlord' for the actual landing, seem astonishingly transparent. Fortunately, all the German spies in Great Britain had either been interned or 'turned' to work for the Allies, and the Germans were so completely deceived about D-Day that the Neptune–Overlord code was not penetrated. The explanation for the choice of Neptune and Overlord was that many high-ranking officers liked the code-word for an operation to have a connotation which would make it easily memorable. Yet for security reasons the ideal code-word was one which lacked meaning in any military or naval context. Thus for an incendiary raid words like 'Fireball' or 'Hot Stuff' would be dangerous: better words would be 'Teacup' or 'Tennis Net'.

Whenever a code-word was chosen it was carefully examined for weaknesses. Was it an anagram of a word which might be linked with the aim? Thus an operation concerning Oslo must not be called 'Solo'. As the war dragged on year after year the supply of suitable words was gradually used up; each branch of the services used thousands and for obvious reasons code-words could not be used twice. The loss of code-books would mean that a whole new family of code-words would have to come into use.

During May 1944 the *Daily Telegraph* crossword included the words 'Utah', 'Omaha', 'Overlord' and 'Mulberry', all vital code-words for parts of the forthcoming invasion of France. On 1 June 'Neptune' appeared. Not surprisingly MI5, as the counter-espionage organization, took a keen interest in this coincidence but eventually decided that it *was* in fact pure coincidence. In 1984 the appearance of the words seemed a little less coincidental. The crosswords had been composed by a schoolmaster who, it is said, used to invite some of his pupils to write words into the pattern to which he would later attach clues. One of those schoolboys was very friendly with American soldiers who were in camp nearby in preparation for D-Day, and according to him the Americans referred to code-words often in their conversation. When jotting down words for the crossword puzzles, the words he had recently heard were buzzing in his mind, and were written down, doubtless without any thought of their significance even if he, in fact, guessed it. The 'boy' recalls the occasion clearly. The crossword compiler is now dead, but in 1944 it seems that he had no idea why such a selection of significant words had appeared in successive puzzles.

The 'Torch' deception had included false trails about landings in the Azores, Malta and even on the coast of southern France. At the same time a constant rumour about an invasion of southern Norway was being floated around. In the event the Germans had no inkling of the 'Torch' landings and had no submarines or aircraft in position to play havoc with the invaders.

'Husky', the Sicily invasion, was a particularly difficult operation to disguise, for originally it involved three separate groups. One group came from Egypt, another from Malta and Tunisia, and a third was made up of troops drawn from Algeria and Britain. All three forces were to be equipped for an assault, so there was no possibility of passing them off as ordinary reinforcements. Three separate sets of deception plans were concocted. The British force was to be issued with English–French phrasebooks, supplied with French currency, and shown models of the coast near Biscay. The other groups, being already in the area, needed less elaborate plans and in their case rumours were carefully spread with the confident expectation that they would be picked up by enemy agents. But there was, in addition, a master deception, code-named 'Mincemeat'. This was the episode of 'the man who never was' of which a full account is given on page 151.

In spite of successful deception the landings on Sicily, when they occurred, were by no means easy. 1st Parachute Brigade had won its spurs by this time, not only in the air but also on the ground. They had suffered 1,700 casualties but had made the enemy pay for them three times over. For Sicily, they were joined to 2nd and 4th Parachute Brigade to form, with the 1st Air Landing Brigade, the 1st Airborne Division.

Air Landing Brigade was given the task of capturing the harbour of Syracuse. Two thousand men in Horsa and Hadrian gliders were towed by Dakotas from 51 US Wing, but unfortunately the American pilots were inexperienced in this form of operation. The weather was bad, the aircraft were fired upon from both sides as they approached their target, some were shot down and in consequence many of the gliders were cast off prematurely. However, it would be unfair to place the entire blame on the aircrews, or even on the original instructions. The villain, not for the first or the last time, was the gale-force wind. But in spite of the mishaps, many of the Air Landing Brigade managed to struggle ashore. A section did succeed in capturing the vital Ponte Grande bridge at the entrance to Syracuse. It was reinforced by another section and a combined total of eighty-seven men began holding the position against attacks by an Italian infantry battalion numbering some 800. Eleven hours later, with only fifteen men left, the brigade was overrun, but by this time had removed the demolition charges and made the bridge available for Allied use when further forces appeared.

This was only one of several airborne operations. The remainder of the British 1st Airborne and the US 82nd Airborne also played a significant part in supporting the ground troops. There were, sad to say, further disasters. 82nd Airborne left Tunisia in 144 aircraft to drop in the forward zone near Gela. The American ground units there had been attacked during the day by German bombers but, in view of the impending drop, the anti-aircraft teams had been instructed not to fire on any aeroplanes which passed overhead later. In spite of this warning, one did; others followed, twenty-three aircraft were shot down, many were damaged, and 229 of the 2,000 parachutists involved lost their lives. However, after this traumatic setback Col. (later General) Jim Gavin rallied the survivors and used them to great effect as infantry when the Germans began counter-attacking.

This is, of course, only a sample of the Allied airborne attacks on Sicily, which were a mixture of disaster and success. Much was learnt from the operation, not least the fact that even when gliders fall into the sea or land in the wrong place, or when parachutists come down miles from their objective, all is by no means lost if the survivors keep calm and resolute and exercise initiative. This was notably demonstrated by Col. Jim Gavin, when he rallied the 504th Battalion with its numbers much reduced and used them to extend the American beachhead. Colonel Gavin was giving a foretaste of the cool determination he would show in supporting the Arnhem operation later, by which time he was commanding the 82nd Division.

The fighting in Sicily ended on 17 August 1943 and on 3 September the Allies began their campaign in Italy. It was hoped that this would be merely a bloodless occupation, for it was known that the Italian leaders wished to make peace. The Germans, however, saw things differently and made sure the Allies would pay dearly for any Italian territory they overran. In the long, slogging campaign which followed, which lasted until May 1945, the parachute regiments found themselves fighting as infantry. They did not, of course, find this particularly disconcerting as every parachutist knows that his ultimate role is ground fighting; he differs from normal infantry in his preferred form of arrival and has learnt specialist skills for that purpose. Nevertheless, when there is no opportunity for parachutists to be employed in their specialist role they fight extremely effectively as normal infantry.

There were, however, certain occasions when airborne attacks were used to great advantage. Sixty men from 6 Para were dropped near Torricella. A number of dummies were dropped with them to confuse the enemy. In view of the inaccuracy of some of the earlier drops, it should be mentioned that British parachutists were dropped by US aircraft with meticulous accuracy in countryside which made precise drops extremely difficult. The aim, which was to prevent the Germans demolishing bridges vital to the Allied advance, was entirely successful.

On the other side of the coin, the Germans brought off a remarkable coup by rescuing Mussolini, who was being held captive in what was thought to be an inaccessible strongpoint in the Gran Sasso mountains. It was certainly virtually impregnable from the ground. However, Otto 'Scarface' Skorzeny was a remarkable German Airborne leader whose tactical appreciations were more akin to SAS thinking than normal German procedures. The place where the deposed Italian leader was imprisoned was a ski hotel situated on a narrow ledge in a veritable eagle's nest. The only approach was by a funicular, both ends of which were guarded by top-quality Carabinieri. A land approach was impossible and descent by parachute or glider extremely dangerous. Nevertheless, a glider attack was thought to be just feasible and accordingly one team landed at the foot of the funicular and overpowered the guards, while the other landed near the hotel. This, though difficult, was not the most hazardous part of the operation: that was still to come. A Fieseler-Storch landed on a makeshift airstrip near the hotel, Mussolini and Skorzeny went on board, and the machine prepared to take off. The shortness of the airstrip required special tactics so German soldiers held on to the aircraft's wings until the engines were fully revved up, then let go. Even then the plane was too overloaded to become airborne and merely spun off the edge into the valley below. Fortunately for its occupants, it then gathered speed as it dived, and was airworthy until it arrived at Rome. One of its wheels had been damaged in its hazardous take-off and the pilot had to make a two-point landing on the Rome airfield.

By now, experience of parachute operations had presented the commanders on both sides with an interesting equation. Did the results justify the coordination problems and the costs? In theory an airborne unit could be kept well behind the lines, then appear at the critical moment, seizing key points and damaging the enemy's communications. This was excellent when it happened but there were a number of variables. Bad weather could blow the parachutists or gliders miles away from their intended objectives, the numbers available might be too few to overcome strong ground opposition, and attempts by ground forces to link up with airborne troops might prove so difficult and lengthy that other tactical plans were disrupted. And, of course, there was always a potential element of jealousy among other troops that the special airborne forces were not doing all that they could to win the war. It was all very well, argued some, to walk around in red berets and then join in for spectacular and glamorous events, but was not the cost of the war really borne by the footslogger who was in the danger zone, always within range of the enemy's guns and aircraft, but not issued with the latest weapons and equipment as the airborne were? The Paras themselves were not blamed for leading such a gilded existence, for as soldiers they were second to none when used in ground fighting; it was the policy-makers and commanders who were the target for criticism.

The invasion of France on 6 June 1944 provided a mixture of success and failure for the airborne units. Each flank of the invasion force was protected by a massive airborne drop during the hours before dawn. The left flank was the province of the 6th Airborne Division under the command of Maj.-Gen. Richard Gale. 6th Airborne was required to be in position around Ranville to block any German counter-attack on troops emerging from the beaches. Meanwhile, a glider-borne force of company strength (100) came down just after midnight and in a brilliant attack secured the bridges over the Caen canal and the Orne river which the Germans had wired for demolition, but which the Allies knew were essential for their link-up. Also on that same night a battalion of paratroops set off to capture the Merville battery. The latter was a strongly-defended gun emplacement, so positioned that its guns could rake the beaches where the Allied forces were planning to land.

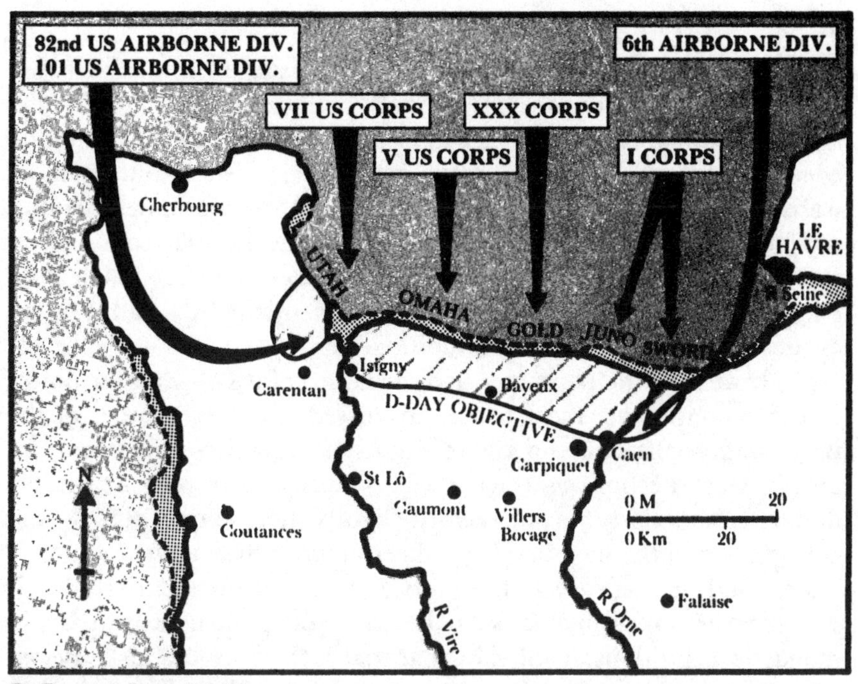

D-Day, 6 June 1944

As is well known, the weather on D-Day was distinctly unpleasant, so much so that the Germans thought an Allied landing was impossible. Gale-force winds make life unpleasant for those on the sea but are seldom disastrous: in the air, for flimsy gliders and for parachutists, they are potential killers. Of the 750 parachutists dropped to capture the Merville battery only 150 successfully arrived in the target area before the assault. The rest of the battalion had been scattered by the high winds, some in fact landing as far as thirty miles away. However, the commanding officer, Lt-Col. Terence Otway, was one of those to arrive on the target zone; he gave the order to attack immediately, in spite of the fact that his force was outnumbered and was assaulting a fortified position. Their enterprise and courage were rewarded in that they succeeded in entering the battery and spiking the guns. The cost in casualties was considerable: by the end their numbers were down to sixty-five.

Perhaps the most remarkable feature of the assault on the Merville battery was the manner in which the planned attack and all its preparations were kept secret. Forty-five acres of farming land in the Vale of Inkpen, four miles to the south west of Newbury, were rented for the preliminary training and rehearsals. Compensation for lost crops was paid out to farmers on a generous scale. In a remarkably short time (seven days), Otway had bulldozers transforming the landscape and making it an exact replica of the countryside round the Merville battery. A replica of the battery itself was built, defences were constructed, barbed wire was laid, and pseudo-minefields laid out, marked 'Achtung Minen!' The local villagers displayed a slightly resentful curiosity at all these preparations but when the whole area became a tight security zone and Otway mentioned that all training exercises would use live ammunition, they gave it a wide berth. Nobody outside the perimeter had the faintest idea of what the object of the exercise was; most people dismissed it as yet another of the increasingly fantastic and rigorous military exercises which country people were becoming accustomed to seeing. The only detectable difference was that this one seemed slightly more extraordinary than the others and the commanding officer madder than most.

Although it was easy to keep intruders out of the security area, it was clearly impossible to keep healthy young men cooped up in monastic conditions, endlessly rehearsing their future task. Before being allowed leave to go to the bars and dance-halls of Newbury they were carefully cautioned about the necessity for absolute secrecy. Not even a hint of the fact that they had a special mission must be dropped: this was merely general training of an exceptionally rigorous type.

Even so, there was no knowing what careless remark might fall from the lips of a parachutist when full of beer and good will or trying to impress a girl in a highly competitive field. As an insurance, Otway borrowed twenty-two pretty young girls from the Women's Auxiliary Air Force and allotted each a territory in Newbury which the Paras would use. They were all wearing civilian clothes and were even given virtually unobtainable silk stockings and scent to make them more alluring. They got on very well indeed with Otway's men, who were quite unaware that these young lovelies were only waiting for the slightest hint of a breach of security and the news would be with Otway within minutes; doubtless the offender would have been a close second. But not a single leak was ever detected, in spite of 'innocent' questioning designed to provoke one. After the final exercise, when they were deemed ready for their purpose, the parachutists were given a forty-eight-hour leave pass. (In the army it used to be said that 'a forty-eight' gave you just sufficient time to get home before it was time to start back: for people living a long distance from their camps and thus subject to wartime delays such as air raids, this was sadly true.)

On this leave there were security police with sharp ears mingling with the Paras on the troop trains, and in the pubs they were likely to frequent. The lengths to which security went in wartime may seem surprising, but it was based upon the slogan which was on hoardings all over the country: 'Careless talk costs lives.'

While 6th Airborne was dropping on to the left flank on 5/6 June, a much larger American airborne force was coming in on the right of the beachhead. Their two airborne divisions (82nd and 101st) produced a total of 12,000 parachutists. Their purpose was to hold off any German counter-attack and leave the way clear for the seaborne troops to move up the Cotentin peninsula and capture Cherbourg. The combination of cloud, gusty wind and anti-aircraft fire played havoc with accurate navigation. Most of the fields were already flooded, but the water on them had been increased when the Germans closed the sluice-gates on the river Merderet; these were never closed except in periods of serious drought, so when the countryside was already waterlogged, it had the effect of transforming swamps into lakes, and isolating whole villages. Although by June the area had been flooded for months, it was not easily detectable from the air and much of the swampland looked like ordinary green fields. When the parachutists came down in the dark, heavily weighed down with equipment, many of them fell on their faces in a few feet of water and mud and were unable to get on to their feet in the treacherous slime. Even those who came down on firmer ground were unable to link up easily, or even discover exactly where they were, for Normandy is characterized by *bocage* – high hedges growing from banks of earth, thus reducing visibility to a distance of a few yards. Nevertheless, the Americans recovered remarkably well, and captured the towns of St Mère Eglise and Pouppeville. One group managed to ambush the commander of the German 91st Division, thereby disrupting the plan to launch a counter-attack on Utah beach. An interesting feature of this drop was that the Germans, unaware that weather and other conditions had caused most of the parachutists to land away from their objectives, were completely baffled by what seemed to them to be an extremely subtle plan. They lost much time in trying to find out what the tactical plan could be.

The D-Day landing was not the only airborne employment in France. On 15 August, just over two months later, the 1st Airborne Task Force dropped in the south of France in order to assist an invasion by ground forces up the Rhone valley. They planned to come up behind the Germans who were battling doggedly on in Normandy.

This move, it was hoped, would enable the Allied armies in the north to break through the German defences and drive towards Germany.

1st Airborne Task Force numbered 9,732 men and had a total of over 1,000 aircraft (transporters, gliders and tugs) to deliver them. There were five US parachute battalions, one US Air Landing Brigade and the British 2nd Independent Parachute Brigade Group in the party. The drop had mixed fortunes, some men landing on target, some twenty miles away. 509th US Parachute Infantry Regiment had the interesting experience of being dropped within three miles of St Tropez, at that time less notable for topless beauties than strong German defences against an expected seaborne assault. The Germans quickly adapted themselves to the unexpected attack from the air, but the Americans came in with such vigour that the German defences were overrun before the seaborne assault came into view. It was a magnificent achievement but not one which could be relied upon to succeed on other occasions. Overall the opposition was light and the airborne forces had little difficulty in occupying essential roads before linking up with the seaborne forces.

The last but one airborne operation in Europe (the last was the Rhine crossing) was at Arnhem and should have been a brilliant success instead of the humiliating disaster it became. The Allies had broken clear of Normandy and, in the north, 30 Corps, commanded by Lieutenant-General Horrocks, had made an astonishing thrust through which it had taken Brussels and Antwerp. It seemed that, if it could now push on even faster and capture the key bridges in Holland, the Siegfried Line could be outflanked and the way to Berlin be opened up. The vital bridges were at Grave over the Maas, over the Maas-Waal canal, over the Waal at Nijmegen, and at Arnhem over the Rhine. While the armies surged forward in the north, and the Americans were making equally good progress in the south, there was a huge airborne force, known as 1st Allied Airborne Army, waiting in England, and urgently wishing to be involved. It included 1st Airborne, the Polish Brigade, the two United States Divisions, 82nd and 101st, and the 52nd Lowland Division, as well as ancillary troops. Command was given to Lieutenant-General F. A. M. 'Boy' Browning, although in fact he was probably the least experienced of the divisional commanders involved.

In retrospect it seems that the plan, code-named 'Market Garden', was over-ambitious. 'Market' referred to the airborne attack; 'Garden' to the land thrust. Books have been written dissecting the details of the operation, but three main factors seem to have been responsible for the failure which led to the destruction of 1st Airborne and delays in Allied progress which enabled the Germans once more to organize a stubborn defence: the first was that there were too few aircraft available for the whole force to be airlifted on the first day, the second that some of the favoured landing areas were waterlogged and could not be used, and the third that German ground opposition was much greater than had been anticipated. This last fact was largely due to luck. Two Panzer divisions were on their way back through the area for a refit after a mauling in Normandy. Although without some of their heavier equipment, they were, nevertheless, still excellent fighting formations. The Dutch resistance had reported the tanks' presence to the Allies but unfortunately their report had not been believed: it was too improbable.

The two American divisions were more successful. 101st Division seized its bridges and held them. 82nd took Grave and high ground near Nijmegen, but failed to hold the bridge over the Waal. However, before the bridge could be destroyed it was recaptured by the Guards Armoured Division and 504 Parachute (US). Meanwhile, 30 Corps was making heroic efforts to push through to the Arnhem bridge. The heart of the problem was that there was only one road through the flooded dykes and the Germans were stubbornly defending every inch of the way.

'Market Garden' was a partial success, for the passage of the Maas and the Waal had been secured. Only at Arnhem, the most ambitious and perhaps the most important point, did it fail. In the event it proved to be 'A bridge too far' and the cost was over 7,000 members of 1st Airborne either killed or captured; a mere 2,000 got away. But it took its toll on the Germans too, for they lost 3,000 in the fighting.

Parachute regiments (in company with the SAS) were used in the Rhine crossing and in the reoccupation of Norway, where there were still 350,000 German soldiers.

One operation, carried out towards the end of the war, concerned the French Regiment de Chasseurs Parachutistes. The 1st Canadian Army was driving through Holland where there were still strong German forces. The 2nd and 3rd Chasseurs were dropped ahead of the Canadians in fifteen-man parties. Their aim was to prevent the demolition of bridges by removing charges, to make contact with the Dutch resistance, and to capture Steenwijk airfield. Needless to say, the tasks involved fierce fighting with Germans whose aim was to prevent these activities, especially the first and last. Nevertheless, the whole operation was extremely successful and supported the theory that airborne drops are probably most effective when they do not try to link up in large numbers. On this occasion, though by accident rather than design, the parachutists dropped through low cloud. Their arrival was therefore unnoticed, a very different matter from floating down against a clear sky on a moonlight night.

Parachutists were, of course, also used operationally in the Far East. In New Guinea on 5 September 1943, the Australians decided to hasten their advance by an airborne thrust, which, though somewhat of an experiment, proved a great success. Among those participating were a troop of thirty-four Australian field gunners. They had been added to the party a mere week before and had not had time for more than one practice jump. With them were their 25-pdr guns. The total number of parachutists in this drop was 1,700 and the operation took the Japanese so completely by surprise that the Australians were able to capture a useful airstrip at Nadzab and make it usable for transport aircraft. Subsequently, several other landing strips were captured. This operation demonstrated that an enemy could first be disrupted, then defeated, if reinforcements were switched rapidly to assist the attacker where needed.

Meanwhile, the development of airborne forces was proceeding in India. General Slim, commanding the British Army in Burma, was quick to appreciate the possibilities of this arm, but was delayed by the shortage of aircraft for delivery. At that time, there were hopes that effective assistance in defeating the Japanese would come from General Chiang Kai-shek. General Stilwell ('Vinegar Joe', as he was not surprisingly called) had been given command of several Chinese divisions, and the need to supply his forces involved a difficult airlift over 'the hump' – the mountain wall which separates China from Burma. (More of this in the next chapter.)

At this moment there came on the scene, with all the force, suddenness and even appearance of an Old Testament prophet, Major General Orde Wingate. He believed fervently that the most effective form of warfare was to drive a deep wedge into and behind the enemy lines. His critics were not slow to point out that, although forces operating behind the enemy lines can do great damage, the effort of training, supplying and eventually evacuating them is not always balanced by the results they achieve.

Wingate's 77th Infantry Brigade was split up into seven columns of 400 men each, with 100 mules per column. The men were a mixture of British, Gurkha and Chinese soldiers and became known as Chindits. A Chindit (or Chinthé) is a model of a lion, based more on mythology than natural history, which the Burmese put outside some of their pagodas as a spiritual guardian. There was little spiritual about Wingate's Chindits. His first expedition in the spring of 1943 achieved results at high cost. Thirty per cent of the force became casualties and had to be abandoned: abandonment in a Japanese-populated jungle meant certain death. Many of those who returned were so disabled by disease and exposure that they were useless for further service. These points were glossed over by Wingate and his supporters, who emphasized the fact that the expedition had demonstrated that the Japanese could easily be beaten in the jungle if will and imagination were present, and that even more could be achieved if adequate air support was provided for future expeditions. Wingate's enterprise and vision excited the admiration of Mountbatten and of Churchill, who was looking for bright, inventive, courageous characters who could bring the war to a rapid and successful end.

In consequence a second raid was sanctioned, this time on an even larger scale, i.e. six brigades – about 20,000 men. An essential item was an adequate supply of light aircraft which could land in jungle clearings and evacuate the wounded: men must not be left to die. General Arnold of the United States Air Force agreed to organize the air component. This led to the establishment of No. 1 Air Commando commanded by Col. Philip Cochran. It included in its 300 assorted aircraft P.51A Mustang fighters, various transports, and 100 Waco gliders. The Mustangs were, of course, one of the great success stories of the war and had overcome the German air force in Europe.

The combined unit, still known as 'The Special Force', consisted of 77th Brigade, now commanded by Brig. Mike Calvert, which was made up of three British and one Gurkha battalions; four other British brigades, of which the commanders were Brigadiers Brodie, Fergusson, Perowne and Lentaigne; and a West African brigade. All the commanders were about to become legendary figures. 'Mad Mike' Calvert, as he was not unflatteringly called, was stupendously brave and resourceful. After adventures with the Chindits he went to the SAS where his training methods are still recalled – and admired. (It is not unusual for unorthodox and daring wartime commanders to be labelled 'mad' by their critics. General Wolfe, conqueror of Quebec, and thus Canada, is a case in point. A contemporary said: 'General Wolfe is mad.' George III retorted: 'Mad is he: I wish he would bite some of my other generals.') There were supporting units, such as Burma Rifles Reconnaissance Force. There was also an American regiment which had been specially trained for deep penetration raiding, but Stilwell had his eye on it, claimed it and acquired it. Under his command it became known as 'Merrill's Marauders'. (More of them in Chapter 4.)

The Japanese had also planned an offensive in Burma in 1944, and when their plans became known to the Allies, General Slim decided to fight a defensive battle in which the Japanese army, at the end of a long line of communications, would be fought to exhaustion and destroyed. As the battle of attrition, which seemed likely to be in the Kohima-Imphal area, would see the heaviest and most important fighting, the other Allied plans were modified accordingly. However, the drive into the Arakan was preserved, and approval was given for Wingate's plans to interfere with Japanese communications in central Burma.

Wingate was not an easy person to work with, as he was inclined to make demands which others felt were unrealistic or impracticable, often both. However, he had an uncanny gift for timing which seemed to be based on instinct rather than intelligence summaries. One of his aims now was to cut the railway line between Myitkyina and Mandalay. His operations were, of course, much more than guerrilla harassments: they introduced the concept of establishing strongpoints, sited initially on jungle clearings, which quickly expanded into well-fortified bases complete with airstrips and a garrison. Their occupants were brought in by glider with their equipment, and from then on were supplied by air. The three best known of these bases were code-named 'Broadway', 'Piccadilly', and 'Chowringhee'.

Before this operation began the Air Commando conducted an extraordinary exercise. The P.51 Mustangs took off trailing heavy hooks; whenever they spotted telephone lines they flew over them and tore them up. One pilot lost his hook but, undeterred, flew his machine through the wires.

However, just before the expedition started out, aerial reconnaissance established the fact that the clearing 'Piccadilly' was unusable: the Japanese had liberally sown it with tree trunks. The first landings were then diverted to 'Broadway'. Here there were problems too, but they were of landing too late, too short, or too fast, and not due to

Japanese interference. Within a day, 'Broadway' was cleared up and made operational. 'Chowringhee' then benefited from the lessons learnt at 'Broadway'. 'Chowringhee' was further south than the other two and Wingate assumed that the Japanese would be quick to attack it, once its presence was known. Therefore, after making use of the base for three days, Wingate ordered that it should be abandoned and all equipment flown over to 'Broadway'. Wingate's intuition proved sound: the Japanese attacked 'Chowringhee' two hours after the British had left.

The next operation was to cut the Japanese communications between Indaw and Myitkyina. This was accomplished in an extraordinary battle organized by Brig. Mike Calvert. He took a battalion of 77th Brigade to a point on the Japanese line of communications near Henu. The ensuing encounter was apparently more like feudal times than modern warfare, for both sides were happy to come to close quarters and fight it out with sword and bayonet. Calvert's men won this spirited battle and set up a new strongpoint, named 'White City', which took its name from the supply parachutes hung up on the surrounding trees. There was already a strongpoint to the south west, code-named 'Aberdeen', which had been established on 22 March.

Wingate was killed on 25 March and Brigadier Lentaigne appointed to succeed him. Lentaigne inherited a complicated situation, with his troops heavily occupied in several different areas. He was fully equal to his military task: what he found less to his liking was trying to cooperate with Stilwell, who was constantly demanding more than was possible and was ungrateful for the superhuman efforts which were made to meet his requests. Eventually when the time came to leave, after two months exhausting fighting, enervating climate, and debilitating diseases, the special force was pulled out. By then it had materially assisted Stilwell's capture of Myitkyina and in addition had delayed and diverted the equivalent of two Japanese divisions from their main task. Perhaps its most valuable contribution had been its effect on Japanese morale. No army likes to feel that the enemy is busy establishing strongpoints behind it on its line of communications. It likes that fact even less if there is any possibility that it might have to make a tactical retreat. In assessing the value of the Chindit operations, the effect on Japanese morale, already somewhat diminished by the difficulties of maintaining long lines of communication in a hostile environment, should not therefore be overlooked, as it often is.

Chindit operations fall into this chapter because they were closely linked with airborne activities, and included parachute drops, glider landings and air supply. Helicopters were then few in number. Subsequently, of course, the development of helicopters has made this type of operation infinitely easier. Had helicopters been available in sufficient numbers in Burma, they could have saved many lives by prompt evacuation of sick and wounded, and supplemented the remarkable achievements of the American Light Plane Force in this field.

Long after the last shots had been fired, the military analysts were still weighing up the pros and cons of the Chindits. It has been suggested that, if they had operated more closely behind the Japanese forward units when their offensives were in full spate, their effect would have been much greater. But no one has suggested that the special force was an entire waste of resources. In relation to what it achieved it was perhaps an expensive project, but in 1944 bold ventures were needed for political and psychological, as well as purely military ends.

Major R. C. Pringle, Brigade Signal Officer, describes his experience with the advance party of the Chindits:

Chalk Serial 15P was one of two Waco gliders hitched to a Dakota tug plane. 15P on the port side was on the short tow, 14P on the starboard side was on the long tow. Eighty such gliders were lined up in pairs on Lalaghat airstrip in Assam, due to take off on 5 March 1944 with American and British engineers and the advance party of Brig. Mike Calvert's 77 Brigade. Their mission was to land 150 miles behind the Japanese lines in Burma and prepare two airfields ready to receive the Dakota aircraft build-up of Wingate's Special Force of Long Range Penetration Groups, the Chindits, starting with 77 Brigade the following night. The Chindits would then attack the enemy from the rear and disrupt their lines of communication. The original manifest for 15P showed six staff officers of HQ 77 Brigade, one USAAF pilot, eight soldiers and the brigade commander's Rover (a pony named Jean). The senior officer in 15P was Lt-Col. Peter Fleming, explorer and travel writer, brother of Ian (James Bond) Fleming. The next senior was Major R. C. Pringle, the Brigade Signal Officer.

The front of a Waco opens upwards on hinges to accept large or awkward loads, jeeps, guns, etc., when the tail is jacked up on stilts. 15P was rigged with a bamboo stall into which Jean was to be backed and securely lashed. As the pony was protesting, the tail stilts collapsed sideways, twisting the framework of 15P which was then declared unserviceable. The first reserve glider was wheeled out. Fortunately, as it turned out, there was no time to rig a stall in it for the pony.

Since all serviceable gliders were already lined up to go, it followed that any reserves would, in varying degrees, be less than 100 per cent serviceable. The new 15P was faulty in two important respects: the intercom with its tug and with its sister 14P on the long tow did not work, and a wheel above the pilot's head used for trimming the attitude in flight was jammed in such a way as to encourage the glider to fly 'nose-up'.

Some enterprising staff officer had discovered that by removing the safety belts more men could be carried on the bench seats than they were designed to accommodate. This was to prove a mixed blessing: to adjust the trim, when the pilot called 'more men up front' to keep the rising nose down, they could quickly huddle round his shoulders; however, if stopping abruptly on landing, the unsecured men with their equipment and weapons would be flung forward into a disorganized heap.

15P was airborne at 2015 hrs. Shortly after take-off Peter Fleming, riding in the co-pilot's seat, noticed that 14P was no longer present. It had 'cut', leaving its long tow rope snaking dangerously near 15P's starboard wing. Had the pilot of 15P known this, he would certainly have 'cut' also.

At 2115 hrs, after an hour's flight, tug and glider crossed the Chindwin river at 10,000 feet, by the light of the full moon. The glider pilot was flying extremely skilfully and courageously, keeping station with difficulty behind the tail light of the Dakota tug, incommunicado in the turbulent conditions prevailing over the 6,000-feet-high Chin Hills, and adjusting his trim periodically by verbal control of his moveable (human) load. At 2140 hrs, despite the fact that most of the passengers were packed into its front end, the glider started soaring upwards and juddering on its tow rope. The pilot thought it was about to pull the tail off the tug so he hit the release lever to cut free allowing the glider, as he said later, to perform a 'loop and half roll'.

The next sensation was of sudden silence. An eerie hiss of air replaced the din of the two Dakota engines which had been a comforting form of contact with the outside world.

The glider spiralled round, with the moon illuminating what appeared to be unbroken jungle below. 'Hang on!' shouted the pilot. To what? Each man was trying to hang on to his large pack and rifle or sten gun, in the absence of seat belts. The pilot spotted a dried-up river bed and very cleverly landed in it between scattered boulders, on sand into which the glider dug its nose and stopped with a jerk. Unbelted men, loose packs, weapons etc., were thrown forward into a heap at the bottom of which were the pilot and the senior officer in charge. It was extremely lucky that the pony had been left behind, as at this moment its presence in the heap could hardly have failed to cause casualties. Fortunately, although some were dazed and shaken, no one was seriously injured. Without doubt, all members of the party owed their lives to Flying Officer Bruce Williams of No. 1 Air Commando USAAF, whose bravery and expertise in handling his unserviceable glider in flight and on landing was responsible for their survival.

All ranks scrambled out in some confusion and, on the orders of Lt-Col. Fleming, formed a perimeter guard and started a bonfire of cipher, signal and other secret documents. While the glider was illuminated by the fire it was attacked by a low-flying fighter firing a burst of exploding bullets – whether it was friend or foe was never known, but luckily it was harmless.

After this the party left the clearing and set off into the jungle at a brisk pace, heading north west along a little-used path for about three hours to get away from the scene of the crash. This brought them to a hill overlooking a village from which came sounds of activity and loud Japanese voices – it was assumed that news of the landing had been received. Certainly the airborne invasion would have been observed passing overhead earlier. The party moved away towards the south west until the moon set at about 0330 hrs, by which time everyone was quite tired and a halt for the night was called.

The next day (6 March 1944) they lay up in a patch of elephant grass and took stock. Everyone had a weapon of sorts, ammunition was plentiful and the party had as much food in 'K' ration packs as could be conveniently carried. Several compasses were available but, incredibly, no maps except 1:1,000,000 'escape' maps of Burma printed on orange silk handkerchiefs.

No one had any precise idea of where they were but it was calculated, from flying time on a line roughly between the take-off airfield and the planned destination, that they were perhaps fifty miles east of the

Chindwin and fifty miles short of their objective. In the event of a forced landing, the orders were to go on if the landing was beyond the Gangaw Range (thirty miles short of the objective) or to march back if landing was short of it. Thus they now had to go back and start again. At least they knew that if they kept going westwards they must eventually reach India.

For the next five days, until 10 March, they marched generally westward through jungle and teak forest, deliberately avoiding paths, villages and clearings, and often following dry stream beds. They saw few signs of life except an occasional woodcutter and, on one occasion, a patrol of fifteen Japanese. The party was glad to have with them the Brigade Medical Officer, Major Faulkner, who had been on the first Wingate expedition; he was able to reassure the other as yet unblooded warriors that, contrary to their nervous conviction that they were, in the words of Wingate, 'a dagger inserted in the guts of the enemy', it was most unlikely that a Japanese soldier would be lurking behind every bush and a sniper up every tree.

On 9 March they were lucky to strike a valley which in the monsoon carried a tributary westwards to join the Chindwin. Occasionally the valley opened up and they could see the tops of mountains which had to be on the west bank of the Chindwin.

At 9 P.M. on 10 March they arrived on an escarpment overlooking the east bank of the Chindwin. In the moonlight they could see a well-used track, which it was assumed would be patrolled, running parallel to the river between them and the sandy shore. They discovered later that they had arrived on the Chindwin some fifty miles east of Imphal, midway between Homalin and Thaungdut, where in a few days' time a division of the Japanese 15th Army was to cross in strength to attack IV British Corps at Imphal and Kohima.

The Chindwin here was slow moving and about 650 yards wide. The east side, lined by fifty yards of sandy beach, was shallow enough to be waded for the first 150 yards. After that, 500 yards had to be swum to reach the west bank, which was steep and jungle-covered.

On 11 March, a quick reconnaissance revealed there were no boats readily available for 'borrowing'. As the party was going to be uncomfortably conspicuous for too long anyway on the wide beach and in the shallows, they did not range far up or down the river looking for boats. The doctor was appointed chief shipwright, and under cover of the jungle a craft of sorts was constructed of bamboo and ground sheets. At dusk it was taken to the shallows and loaded with packs and weapons. After a while it was realized that the craft had been aground for some time. It was pushed to deeper water, where it just floated with hardly any freeboard. It proved so unstable that water was too easily shipped in over the side and it promptly sank.

Major Pringle, who in happier days had been captain of swimming at the Royal Military Academy, Woolwich, and who had built canoes as a boy, took over the boat-building. He recollected Archimedes and reckoned that by lashing in the contents and turning the craft upside down, sufficient air would be trapped to enable it to float like an upturned boat unless rocked violently to let the air out. This theory worked. Five non-swimmers wearing Mae Wests launched the craft upside down through the shallows with orders to hang on to the sides and kick their legs, while Major Pringle steered the vessel slowly through the remaining 500 yards of deep water to the west bank. One signalman left the security of the raft and swam ahead supported only by his Mae West. He was heard choking in the darkness and was never seen again. Only a limited search was possible without abandoning and losing sight of the raft and the four remaining non-swimmers.

Luckily, the lengthy activities on the water's edge and the slow crossing had not attracted any enemy attention. However, on returning to the east bank with the Mae Wests and ground sheets to enable a second batch to cross, Major Pringle found the beach deserted. The rear party, who could all swim if not heavily laden, had crossed in the dark leaving most of their kit on the beach. Major Pringle then made up another float of packs and assorted weapons and swam it to the west bank. By now it was after midnight and all concerned were very cold and wet, so the party sat round a large camp fire to get warm and dry out – Col. Fleming having decided the successful crossing by all except one soldier outweighed the risk of being surprised by an enemy patrol.

Next day Major Pringle with another officer volunteered to cross again to retrieve more kit, especially boots, which had been left behind by the poorer swimmers. These officers returned with another assortment of kit at about 0900 hrs on 12 March. (For his efforts in swimming the Chindwin five times, on three occasions transporting arms and equipment, Major Pringle was later awarded a Mention in Despatches.)

The whole party set off at 1030 hrs going north along the west bank of the Chindwin, looking for the first opportunity to strike westwards towards India through the jungle-clad steep hills lining the river. After a mile or so they came across an observation post manned by the Frontier Force Regiment who directed them back (southwards). After two hours they met a British patrol and were conducted to, and made welcome by, Battalion HQ 1 Seaforths for the night of 12 March.

On 13 March, the party marched twelve miles over a pass in the Naga Hills to roadhead, thence by truck to Tamu. The following day a Dakota flew them to Imphal, which at that time also contained Advance HQ Special Force and Rear HQ 77 Brigade. After a couple of days' rest another Dakota flew the party (two weeks late) into Burma to their original objective, the landing zone code-named 'Broadway', which by now had been converted into a defended airfield and stronghold 150 miles inside Japanese-held territory. From here a short light aircraft trip delivered them to HQ 77 Brigade, by now established seventy-five miles north of Mandalay with other columns of the Brigade, in a road and railway block code-named 'White City' across the main line of communications to the Japanese 18th Division opposing General Stilwell's American/Chinese forces.

In April 1944, HQ 77 Brigade was located in 'White City', the codename of a stronghold covering an area of some 1000 by 800 yards of jungle-covered high ground containing a variable garrison of columns of up to two battalions' strength. The stronghold was established and supplied by air as a block on the road and railway behind the enemy lines in Burma, about seventy-five miles north of Mandalay and thirty miles south of the northernmost railhead at Myitkyina. This road and railway had been the main supply line to the Japanese 18 Division which was opposing the advance by Gen. Stilwell's forces down the Ledo road towards Myitkyina.

Wireless communication by night with columns patrolling round the block was often unreliable due to electrical storms and jungle screening. To improve matters, Major R. C. Pringle was ordered to find out if the railway signalling system could be used to establish points from which patrols up and down the railway line could report in by telephone to Brigade HQ in 'White City'. Accordingly, an *ad hoc* line detachment was assembled comprising Major Pringle, two wireless operators (volunteers) — Corporals Hargreaves and Halliday, a Gurkha mule driver, and the unit's most docile mule laden with cable and miscellaneous line stores.

The party set off in daylight through a gap in the barbed wire and mined perimeter, and connected a telephone in the command post by field cable to the most useful-looking pair of heavy galvanized iron wires on the nearest standing pole. The overhead route poled alongside the railway line had been largely destroyed by bombing, which felled the poles, or tore down the wire. Parts remained standing or sagging, but most was lying on the ground.

By trial and error, a working circuit of sorts was established by hauling up sagging bays and patching breaks in the overhead wire with lengths of field cable. Periodic ringing back to test the line confirmed a circuit was working, despite the incorporation in it of various lengths of uninsulated open wire lying on the ground.

In a Chindit unit there was normally no provision for line laying, apart from improvisation using line stores specially requested by air supply drop to a HQ stationary long enough to warrant a few simple hand-laid telephone links. There was certainly no sophisticated ratchet tensioning equipment for regulating sagging bays of permanent line, or even ladders for reaching the lowest steps on the poles.

The unfamiliar sight of an isolated British line party at work aroused curiosity and quite soon an audience collected of Burmese from the jungle. It could just as easily have been an audience of Japanese, since clashes were continually occurring in the neighbourhood as the enemy attempted to dislodge the stronghold.

The railway embankment ran across open paddy fields along the edge of the jungle-clad foothills of the Gangaw Range. There was no cover from view and the party half expected to be fired on at any time by an unseen patrol in the trees. Climbing poles and hauling up wires along the side of the railway in the open was uncomfortably exposed and slow work.

After about three miles, on generating a ringing call to test the line on completion of a joint, Corporal Hargreaves was surprised to hear a voice answer in Japanese. Luckily, 'White City' did not answer in English. By some trick of crossed wires or possibly by induction between open wires lying parallel on the ground, a connection which gave rise to clear overhearing had been made to the local Japanese telephone network.

Since there was no merit in continuing to build a party line to be shared with the Japanese, Major Pringle decided there should be no more ringing or talking in English on the 'patrol line' but that, as quickly as the mule would walk, the party would return to base and report.

The Brigade Intelligence Officer was delighted with the situation. It transpired that they had overheard the Japanese using their static civil telephone network, based at Mogaung, to pass routine messages and situation reports. On learning this from Special Force HQ, General Stilwell flew two 'Nisei' (American-born Japanese) into 'White City' to listen on the wiretap using a more sensitive American telephone (type EE8) and act as translators.

For ten days a good deal of important information was derived from the telephone traffic and 'operators' chat' overheard in this way. Eventually, repairing some cables cut by shelling gave the game away. The Japanese probably heard an English voice testing one of their lines, for they went quiet and were never heard again.

It must be one of the more unique feats of military signalling in war for a signal officer to connect his Brigade HQ to the telephone exchange of an enemy in the field.

4: *Ground Attack*

The proper designation of Merrill's Marauders was 5307th Composite Unit (Provisional) United States Army, but it soon suited everyone to call them after their talented and versatile commander, Brig.-Gen. Frank Merrill. The role the Marauders played can best be appreciated by a brief sketch of the events which led to their being employed in the area.

When the Japanese had launched their attacks (before declaring war) in South-East Asia in 1941, they had scored immediate successes, notably at Pearl Harbor, in Hong Kong, in Malaya and in what is now Indonesia. They had pressed on through Burma, and by the end of May 1942 controlled the whole country. By then the British troops had been driven back across the Chindwin river to India, and the Chinese armies back to China. In the first stages of the 900-mile retreat, Lt-Gen. William Slim took over the much battered Burma Corps and made his plans to eject the Japanese from the territories they were overunning. In their victorious advance the Japanese had captured the vital Burma road, through which the Allies had been supplying China. The loss of the Burma road was a great setback to the plans for keeping the Chinese armies adequately supplied and thus able to continue their long campaign against the Japanese. (Hostilities between the two countries had been going on intermittently since 1931.)

The commander of the Chinese troops in Burma was General Joe Stilwell. Stilwell was a veteran of World War I and a number of other campaigns too. He spoke fluent Chinese and was, among many other assignments, assistant to Chiang Kai-shek. He did not care much for his allies, and referred to General Chiang Kai-shek as 'the peanut', and to the British as 'the goddammed limeys'; although his social qualities fell somewhat short of the diplomatic, his courage and endurance were of a high order. In 1942, at the age of sixty, he marched 140 miles through the jungle, all the while trying to rally the troops under his command. With the loss of the Burma road, all supplies to China had to be flown by the difficult and dangerous route known as 'over the Hump'. Stilwell never wavered in his conviction that the principal object of fighting in Burma should be the reopening of the Burma road. This was eventually achieved, and in 1945 the road was officially renamed the 'Stilwell Road'. Stilwell, sad to say, did not live long to enjoy his triumph, for he died in 1946.

A key point in the strategy for reconquering the Burma road was Myitkyina, where there was an airfield used extensively by the Japanese. The airfield was a problem in more ways than one, for it enabled the fighters to threaten any American supply planes which did not fly well to the north and then turn south east. In order to make the best use of the Burma road when it was recaptured, an ancillary road was now begun in the north. In theory this road-building would be screened by advancing Chinese divisions, but when these encountered the Japanese 18th Division, veterans of the Singapore campaign, the advance was halted.

However, Stilwell, in spite of being frustrated by Chiang Kai-shek, galvanized his Chinese troops into action. (It was an astonishing innovation for a foreigner to be commanding Chinese troops.)

When the 5307th appeared in Burma, Stilwell immediately realized that the regiment was exactly what he was looking for, and insisted he had it in his command. He himself appointed Merrill. Merrill had begun his army career as a private soldier at the age of eighteen; in spite of being short-sighted he had subsequently been accepted for officer training at West Point. He also acquired the degree of Bachelor of Science from the Massachusetts Institute of Technology. Even more relevant to the present circumstances was the fact that he had been assistant military attaché in Tokyo, had learnt Japanese, and taken the opportunity to accompany the Japanese army when it was on manoeuvres.

The Marauders had completed hard commando-type training and had been carefully briefed on the techniques of survival in the jungle. They learnt that they would be working closely with the Kachin Rangers. The latter was a secret unit which had been formed in 1942; officially it was Detachment 101 of the Office of Strategic Services (OSS – US equivalent of the SOE). The Kachin Rangers was made up of a number of North Burma hill tribesmen and some accompanying British and American soldiers. They were invaluable for producing intelligence and also operated effectively as guerrillas.

The area in which the Marauders began their operations was unfriendly to man and beast. To the north are the Himalayas, but from the Himalayas there branches (to the south west) another range some 10,000 feet high, known as the Patkai mountains. There are other mountain ranges too: the Kumon (also 10,000 feet) and the Jambu Bum are the largest. The vegetation is a mixture of tall trees (about 100 feet high), bamboo rain forest (a tangle of densely-growing trees and rotting vegetation: broken bamboo is as sharp as a razor and cuts from it invariably fester), and six-feet high Kunai grass, also very sharp. It is hot, humid, muddy, full of insects and often very misty. The most loathed parasite was the leech which seemed capable of penetrating anywhere. Malaria and dysentery were commonplace. The dampness made clothes rot – mould could appear on boots overnight – and weapons rusted unless meticulously cleaned. Most of the towns were no more than villages but Myitkyina housed 8,000 people.

During the heaviest part of the monsoon all tracks would become small or large watercourses, the level of rivers would rise twenty feet almost overnight, and movement would become almost, though not quite, impossible. In such conditions, only the hardest, best-trained, most highly motivated soldiers win their battles. The Marauders were just that.

Their technique here was to appear where least expected, exploit surprise, kill Japanese, and move on. Gradually they probed and squeezed the forward units of the Japanese, forcing the latter to withdraw to tighter, less vulnerable positions. But the Japanese 18th Division was fully deployed and Stilwell decided that it was feasible to cut it off, or at least the advance units. The Kachins were excellent guides and in consequence the Marauders were able to infiltrate and cut off, to force the Japanese on to the defensive and to disrupt their plans for a renewed offensive. One detachment of the Kachins was known as Ma Proph Pum (the Lightning Force) and these were expert at all forms of guerrilla warfare. But not least of the Marauders' assets was the fact that they were regularly supplied by air drops. However, as the Marauders and their Chinese allies came nearer to Myitkyina, the going became very hard indeed. The Japanese were now fully alert to the danger of their position and counter-attacked vigorously as their opponents closed in towards them. The summer of 1944 saw some Japanese pressing desperately forward to capture Imphal and Kohima in the west, which they failed to do, and others engaged in a slogging match with Stilwell's Chinese.

Stilwell's objective was still Myitkyina, even though he was told that if it was captured it would soon have to be given up. In spite of this, he managed to persuade Chiang Kai-shek to give him two more divisions: the fact that Mountbatten gave his support was also a considerable advantage. The Japanese 18th Division had now been reinforced and was at full strength.

The final stages of the attack on Myitkyina have been compared to the battle for Cassino which was another long slogging fight. When the town eventually fell, the general who had held on for three months committed hara-kiri. A number of his men followed his example. By then many Japanese soldiers had been withdrawn from the town to fight elsewhere; only 187 were left at the surrender and most of those were in hospital. Capturing the town had cost the Allies 6,000 casualties. As we saw earlier, the Chindits had been kept in the jungle to assist in the capture of Myitkyina, and this had been in contradiction to normal British practice. Hard-won experience had shown that the effective life of a unit operating in the jungle was three months; if it was not withdrawn and rested after that period it could quickly reach a point at which it could never again be a fully efficient fighting force. The Chindits had stayed a month beyond the time limit, and the results confirmed the diagnosis. Most of the men had lost two or three stones in weight, had had an average of three attacks of malaria, and suffered from various unpleasant forms of skin and intestinal ailments. The Marauders were, if anything, in a worse state. They had performed well, and had many successes, but by the concluding stages of the siege of Myitkyina it was necessary to declare as fit for service any soldier who could walk and fire a gun. Physical deterioration was unfortunately accompanied by a similar drop in morale. In their 'rest-camp', where they were meant to be convalescing, they temporarily restored morale, though nothing else, by drinking large quantities of brandy mixed with marijuana. With the wisdom which comes long after the events, it was decided that two main reasons explained why the Marauders had done so well initially, yet failed to last. The first was that – as with the special force – they had been kept in the jungle too long; the second that they had been misinformed. When they had been embodied and trained, they had been told they would be given a short, strenuous mission and then returned to the United States. In the event, they were given a long mission which was far more strenuous than they or anyone else had anticipated and were kept in the jungle until exhaustion and disease caused them to fall to pieces. However, in bad shape though they were, the Marauders were still in at the finish.

The special forces which served in Burma had good reason to be embittered, although not many were. Not for nothing was Slim's 14th Army known as 'The Forgotten Army'. It fought in a territory which no one in Europe could begin to comprehend and its victories were at places which were unpronounceable and shown on few maps. Special force operations had the additional disadvantage that journalists could not report them – even if they could get near them – until they were over, but those who took part returned to normal life with bodies damaged by disease and often, unknown to the owners, harbouring lethal pests which would manifest themselves later. Doctors who knew anything of tropical medicine were rare in Britain and the United States, and tended to be unsympathetic about vague symptons which they had never encountered. Disablement pensions were often withheld, and illness blamed on other causes. The Americans were much more prescient in recognizing the disabling after-effects of service in the jungle: only some forty years afterwards did the British pension authorities grudgingly admit that the degree of damage to men in the tropics had been underestimated and that victims should have been compensated; by the time that happy note was struck, many of those most deserving of help had already died without receiving it.

This survey of the special forces which were either delivered or supplied by air, has taken us a long way from Europe, to which we must now return. The first special forces raised for secret raiding missions were the Commandos. On 18 June 1940, Churchill wrote a minute that Britain should have 'at least twenty thousand Storm Troops or "Leopards" drawn from existing units, ready to spring at the throats of any small landings or descents. These officers and men should be armed with the latest equipment, Tommy guns, grenades, etc.' In the event, the Commandos were never required to 'spring at the throats' of enemy landing parties, but instead made landings on Axis-held territory.

There were in June 1940 only forty Thompson machine-guns (Tommy guns) in Britain, and no ships at all suitable for raiding. But the brain behind the commando idea was Lt-Col. Dudley Clarke, Military Assistant to Sir John Dill. Sir John Dill was Chief of the Imperial General Staff, a designation which meant that he was the commander of British land forces. The title dates back to the days when the British commander-in-chief also commanded the armies of the British empire. The term became obsolete during World War I, but the word 'Imperial' lingered on till well after World War II.

There was nothing obsolete about Dill, still less about Clarke. Dill was a forceful, imaginative character who was respected far and wide, particularly in America. Clarke was an inventive genius. Both were accustomed to getting things done. The day after Dunkirk ended, Clarke thought that commando-type raiding should be the next step. He explained his thoughts to Dill. Dill took them to Churchill. Churchill gave appropriate instructions. Within four days of Clarke's brainwave, the Commandos were in the planning stage. Churchill's statement came ten days later. The word 'Commando' was taken from the Boer War where the Afrikaners had put a number of highly mobile units in the field under this name, which had given enormous trouble to the 250,000 British and Dominion troops who tried to catch them.

The first two British Commandos, 1 and 2, were drawn from the members of the Independent Companies which had been formed to fight in Norway earlier in the year. (The fact that they had had little success was no fault of theirs.) All were volunteers. However, it was not sufficient merely to wish to be a commando. A man had to be selected from the volunteers and then trained vigorously. There was no room for half measures. Many of the recruits came from Territorial army units, but a good sprinkling were regulars. Among those joining at the beginning were Robert Laycock, John Durnford-Slater, Ronnie Tod and Peter Young. Almost every unit in the British army was represented in the Commandos. Nineteen days after their formation they launched their first raid. It landed near Le Touquet on 23 June 1940, and though not an outstanding success showed that the Commandos were more than a symbol of resistance: they were a dangerous force and would become ever more dangerous in the future. This raid was commanded by Ronnie Tod (then a major), was 120 strong, and bore the misleading title of No. 11 Independent Company. The raiders were carried in RAF Air/Sea Rescue craft. The bows of these ships rode high out of the water and this gave them too high a profile for them to be suitable for raiding.

Accompanying the party was Dudley Clarke himself. He became the first – though not serious – casualty, for a German bullet nearly took off his ear. He therefore acquired the interesting distinction of being not only the man who had 'invented' British Commandos, but also the first casualty to be wounded with them.

The Commandos on this raid had split into two groups: the one which included Dudley Clarke had intended to raid Boulogne harbour but was spotted (by a searchlight), sheered off, and landed further along the coast where it ran into a German patrol. The other went ashore four miles south of Le Touquet and attacked a fortified building. In the process they killed two German sentries. The building was too well fortified for them to capture it with the weapons they were carrying, so they then withdrew. They had made their point: they were in business.

Three weeks later the raid on Guernsey, on a larger scale and more organized, took place. Unfortunately it failed to encounter the enemy or any suitable targets before it withdrew. The only barracks it had reached was unoccupied. The raiders were fired on by the Germans as they left, but no one was hit. The raid produced no material gains, but provided an interesting example of how much can go wrong unexpectedly. In fact, everything which could go wrong seemed to do so on that trip. The weather worsened rapidly, navigation was faulty, communication was erratic, and the islanders they met were too scared to talk (assuming the Commandos were Germans in disguise, setting a trap). But a few disasters in the early stages are an ideal preparation for a special unit which has every intention of profiting from its mistakes.

One result of the Guernsey raid was that Combined Operations (which included Commandos) was put in the charge of Admiral of the Fleet Sir Roger Keyes. Keyes was a fearless and dynamic character who had organized a hazardous raid on Zeebrugge in March 1918. Earlier he had fought with great gallantry at Gallipoli. The next few months were, in the words of Peter Young, 'one long story of hope deferred'. As soon as Keyes had arranged an operation and had the men trained for it, it was cancelled. At one point the capture of the Azores was the objective, then, after that, the next target was Pantellaria, a small island in the Mediterranean.

During late 1940 and early 1941 the Commandos, which had begun with such high hopes, seemed likely to end in disbandment. Churchill pointed out that German victories in France had been achieved not by the mass of the German army but by élite spearheads, but even this did not break down the wall of opposition. Commanders of orthodox regiments hotly denied that commandos could do anything their own men could not do, and administrators in the War Office, regarding these new creations with suspicion, frustrated attempts to get special weapons, equipment and facilities. But on 3 March 1941 the log jam broke, and a party consisting of Nos 3 and 4 Commandos (a total of 500), fifty-two Royal Engineers, and fifty-two Norwegians, set off for the Lofoten islands, off Norway. The raid was commanded by Brigadier Haydon. The troops were conveyed in two infantry landing ships, the *Princess Beatrix* and the *Princess Emma,* and were escorted by five destroyers. The objective was the four ports of Stamsund, Henningsvaer, Svolvaer and Brettesnes, where there were fish processing stations from which the Germans were obtaining fish oil – and thus glycerine. Glycerine was used in the manufacture of explosives, so this was a very worthwhile expedition for that fact alone. The Commandos were encouraged by the Norwegians, who helped them even though they were storing up future trouble for themselves. Three hundred and fifteen Norwegians returned to England with the Commandos, and so, less willingly, did 210 German prisoners and sixty collaborators who had been identified by the Norwegian police. The only opposition was the weather, which was paralysingly cold, and a German armed trawler which tried to make a fight of it with one of the destroyers and ended up in flames. At the end of the day twelve ships had been sunk, eighteen factories demolished, and 800,000 gallons of petrol and oil burnt. But, although Hitler had demanded ruthless measures against Commandos and all who helped them, the Germans, when they returned in force to the ports, limited themselves to burning a few houses.

The greatest achievement of the Lofoten raid, and which made it of the utmost value for the eventual Allied victory, was one which could not be disclosed until over thirty years later. The Commandos brought home some spare Enigma wheels (see Chapter 5). They were of vital importance in the decrypting operation of the German Enigma machine.

The next raid took place in August of the same year. Spitzbergen was an important centre of coal production, and was being fully exploited by the Germans. The raid here was on a large scale and incorporated both Canadian and Norwegian troops. Here again the local people were friendly and helpful, even though they were destroying their own livelihood. Huge stocks of petrol and oil and 450,000 tons of coal were destroyed. Eight hundred Norwegians returned with the raiders.

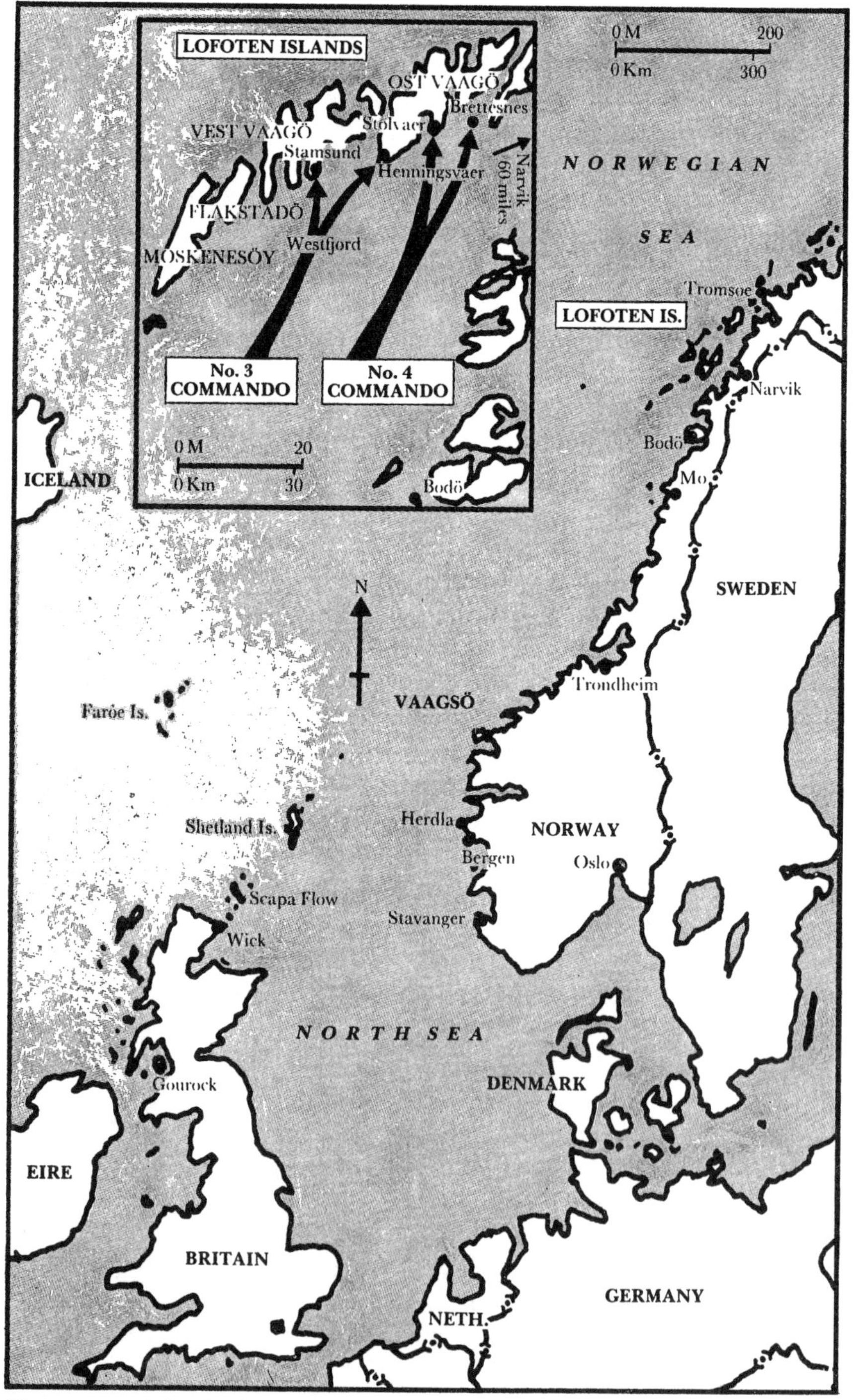

Norway and the Lofoten Islands

Minor raids on the French coast, of no great military significance, followed, giving the Commandos a chance to put training to use. In October 1941 Admiral Keyes was succeeded by Lord Louis Mountbatten. Mountbatten was a younger man, and probably had more influence on the War Office. Keyes was a Member of Parliament and now made the best use he could of his position to help the Commandos.

A more ambitious raid took place at the end of 1941. There was known to be a German garrison at Vaagso in Norway thought to be about 250 strong, well armed, and under the cover of three German airfields. It was thought that if this port could be raided successfully, not only would large quantities of valuable German stores be destroyed but the Germans would overreact and station large garrisons in other Norwegian ports. Those garrisons would never be used, but by being immobilized in these distant spots would be unable to fight in more important areas. The raiding force included a cruiser, four destroyers, two infantry assault ships, a submarine (to assist in navigation), and 576 soldiers. The RAF would provide fighter cover from the German air force if needed and also arrange for appropriate bombing and smoke-laying. The area round Vaagso had been carefully fortified by the Germans, particularly on the islands of Maaloy and Rugsundo.

On the approach the convoy ran into a force-eight gale off the Shetlands. Although this delayed the expedition, it was not a disaster. Their arrival at Vaagso was silent and unexpected: at first the Germans could scarcely believe their eyes. However, they soon recovered and put up a stout fight. Maaloy, considered to be the toughest nut to crack, fell in eight minutes. The leader of the troops of No. 3 Commando, which captured Maaloy, was Maj. Jack Churchill; he gave a demonstration of the courage and style he would display in other raids, which caused his nickname to be 'Mad Jack'. He landed playing 'The March of the Cameron Men' on his bagpipes, but soon abandoned bagpipes for claymore and pistol. Churchill reached the German commander's office and was searching it for useful intelligence information when he was wounded by a demolition charge. His wounds, though painful and incapacitating, were not serious enough to keep him out of action for long. Among others to distinguish themselves on this raid were Peter Young, John Durnford-Slater, Arthur Komrower and Denis O'Flaherty. However, it is only fair to say that on this fast-moving occasion everyone contributed a handsome share and some were killed in the process. In the final stages the Germans were putting up a very tough resistance indeed.

The British warship sank over 15,000 tons of enemy transports, and destroyed shore batteries with shellfire. The Germans were believed to have had some 120 killed and many more wounded; ninety-eight prisoners were taken. Seventy Norwegians took advantage of the presence of British ships to join their own government's army in exile.

But the most valuable effect of the raid was that it confirmed Hitler in his belief that the Allies were about to return to Europe by invading Norway. Although this piece of self-delusion was not shared by his staff, they did not think it would be in their own best interests to oppose it. In consequence, at the time of D-Day in June 1944, the Germans had 372,000 troops in Norway. They included some of the best German infantry divisions. What effect this reservoir of manpower could have had in the Western Desert, on the Eastern front or in Normandy on D-Day, one shudders to contemplate. Hitler's delusion was, of course, sustained by skilfully planted pieces of information and the circulation of rumours. In World War II campaigns and battles were influenced to an astonishing extent by deception and propaganda. In all wars there is an element of deception, even if it only involves catching the enemy by surprise, but the psychological warfare experts of World War II not merely misled the enemy over the time and place of the next attack, they supplied him with so much false information that when that attack occurred many of the troops who should have been there to resist it were wasting their time and energies in garrisoning remote and unimportant places. The Germans wasted thousands of men in Norway and the Greek islands, but it should not be forgotten that the Allies left a large number of troops in the United Kingdom after all danger of a German invasion was past.

In the Mediterranean Robert Laycock's 'Layforce', consisting of 7, 8 and 11 Commandos, was joined by the remnants of 50 and 52 Commandos, which had been raised locally for small-scale raiding. This strong force was then ordered to raid Bardia, a port on the North African coast which was in enemy hands. The raid produced a series of unforeseeable disasters. First, the submarine which had been detailed to act as a beacon to guide in the ships was attacked, regrettably, by Allied aircraft. Secondly, Captain Courtney, founder member of the Special Boat Squadron, who was to show a navigational green light, had his folboat wrecked as he was launching it from the same submarine. By one of those miracles the navy seems able to produce when needed, the boats still got in, though a little late. Once ashore they found targets difficult to locate, although four guns of a shore battery were destroyed and a dump of tyres set on fire. However, as in Norway, the Germans overreacted and, assuming that this raid must be the reconnaissance for a larger landing, took an armoured brigade out of their main dispositions and stationed it at Bardia as a reinforcement. Its presence there was totally unnecessary: so far from capturing Rhodes, Layforce now found itself despatched to help in the defence of Crete. Here, although under intensive bombardment, they could not fail to notice the nonchalant and flippant courage of Evelyn Waugh (previously known for his cynical, witty novels and bon viveur attitudes). But Layforce had little to be cheerful about: out of the original force of 800, 600 became casualties.

Fortunately, No. 11 Commando had not accompanied the rest of Layforce to Crete, but had been sent to Cyprus. It was now available for use in Syria, where the Vichy French commander, General Dentz, had allowed the Italians to establish airbases. The Australian troops who had invaded from the north in order to remedy this state of affairs were held up on the Litani river by determined Vichy French opposition. No. 11 Commando, which included Geoffrey Keyes, son of the admiral, was given the task of assisting the Australians by landing on the Syrian coast and coming inland on the French side of the river. In the event, they misread the coastline and landed on the wrong side, but at the price of 123 casualties enabled the other troops to cross the river.

Apart from raids on enemy-held Tobruk, there was now little for Layforce to do. The navy, desperately hard-pressed with its many tasks in the Mediterranean, could not spare the shipping to transport commandos to raiding targets. Some of Layforce joined David Stirling and became the SAS; most of the remainder returned to their original units. However, one small raiding force was retained and this made the enterprising, though ill-fated, expedition known as 'The Rommel Raid'.

The Rommel Raid was timed for 17/18 November 1941, a date which coincided with the first SAS air drop, which was an almost total disaster, and the beginning of General Auchinleck's offensive to relieve Tobruk. The commandos' objective was no less than the capture of the German commander himself, Rommel, the 'Desert Fox'. It was based on the assumption that he would be in a house at Beda Littoria, a point twenty-five miles inland from the landing point at Hamma. The chances of removing the German general, or even getting away themselves in the aftermath of the battle around his house, seemed extremely slight; it was realized that at best it might result in Rommel's death and the loss of most, if not all, of the raiders.

The progress of the raid showed that this sort of event is conducted more comfortably and successfully in film or television drama than in real life.

The Commandos were carried in two submarines, *Torbay* and *Talisman*. On arrival at the chosen point on the desolate coast they discovered a heavy swell was running; this made embarking from submarine into rubber boats extremely difficult, and the process of launching without being overturned and losing all stores, a matter of luck rather than skill. Those who succeeded in landing in the right spot were soon marching in steady rain over muddy tracks. Their only maps were of Italian origin and were, apparently, far from accurate. The exact sequence of events when they reached the target house has never been clearly established, but it seems that when the commandos entered the building unobserved, they encountered heavier opposition than they had anticipated. Keyes was shot and died immediately. Apparently, he had opened the door of a room full of German soldiers, to roll a grenade in, but a German reacted more quickly than expected and fired accurately. The Rommel Raid was studied very carefully subsequently by the SAS, who also engaged in this type of attack, and they afterwards made sure that none of their men would ever frame himself in a doorway if an alert enemy was expected to be inside. Keyes was awarded a posthumous Victoria Cross. The Germans buried him with military honours.

After the raid the Germans pursued the raiders to the beach where brisk fighting took place. Eventually all but two, Colonel Laycock and Sergeant Terry, were killed, wounded or taken prisoner. Laycock and Terry managed to evade their pursuers and after a further hazardous journey made their way overland to the British line at Cyrene.

The irony of this enterprising and courageous raid was not known till later. Rommel was not at the house which was attacked, and in fact had never used it. It was used solely as headquarters for German and Italian supply services. But even if it had been his headquarters he would not have been in it that night: he was in his own front line, where he expected a British attack. (At one time it was reported that Rommel was in Rome that night attending a birthday party, but that story was not true.)

It was now the turn of No. 2 Commando to get a whiff of grapeshot. The unit, commanded by Lieutenant-Colonel A. C. Newman, was not without experience of battle, for two troops had been at Vaagso, and some men had seen action before joining the Commando, but it had not yet had its own special assignment. The one it now received made up for all previous disappointment.

St Nazaire was one of the major ports on the west coast of France. It had a dry dock large enough to hold the biggest battleships. If the mighty *Tirpitz* set off from Norway into Atlantic waters and began a career of destruction of Allied shipping, St Nazaire would obviously be its main base. But if the use of St Nazaire could be denied, the *Tirpitz* might think very carefully before risking the fate which had overtaken the *Bismarck,* which had been sunk after a dramatic chase.

The task of putting St Nazaire out of action was daunting by any standards. It was 250 miles from the nearest British port, thus making an unobserved approach to it somewhat unlikely. The port itself was six miles upstream from the mouth of the river Loire. Its enormous importance was appreciated by the Germans, who were building U-boat bunkers there in which their submarines would be shielded from aerial attack by many tons of concrete. It was protected by a variety of guns and trained troops: it has been described as the most heavily protected fortress in the world.

The aim of the raid was to destroy the dry dock and to make the submarine bunkers unusable. It was a formidable task for a small force of 235 (later increased by thirty). This included 150 men from No. 2 Commando and a demolition party, numbering eighty, which had been drawn from six other commandos. The raid was timed for 28 March 1942. Although intensive preparations for it had begun a mere month before, the commandos concerned had all been training for two years in movement and attack by night in exceptionally difficult conditions, and in using their initiative in disconcerting situations.

The naval side of the operation was commanded by Commander R. E. D. Ryder, who would later earn a VC for his part. Newman chose a number of Frenchmen for the expedition, feeling that their appearance would make them less recognizable as they set about their deadly errands. The Admiralty produced an expendable destroyer for the expedition, a former American craft, the *Buchanan,* which had been rechristened HMS *Campbelltown.* This, crammed with explosives, would be used to ram the gates of the dry dock. The raid was rehearsed at Devonport dockyard and in that rehearsal so many things went wrong that it looked more than ever like a suicide mission. Any optimistic views that it would be all right on the night were consider-

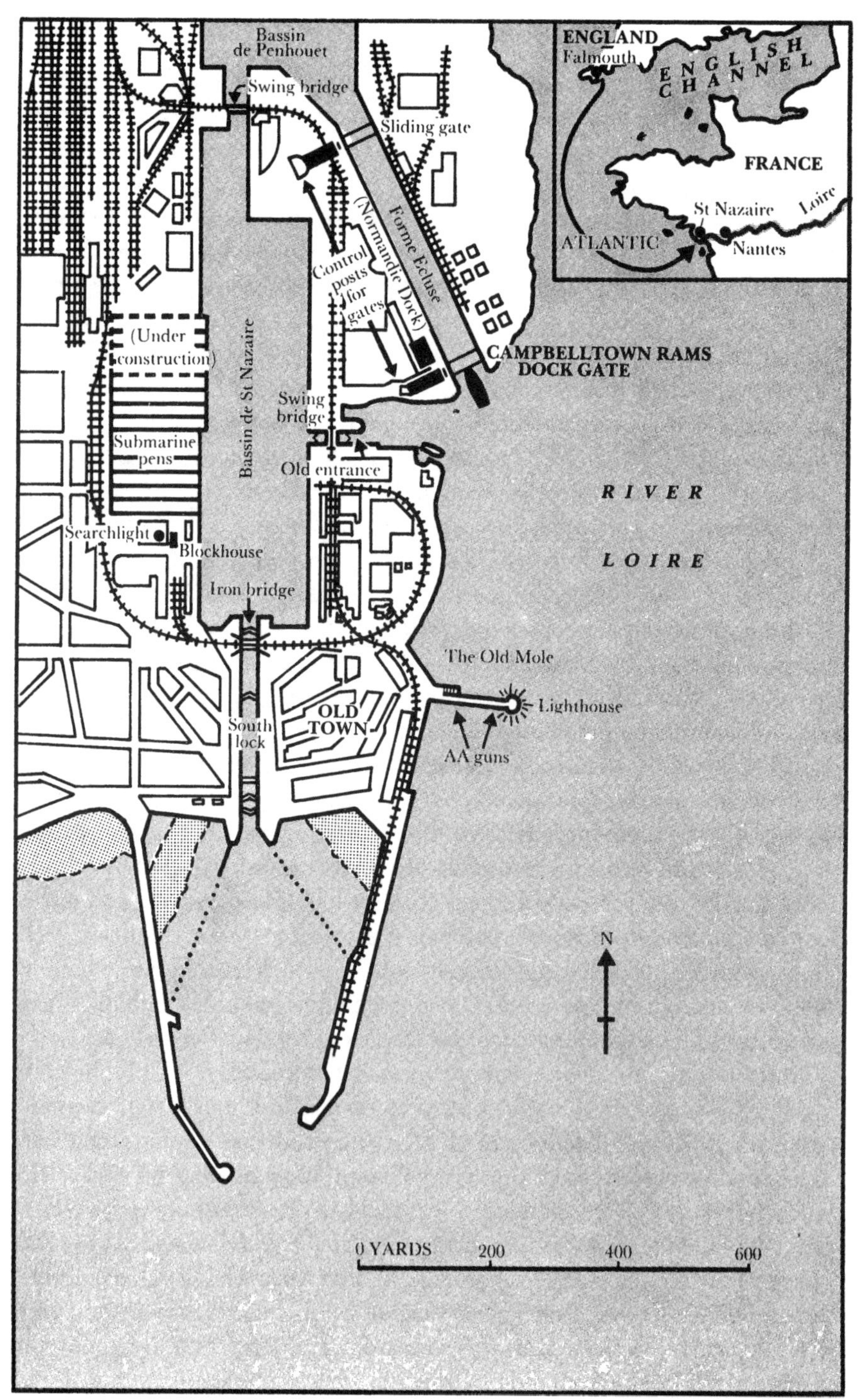

The Raid on St Nazaire, 28 March 1942

ably modified by aerial photographs which showed St Nazaire to be more strongly defended than it had been when the raid had first been planned.

The expedition set off on 26 March 1942 in a varied assortment of craft; two Hunt Class destroyers in addition to the expendable *Campbelltown*, a motor gun boat (MGB) and a number of motor launches which were heavily loaded with extra petrol. The weather was rough, which made life in the motor launches less than pleasant. Although they encountered a German submarine on the way out, and greeted it with depth charges, there were no other hazards. When reasonably close to the port they took up assault formation: the MGB led, *Campbelltown* came close behind, two columns of seven motor launches followed, and a motor torpedo boat (MTB) brought up the rear. They flew German colours as they crossed the mud flats safely at high tide, but had difficulties when they were picked up by two searchlights from the shore. On receipt of an enquiry about their presence and purpose, they signalled that they wanted to bring in two ships damaged by enemy action; this was reasonable as the RAF had just bombed the port. Needless to say these negotiations were conducted in German, using German code-words which had been acquired. The ruse was not entirely successful, for shelling which had begun when the searchlights were switched on, still continued sporadically. However, *Campbelltown*, which had been modified to make it resemble a German torpedo boat, was already slipping past the big German shore batteries at a speed raised to nineteen knots. The Germans, far from convinced about the legality of its presence, opened fire with more determination than accuracy. *Campbelltown* responded by pulling down the German flag and hoisting the White Ensign.

As the Germans increased their fire in the general direction of the raiders, many of their shells found targets in their own ships. *Campbelltown* surged forward and at 1.35 A.M. crashed into the lock gates. The commandos on board then raced to the shore, each party aiming for its allotted target. They were joined by other parties from the motor launches, although many of these had been less fortunate than *Campbelltown* on the way in. There was no shortage of targets. The bridges connecting the various sections of the harbour, the submarine pens, the pumping and winching stations and inner lock gates all required attention, and received it. All this was not done without casualties; one launch containing a demolition party was hit by enemy fire as it came in to land; its occupants were either drowned or burnt to death. The Germans, now recovering from the first shock of finding commandos among them, responded ferociously. All round the dock there was fierce hand-to-hand fighting, sometimes in the dark, sometimes lit by blazing wreckage from where the demolition parties had done their work.

Now that the main task was accomplished the next problem, for the survivors, was to avoid being captured. It was obvious that there was no hope of getting most of them away by sea. When their tasks had been accomplished, some fifty commandos rendezvoused with Colonel Newman at the prearranged spot. Many were wounded. They had hoped to be taken off by motor launch but it soon became clear that the surviving boats would not be able to reach them and would be hard put to get to safety with those they had already taken on board. Newman ordered his party to split into small groups and to try to reach Spain on foot. A group of twenty under Newman, most of whom were seriously wounded, took temporary refuge in a cellar but were surrounded by German soldiers and eventually had to surrender. However, five members of another party did manage to slip through the German lines. Against all probability, with the German naval and air forces fully alerted, the MGB and three motor launches actually made their way back to Britain, using up all their fuel on the way and even shooting down one German aircraft which came to investigate them.

This is necessarily a very brief account of a raid in which there were many hard-fought minor actions. From the commandos' point of view the happiest note was struck by the success of the *Campbelltown*. On the morning of 29 March its presence, jammed in the lock gates, was a source of interest to the Germans, and forty officers went on board, while some 400 German soldiers watched from the quayside, and speculated on what it had been aiming to do. Their doubts were resolved when the five tons of explosive hidden in her bows went off, killing occupants and onlookers alike.

It was not the only unwelcome surprise left by the commandos. The following day two more delayed-action charges exploded in the submarine pens. Unfortunately in the ensuing panic the Germans fired on French civilian workers, killing 300. They also shot a number of their own workmen, confusing their uniforms with those of British soldiers.

But the cost was high on the British side, too. Thirty-four officers and 151 sailors were killed from the naval party, and thirty-four officers and 171 commando soldiers were killed.

It should not be overlooked that the five who succeeded in escaping could not possibly have done so without French civilians who helped them at considerable risk to themselves. They were given money and advice, and were never refused food or shelter for the night. A major problem was crossing the Loire, which was the accepted boundary between occupied and unoccupied France, and was thus watched carefully by German sentries. The commandos were assisted by a friendly farmer, who sent his daughters to bicycle in an immodest way over a bridge, while the commandos swam across 100 yards downstream. The commandos were not observed, but the girls were watched carefully.

Five VCs were awarded for this raid but two, sadly, were posthumous. The dock was out of action for the remainder of the war. In many ways, such as in the use of motor launches, this raid bore a close resemblance to the raid on the Zeebrugge peninsula in 1918. Both were regarded as impossible before they took place.

From the commando point of view the main value of the raids on the Lofoten islands, Vaagso and St Nazaire, was that they established the unit's credibility. The military requirement was now seen to justify the existence of a specialist force to be used in swift, secret operations. The next assignment, therefore, came quickly after the St Nazaire raid. Madagascar (now Malagasy Republic) was still nominally under Vichy French control, even though the French had no possibility of making use of it. A far more serious prospect in May 1942, when the Japanese had completed their conquering tour of the Pacific from Hawaii to the Indian Ocean, was that the Imperial Japanese Navy would land and take possession. If so, they would be firmly based on the Allied main supply route to Egypt and India. In 1942, any convoys of Allied shipping which entered the Mediterranean ran the gauntlet of German and Italian bombers based on Sicily, Italy, Crete and Greece. In consequence, the use of the Cape route was inevitable. The possibility of this strategic point being in Japanese hands was too appalling to contemplate.

The task of capturing Madagascar was allotted to No. 5 Commando and certain other units. The island, which is the fourth largest in the world, had a population of under 8 million and an area of just over 200,000 square miles. The commandos landed on 5 May, rounded up the German agents on the island, and occupied the key points

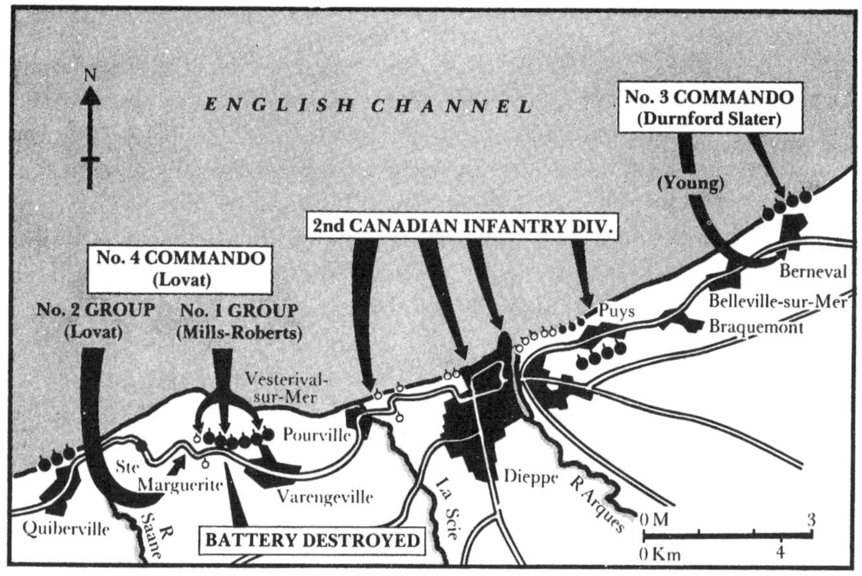

The Raid on Dieppe, 18–19 August 1942

including the capital Tananarive (now Antananarivo). Resistance was minimal. The main prize was the naval base at Diego Suarez (now Antsirane).

Important though the taking of Madagascar was, it was a minor skirmish compared with the events at Dieppe on 19 August of the same year. Dieppe was, as is now well known, a costly disaster *as a raid* but in terms of invasion experience was extremely valuable. Before Dieppe, the American chiefs of staff, and a number of other people too, believed that a landing in France was a necessary and feasible operation which should be undertaken in the near future. Others who held this view were armchair strategists, usually of left-wing opinions, who thought an invasion attempt should be made in order to take the pressure off the Russians who were fighting Germany on the Eastern front. The raid included many more troops than the usual Commando complement. Two Canadian infantry brigades and a tank battalion would also be involved. The commandos' task was to destroy two coastal batteries which the Germans had installed in order to make a sea landing excessively dangerous, if not actually impossible. An estimate of the problems involved may be made fairly accurately from the fact that capture of these batteries by airborne assault was considered too difficult.

No. 3 Commando was allotted the task of capturing the battery at Berneval, No. 4 Commando was assigned to Varengeville. Lt-Col. the

Lord Lovat was in command of No. 4, Lt-Col. John Durnford-Slater in command of No. 3. For the assault, each Commando split into two groups. In No. 4 Commando, Mills-Roberts took the group which landed on the shore in front of the target battery, while Lovat took the group which landed further west, then hooked round to assault the battery from the landward side. In No. 3 Commando Durnford-Slater took the shorter approach, while Peter Young led the attack which hooked in from the landward side. In both assaults the group making the more direct attack was expected to engage the attention of the enemy and encourage the belief that the only threat was coming from that direction. In No. 4 Commando, Mills-Roberts's group numbered eighty-eight men, while Lovat's had 164. For the moment we will follow the fortunes of No. 4.

Like all the Commandos, this one had trained so long and thoroughly at Achnacarry in Scotland that climbing cliffs, crossing freezing rivers, blowing up targets and surviving in conditions which before the war would have been deemed impossible were now second nature. They were very hard and dedicated men, though by no means lacking a sense of humour. As live ammunition was used in exercises, and some forty people were killed while training at Achnacarry, a sense of humour was not the least important military requirement.

The commandos set off on their journey at 1 A.M. and arrived off the French coast at 4.30. Here came the first setback. Searchlights were sweeping the sea and picked out the oncoming craft. Fortunately an air attack was then delivered on to the town defences and, as it hammered the German positions, the commandos lost no time in covering the remaining distance to the beachhead. Surprise, alas, had been lost. This boded ill for the main assault, which was still in mid Channel. Mills-Roberts's detachment had been allotted a gully in the cliff which, not surprisingly, was found on arrival to be full of wire. This was demolished by a Bangalore Torpedo (a weapon designed to be inserted under barbed wire to blow a gap in it). The noise of the explosion was apparently not noted by the Germans above, who may have assumed it came from further along the coast. The Commando moved swiftly past houses and through scrub to come out in front of the battery which was now firing salvo after salvo in the direction of the approaching Canadian assault force. Mills-Roberts's soldiers took up positions where they could see and not be seen and began sniping at the German gunners. After their first casualty, the Germans began to rake the surrounding area with a 20mm gun firing phosphorescent shells and a heavy machine-gun. These were soon joined by mortars. The commandos, although scarcely comfortable, were making the Germans even less so by the fire from three Brens and a 2-inch mortar. A lucky shot from a commando mortar set alight a stack of cordite. However, the raiders were still hard pressed, and were much relieved when the RAF put in another swift attack on the German positions.

While this was going on, Lovat's force had landed, made its way through wire defences on the beach, been fired on by machine-guns and mortars, and climbed the cliff at a speed which broke all previous records. A pillbox on the cliff was dealt with by a shower of grenades. The country behind the cliff top was wooded and marshy, but gave some cover. This enabled them to work round to the rear of the battery and reach a point less than a hundred yards from the position. A well-aimed shot killed a German soldier on the observation tower and then the commandos moved in under the cover of smoke. They encountered an infantry platoon of some thirty men and with a brisk burst of fire killed them all. However, getting inside the building proved extremely difficult, for there were now German soldiers ready for battle at various points on the way. The commandos began to lose men. At this point Capt Pat Porteous took the lead for the final charge. He was wounded in the wrist, but killed his assailant with a shot from the pistol he was carrying in the other hand. He carried on, though wounded again, this time by a shot through the thigh. Nothing seemed to stop Porteous who then led bayonet charges into the gun pits. His Troop Sergeant Major, Portman, accompanied him until his heel was removed by a grenade burst. But the painful wound, gushing blood, did not deter Portman. Forced to sit, for he could no longer walk, he took carefully aimed shots at the enemy soldiers. The Germans fought stubbornly, defending every inch of the buildings, but the commandos were in no mood to be stopped. At a cost of twelve killed, four missing (doubtless killed too but unidentifiable) and twenty wounded, the commandos captured the battery, killed 150 Germans and destroyed the guns. Many of those who took part were awarded decorations: Porteous received a VC. Porteous, incidentally, is no fire-eating warrior. In civilian life he is quiet and self-effacing.

There was an unnerving moment when the commandos were about to demolish the guns. A German aircraft came overhead to investigate and to drop bombs if needed. Lovat waved at the pilot cheerfully as if to indicate that he was one of the defending Germans and they had now disposed of their attackers. Reassured, the pilot waved back and flew off.

No. 3 Commando was not quite so lucky. Again the Commando split into two groups, the one landing on the beach being under the command of Durnford-Slater himself, the other under Maj. Peter Young. The battery was known to be strongly defended and to contain at least 200 men.

The Commando had an unpleasant run-in, for the assault ship which should have carried them was not available, and the entire journey was made in wooden landing-craft known as Eurekas. Each of them could carry eighteen men uncomfortably. It was a tradition of the Commandos not to be seasick, but crossing the Channel in flimsy assault boats tested the credo sorely during the seventy-mile journey. An added interest was the fact that the destroyer escort which should have accompanied them all the way left them after a short time to investigate another matter. At 3.45 the twenty wooden Eurekas, already hard put to complete the journey in the prevailing conditions, ran into a German coastal convoy. The ensuing gun battle left the Eurekas no better for the experience. However, Young's boat had survived and at 4.50 A.M. he landed on the beach at his appointed spot. As he did so, he observed with satisfaction that the defensive trenches they had expected to be full of German soldiers were still unoccupied, and would not have to be fought over. They moved swiftly to the gulley in the cliff. It was full of barbed wire but, as Young expressed it, 'The German officer who had been responsible for wiring that position had made such a good job of it that he had created a sort of mattress of wire which we could walk on.' It was not a comfortable or rapid climb, but it was possible. As they moved inland, they came to a notice board and moved round to the other side to read what it said. The message was simple: '*Achtung Minen*' (Beware mines). They had walked through a German minefield.

From the cliff top they could now see five other landing craft approaching the beach. If their occupants succeeded in landing and climbing the cliff, this would give the commandos a total of ninety-eight. As the Germans were known to have 200 in the battery and the original commando plan had been to assault it with 450, Young estimated his chances of doing the job unaided with his eighteen; he decided that the only possible policy was to rendezvous with the others at the top of the cliff and moved to where he thought he would meet them. Unfortunately, this led them into the view of a German machine-gun crew. Young then tried other means of approaching the battery, but a stealthy move through an orchard was greeted by rifle fire. He decided they should conceal themselves in a neighbouring cornfield and open fire with rifles and Brens from that position. Visibility was poor and vulnerability high, and Young doubted if they were doing much damage, particularly as the battery was now firing steadily in the direction of the sea. He sensed that the commandos regarded a cornfield as adequate for temporary cover, but unsatisfactory as a defensive position, so Young reassured them that standing corn would stop a bullet as effectively as a brick wall. In the absence of scientific tests they believed him – reluctantly. As Young said: 'They didn't have a choice.'

After a time the rifle fire in the direction of the commandos stopped and they presumed the Germans had either forgotten them or assumed they had withdrawn. A few minutes later they realized it was not so, for the Germans in the battery had traversed one 6-inch gun and were firing in their direction. Fortunately for the commandos, the elevation could not be lowered far enough, and the shell whistled overhead. Several others followed, but without doing any damage except to the distant countryside. The commandos, who were now running short of ammunition, decided it was time to leave. They suspected that the Germans might soon begin more thorough retaliation, perhaps by sending an armoured unit to look for them. They climbed down the cliff and found their craft waiting. Young had reached his objective, inflicted casualties on the enemy, and retired without losing a single man.

Others were not so lucky. The boats which Young had seen following landed but quickly ran into strong opposition. Heavily outnumbered, they sustained a number of casualties and with their retreat cut off were compelled to surrender. The only positive gain from the assault on the Berneval battery was that none of the shells fired from it hit any of the ships bringing in the main party. Undoubtedly the attention of Young's party must have been a distraction, even though it was unable to stop the firing completely.

There were other Commando units in the operation: 'A' Commando, Royal Marines, one detachment from No. 10 Inter-Allied Commando, and a detachment from the US Rangers.

As a whole, the raid was a disaster. The Allies had 3,670 casualties, lost a destroyer and many landing craft, twenty-nine tanks and 106 aircraft. The Germans lost a mere 591 men and forty-eight aircraft. But Dieppe provided lessons. The first was that absolute secrecy must be preserved before any assault or invasion. If not, the enemy will be alert and watchful, even if they do not know exactly when and where an attack will come. Second was the fact that beaches must not be too steep for tanks to climb. Third was the fact that ports could not be taken by frontal assault without appalling losses. In 1944 all the ports were taken by landward attack, notably Cherbourg. The D-Day landings were made over open beaches, and the invaders brought their port facilities – the Mulberry harbour – with them.

It is said of the army somewhat cynically, by those in it, that as soon as planners have planted the seeds they start digging them up to see how they are growing. As anyone with any experience of army organization (or disorganization, some would have it) knows, periodically everything is changed and not always for the better. If the changes are not made by the commanding officer they are made by some remote committee in the War Office which seems to believe that the best perspective is obtained by not clouding one's mind by too many facts. The Commandos, having justified their existence as secret raiders and pre-assault troops, might well have expected that role to continue. Needless to say, it did not: instead they were put to other uses. Some found this change of role a disappointment and went off to join other enterprising units, such as the Special Air Service and Special Boat Squadron. Many good men were lost to the Commandos in this way, but who is to say that their talents were wasted?

The general pattern of commando development between 1942 and 1945 was that the small raids became smaller (in numbers employed) and the larger forces more orthodox. Small-scale raiders were very active in 1942. By that year it was realized only too clearly, from the unfortunate experience of the Royal Navy in the Mediterranean, that there had been a disconcerting development in underwater warfare. This lesson had been learnt from Italian frogmen who attached limpet bombs below the waterline of ships whose crews imagined they were resting in safe anchorages. The navy's reaction was 'What anyone else can do, we can do better' – and proved it. But credit for pioneering these activities also belongs to the Commandos, for 101 Troop (Army Commandos) had been developing similar skills since 1940. 101 Troop was led by Captain G. C. S. Montanaro and practised the arts of canoeing, underwater swimming, camouflage, infiltration, and not least the technique of attaching magnetic mines to ships below the surface. Montanaro was also an expert on explosives. 101 Troop learnt and imparted many lessons but had a short life and was eventually disbanded to become part of the 1st Special Boat Squadron. In its brief life it had proved the need for the specialist skills it had developed. In consequence on 11 April 1942 Captain Montanaro and Trooper Preece had used a canoe to enter Boulogne harbour where there was a medium-sized German tanker, and attached limpet mines to it. These blew away enough of the hull to make the tanker's stay in the harbour a lengthy one.

Small-scale raids were not popular with the higher command, for it was thought they wasted valuable resources and were almost as disruptive for Allied forces as they were for the enemy. They were, however, a godsend to adventurous and restless young men who became infinitely bored with routine soldiering and training exercises in the years after Dunkirk. For those who went to the Middle East and Far East there was no lack of action and experience, but for those necessarily kept at home life could be very tedious.

One of the outstanding characters in smaller-scale raiding was Capt Gus March-Phillips. He was an unconventional species of regular officer. He had, in fact, become so bored after a short spell with his regiment in India that he resigned his commission and became a novelist and journalist. He was a first-class rider, swimmer, shot and small-boat sailor. Somewhat unusually for a person of his chosen way of life, he was very religious. In appearance he was strikingly good-looking (apart from a broken nose), was a stickler for appearance (except when in disguise), and exuded such charisma that his men thought he had almost superhuman powers. At Dunkirk he had made the acquaintance of Geoffrey Appleyard. Appleyard had had a Quaker education but was not pacifist. He possessed a variety of interesting qualifications. He had a Cambridge degree in engineering with first-class honours, he was a skiing blue of international standard. He is believed to have introduced water-skiing to Britain; some say that he invented it.

When March-Phillips was training with the commandos in Scotland he and his colleagues bought (from their own money) a 32-foot boat, and used this for training. March-Phillips, like most of the best soldiers, was very keen on the use of intellectual abilities. (Some commanding officers regarded intellectual soldiers with suspicion and dislike and put them on duties in which their special abilities could not be used.) March-Phillips therefore set thc unit, not merely the officers but the soldiers too, the task of writing essays on raiding techniques. One essay was outstanding, according to Patrick Howarth (himself a Special Agent). The author was J. A. Nasmyth, fresh from Oxford

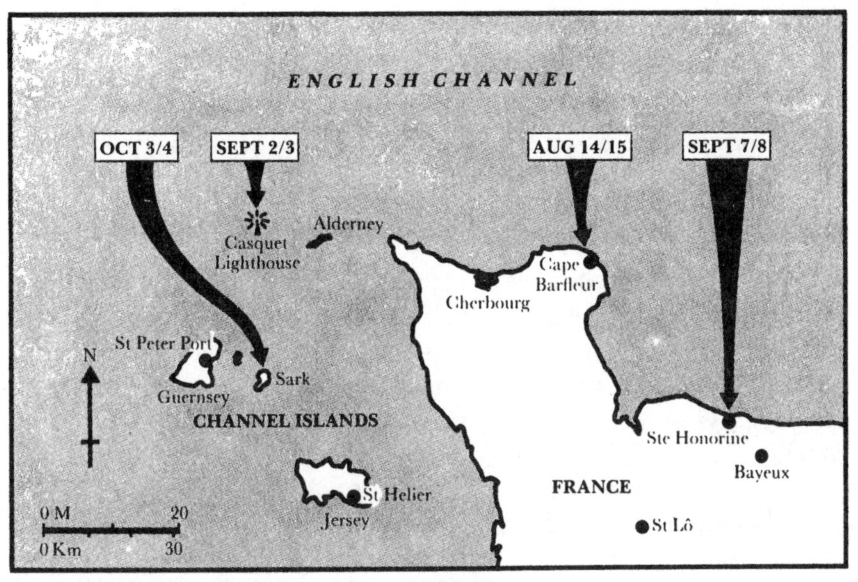

Sorties by Special Raiding Force in 1942

and subsequently to serve with the 7th Hussars. After the war he joined H. M. Treasury and later became very successful as an oil executive. Nasmyth's paper included all the points which it seemed necessary for members of Small-Scale Raiding Parties to know.

The unit soon demonstrated how small-scale infiltration could be used when Appleyard and a Frenchman, André Desgrange, travelled to the vicinity of the French coast by submarine, then disembarked into a canoe. With this they went ashore to collect two agents. The task was not easy because the agents had been so anxious to avoid being spotted by the Germans that they had not dared give any recognition signals. Only when Appleyard walked up and down the beach shouting and waving a torch were their fears sufficiently allayed to convince them their rescue was genuine. Another member of this enterprising unit was Anders Lassen, whose subsequent career with the Special Boat Squadron has already been described.

From now onwards the Small-Scale Raiding Force, as it became known, was extremely active and crossed the Channel several times a week. The skill with which the boats were handled by soldiers irritated the navy and the success of minute forces annoyed commanders of larger units which felt that the independent operators were getting more than their fair share of excitement and credit. It is now well known that the Germans found these pinprick raids disconcerting and annoying. Sentries were either kidnapped or found dead. Although the German High Command did not see these raids as a serious danger, they visualized a time when they might become one. As long as the commandos had a fair share of luck they would get away with their daring adventures. The unit were in training at Anderson Manor, ten miles from Poole. It was thus extremely convenient for operations mounted from Wareham, Portsmouth and Portland.

On 2 September 1942 the raiders took as their target the Casquet lighthouse, Channel Islands, which the Germans were using as a naval signalling station. Here they achieved such complete surprise that they took all seven of the occupants prisoner without suffering a single casualty themselves. A major prize was obtaining German secret naval codes.

The next raid was a total disaster. It took place at Port-en-Bessin on the night of 12/13 September 1942. Port-en-Bessin is a small harbour on the Normandy coast which was destined to see more fighting after the landings on D-Day in 1944.

As happens sometimes on these occasions, the actual details still remain cloudy though the results, sadly, do not. Appleyard could not take part in the landing for he had broken a bone in his foot during the re-embarkation after the Casquet raid: however, he was able to navigate the MTB in which they travelled to their destination. Almost immediately after landing March-Phillips and his men ran into a German patrol. There were ten commandos to seven Germans and the Germans were all killed without loss to the commandos. Unfortunately, however, the noise had alerted other Germans in the district and they hastened to the spot. Although the raiders managed to re-embark they had scarcely travelled a few yards before they were caught in a burst of fire from the shore. March-Phillips was killed, as were most of the others. One man, Hayes, who was an exceptionally strong swimmer and had had the good fortune not to be wounded, swam along the coast, landed and found a French family which passed him to the Resistance. He was smuggled through France to Spain. There, however, he was caught by Franco's police who were anxious to find favour with the Germans at this time. They sent him back to Paris; he was interrogated by the Gestapo, and shot nine months later. The Frenchman Desgrange was also captured but, after being tortured, escaped. The other members of the unit were captured. It seems possible that the Germans did not believe that Hayes was a member of the commandos but assumed he had come ashore with them to act as a spy. Although the Germans were under orders to shoot captured commandos, they did not always do so: had Hayes been captured with the others he might have survived the war.

A more successful – in fact, very successful – raid took place on the night of 3 October. This party included four members from No. 12 Commando; among the participants was Anders Lassen. The objective was the island of Sark. The raiders were led by Appleyard; he did not find climbing the cliffs easy, as his foot was by no means fully recovered. Lassen was sent forward to gain what information he could. He encountered a woman (a fact which subsequently gave rise to much derisive comment, as Lassen spent much of his time encountering women) who proved to be a mine of information and enabled the raiders to capture five Germans in their sleeping quarters. Four of them subsequently tried to break away and escape; the fifth seemed glad to have saved his life by not doing so. He provided so much valuable information about German plans that Appleyard was given a DSO for the raid. Another member of this party was Philip Pinckney, the SAS survival ration expert. All were killed on later expeditions.

While March-Phillips/Appleyard's Small-Scale Raiding Force was operating, other raids were being mounted by the various Commando units. Some of these had little to show for their efforts. The most successful, in terms of results, was the one by No. 2 Commando on 20 September 1942. The commandos, commanded by Captain G. D. Black and Captain B. J. Houghton, were accompanied by some Norwegians; their objective was the hydro-electric power station at Glomfjord in Norway. This was a target of great importance, for it supplied power to the largest aluminium manufacturing plant in Norway. The raiders travelled out on a Free French submarine, had an extremely difficult journey through mountainous country, but successfully blew up the station and a pipeline. Then their luck deserted them, for they ran into a strong German force. Both the commanders, Houghton and Black, were wounded. They were subsequently shot by the Gestapo.

From 1943 onwards the need and opportunity for commandos to carry out small-scale sabotage or 'butcher and bolt' raids became extremely limited. It therefore seemed better for specialists, such as the SAS and SBS, to be left to carry out these tasks and for the commandos to turn to a more conventional infantry role. The presence of Commando units on a conventional field of battle had two advantages: one was that it provided a nucleus of highly-trained, resourceful and experienced assault troops; the other that its presence stimulated other units to match themselves against it. However, the change in the commandos' role from amphibious raiders to land-based infantry provided certain logistical problems. For their new employment they needed heavier weapons, more signals, more administration back-ups, even more cooks. In addition, the commandos, by virtue of the determined way they approached their tasks, needed more replacements: their casualties were higher than those in many units. Commanders of more orthodox units were less than enthusiastic when commandos requested facilities to recruit from their own experienced and battle-hardened troops – and expressed their views forcefully. The fact that David Stirling was always on the look-out for likely members of the SAS did not help matters either.

At this time the higher command, which found the presence of numbers of semi-independent units an irritation and an embarrassment, decided to put them all into one group – the Special Service Group. This also incorporated the Royal Marine Commandos. The fact of there being both army commandos and Royal Marine Commandos requires some explanation. Because the Royal Marines were fully trained in the art of amphibious warfare it was vital, during dark days of 1940 (when the army Commandos were formed for raiding) that the Royal Marines should be available intact, as part of Britain's defence against invasion. The Marines were a regular formation actually in being: the army Commandos were volunteers learning by trial and error. The Marines, not surprisingly, regarded the encroachment of the army on their specialized territory with a mixture of scorn and suspicion – initially. However, as the two units learnt more about each other and worked together, these earlier feelings of distrust were replaced by warmth and goodwill. Their first full-scale joint operation was in Sicily, but the other large Commando operations mainly fall outside the province of this book. Nevertheless, the performances of the commandos in North Africa, Sicily, Italy and Burma contain innumerable examples of the determined, close-quarter fighting which had been a feature of the earlier raids, and make riveting stories.

However, while considering the activities of raiders and small-scale forces during the early days of the war, we need to mention the intrepid canoeists who became well-known to the public as 'The Cockleshell Heroes'. (They themselves disliked the name intensely.)

The history of small water-borne raids is complicated: the armed forces contained hundreds of keen canoeists, climbers and small-boat sailors. Those in the navy had more opportunity than most to practise their skills but, as the Small-Scale Raiding Force indicates, the Commandos were also active performers. At home, Major E. G. 'Blondie' Hasler was commanding the Royal Marine Boom Patrol Detachment. The innocuous term 'Boom Patrol Detachment' was used to cover its real activities. Most people knew that the entrance to harbours was protected by booms and it seemed entirely natural and un-secret that there should be a body of men responsible for inspecting and maintaining these useful devices. In fact, Hasler and many like him were engaged in experimenting on how to pass enemy booms, how to enter hostile waters and how to attack warships which imagined they were lying safely in well-protected anchorages. The story of these canoe-borne raiders is a tangled one, partly because some of the UK pioneers were posted to the Middle East and back again. At the same time an independent Special Boat Service was gradually coming into being in the Middle East and proving itself with quick, lethal raids. For the moment we shall leave the development of small-scale undersea warfare (which eventually embraced a variety of other activities and devices) and continue with land-based units.

When the United States entered the war on 8 December 1941, the other Allies had already acquired fighting experience in France and elsewhere. The Americans had vast resources and unlimited enthusiasm, but lacked this experience. General Marshall, the US Chief of Staff, was anxious that this deficiency should be remedied as soon as possible, even though on a small scale. He looked around for the most experienced and successful British soldiers and his attention was quickly drawn to the Commandos. They seemed to be experts in a form of warfare which would be of the greatest importance when Europe was invaded again. In the minds of the American high command that invasion would not be long delayed: many envisaged it taking place in 1942 or in 1943 at the latest. As mentioned earlier, the Dieppe experience, which showed the enormous practical difficulties of making an opposed landing, soon put an end to such optimism. However, nothing caused the American military pundits to change their view that the main thrust must be over the Channel and straight to Berlin; Churchill's ideas of thrusting up through 'the soft underbelly of Europe', i.e. the Balkans, met with a very chilly reception.

Command of the American Commandos was given to William O. Darby on 8 June 1942. Darby was thirty-one, and a West Point graduate who had been commissioned into the Field Artillery. He was a progressive military thinker and had already put his own troops through their paces in amphibious landings in training long before America entered the war.

The regiment, to be known as Darby's Rangers, began its active existence at Carrickfergus, Northern Ireland, on 19 June 1942. It consisted entirely of volunteers and was attached to the British Special Services Brigade for training and control. Although lacking wartime experience, Darby's Rangers soon earned the respect and liking of their British counterparts. The Rangers were a complete cross-section of American soldiery, and even included a lion-tamer. Officers trained with the men, and always took the lead. Every moment of the day was occupied; there was no spare time. A typical exercise was a three-day march followed by combat. The last day of the march was the most gruelling and included experience of live firing and abseiling down cliffs. But, as their instructors pointed out, this is the way it is with special forces. The enemy will see that your approach is as difficult as possible, particularly in the final stages, and will not provide you with a comfortable rest period just before your attack begins. Furthermore, special forces engaged in secret warfare need to be trained not only to approach a difficult target and destroy it, but also to return, often carrying heavy burdens, in spite of the fact that an enraged enemy will now be looking for them with large forces.

The Rangers had their baptism of fire at Dieppe on 19 August 1942, but this involved only six officers and forty-four other Rangers. Forty of them joined No. 3 Commando, six joined No. 4, and the remaining four were with the Canadians. The assignments of the two Commandos have already been described. The Rangers suffered when the convoy ran into the German E-boats; seven were listed missing, presumed dead, seven were wounded.

One lesson learned from this experience was that any Ranger must be ready for, and capable of, command. A system in which command could only be exercised by an officer was vulnerable, for when the officer and perhaps his second-in-command were out of action, someone else had to lead. In consequence, in training, officers would fall in with the ranks and let a Ranger lead; often he was an NCO but on occasions could be a private.

An unusual feature of commando training in the early days was giving each man a billeting allowance allowing him to find his own accommodation. All he had to do then was to be at the place he was required to be, at the right time. There was no barrack-room life or inspections; self-maintenance was the order of the day. There was some slight apprehension among American officers when this was applied to the Rangers who were not accustomed to living outside barracks; there was a feeling that when not training the Rangers might be rowdy and upset their civilian hosts. In the event the fears proved totally misplaced and would-be critics of the Rangers were put to rout by their landladies.

The Rangers' first full-scale operation took place in the 'Torch' landings on North Africa on 8 November 1942. By this time they had completed their training (if a commando can ever be said to have completed his training) in the wilder parts of Scotland. Five hundred and seventy-five Rangers were given the task of knocking out coastal guns which would otherwise play havoc with the main landings. They were transported in three ferry boats taken from the Glasgow to Belfast run – the *Ulster Monarch, Royal Ulsterman,* and *Royal Scotsman.* Like all passenger ships converted to troopships, they did not err on the side of luxury. The target batteries were at Arzew (two), at Fort de la Pointe, and at Batterie du Nord, overlooking the harbour. The Rangers stormed all four successfully with very low casualties: four killed and eleven wounded.

The Rangers' next important assignment was in Tunis in February 1943. Here they captured Sened, which was defended by the élite Italian regiment, the Bersaglieri. In Tunisia it became clear that the Rangers, like the Commandos, included men of unusual characteristics. Lt Stan Farwell took size 14½ boots. When his supply wore out, he discovered that there were no others available, as the US Army does not normally cater for men with enormous feet. Undeterred, he used house slippers, in which he marched and fought. On one occasion, when the supply of tyres for jeeps was running low, Farwell went behind the German lines by night and collected a tyre from a wrecked German jeep – 'creeping around after dark in slippers', as someone expressed it.

The success of the Rangers led to the creation of several more battalions. They took part in many battles, notably at El Guettar in Sicily, at Sorrento and at Anzio. As with most units, they were sometimes successful, sometimes badly mauled. The 1st, 3rd, and 4th Battalions were in the Mediterranean and the 2nd and 5th took part in the Normandy landings, and the 6th went to the Pacific, first to New Guinea, later to Leyte and Luzon. Probably the outstanding feat of the Rangers during the war – and it was a feat of which anyone might have been proud – was the assault on Pointe du Hoc in June 1944.

The two American landing points on D-Day were Utah beach and Omaha beach. Both beaches were threatened by a heavy German coastal battery at Pointe du Hoc, a position three miles west of Omaha at the top of a sheer cliff 100 feet high. A visitor might well consider an assault on such a strong position would be impossible but, fortunately, that was not the view the Rangers took. At 7 A.M. three companies arrived at the foot of the cliffs. By means of rockets they shot up grappling irons with rope ladders attached and, as two destroyers standing off the coast gave them covering fire, they scaled the cliffs at top speed. The German defenders, unaware of what was happening on the cliffs below, stayed in their trenches to avoid the shelling by the destroyers. When the Rangers arrived they were astonished to find that the guns had already been moved from the casemates. The whole area had been badly battered by previous bombing attacks (but still looks formidable, even today). Half a mile inland the Rangers found the missing guns, undamaged and with plentiful ammunition. There were no German gun crews or soldiers to be seen on this side. Why those guns, which could have done incalculable damage, were neither manned nor fired, is one of the great mysteries of the war. There were plenty of Germans in the surrounding area and the landings had already begun. The only explanation seems to be that the guns had originally been installed at enormous trouble but had attracted such constant attention from the RAF that the first position had been abandoned and they had been repositioned further inland, heavily camouflaged. But, it seems, the crews who should have been manning them had never been sent; it was the sort of mistake that can happen all too easily when the higher command has too much to think about, but it was a mistake which cost the Germans dear. The fact that the guns were not operational in no way diminishes the Rangers' feat in reaching them. Had the position not been reached (and it could only have been reached the hard way they chose) and then destroyed, it could still have been used when its presence had been remembered. Heavy shelling from Pointe du Hoc, even in the later stages of the landing, would have had a devastating effect.

Another company of the Rangers was to make itself very useful a few hours later on Omaha. As is well known, the American landing on Omaha beach came close to total disaster. Casualties mounted steeply even when the assault parties were well out to sea. Those who managed to land were pinned down on the beaches and suffered further heavy casualties. Just after 10 A.M. the Germans put in a sharp counter-attack which, if it had not been checked, would have pushed the Americans right back to the edge of the beach, and then off it, in this sector. The counter-attack was held by a mere 200 men, a mixture of Rangers and the remnants of 116 Battalion. With the situation along the whole of Omaha beach so delicately poised, a successful German counter-attack could have had fearsome consequences.

Perhaps the most extraordinary of the special forces (and the smallest) was the one which became known as 'Popski's Private Army'. 'Popski' was Lt-Col. Vladimir Peniakoff, DSO, MC. His parents were Russian, but he had been born in Belgium. He had been taught English as a first language, had been privately tutored, then sent to Cambridge. However, when World War I broke out, Peniakoff decided that training for a commission in the British army would take too long, so he enlisted as a private soldier in the French army. In this he served for four years, 'enjoyed it mildly, and acquired a knowledge of the French way of life and a distaste for French people which increased considerably in later years'. After the war he settled in Egypt and became a sugar manufacturer. Here he seems to have acquired a 'distaste' for a number of other nationalities too.

While in Egypt Peniakoff took every opportunity for adventurous recreation. He learnt to fly and he taught himself navigation, travelling by car over vast distances in the desert. The latter practice required expert ability in navigating by the sun and the stars. For this he relied heavily on findings made by Maj. Ralph Bagnold and others. Bagnold and his friends had crossed vast tracts of barren desert which had previously been considered impassable by virtue of the lack of landmarks and areas of soft sand which trapped vehicles. The lack of landmarks was overcome by navigational skill; being trapped in the soft sand was avoided by use of steel channels (portable metal strips enabling a vehicle to climb out of treacherous places), and overheating by the water condenser which prevented engines boiling dry. Peniakoff obstinately and foolishly refused to let anyone know in which direction he was heading when he went off on his long trips. He did this because he wished to become entirely self-reliant. One of the drawbacks of this rash policy was that he had to carry almost as many vehicle spares as there were parts to the Ford car in which he made the journeys.

At the start of World War II he was forty-two, and weighed nearly fifteen stone. When he went for a medical test, necessary for renewing his pilot's licence, he failed it. Neither the navy nor the RAF was interested in the offer of his services; the army would have taken him, but the fact of his being born in Belgium made him a neutral. Then the Germans invaded Belgium. After a delay of six months he was commissioned on the General List of the British army and posted to the Libyan Arab Force.

The Libyan Arab Force numbered some 3,000, and included Arabs of every nationality and belief. For the most part they were warlike, though extremely undisciplined. The exact numbers in the force were never known. The Arabs were armed with captured Italian rifles; the most recent dated back to World War I. Ammunition was plentiful, though unreliable. The other British officers in the force seemed to be people whom no one else wanted: as one was in the habit of being drunk for days on end, and another used to tell his Syrian girlfriend all the force's plans, neither gave Peniakoff much confidence in the future of the unit. Fortunately, they were replaced before the first action. Soon the force was justifying its existence; Peniakoff's abilities were now recognized and he was given command of a new unit, the Libyan Arab Force Commando.

The Commando's role was to recruit more Arabs, to build up an intelligence network, and to blow up enemy petrol dumps. Of these the most important was the creation of the intelligence network. Peniakoff selected a group of twenty-four soldiers, all Arabs except for a British sergeant, for the headquarters he proposed to establish well inside enemy territory. With the help of the LRDG, who were always ready to cooperate, he set up this forward post.

Peniakoff found a useful source of information in the Italian-speaking Arabs who worked in Italian headquarters and messes. These servants were treated with contempt by the Italian officers, who discussed military plans openly, unaware the Arabs present also understood Italian. The Italians also left documents on tables where Peniakoff's men read them without trouble. Peniakoff found that his pre-war travels had given him a familiarity with the desert which was now proving very useful. 'I reached Qaret Um Alfein before dawn, roused Sa'ad Ali Rahuma and set out to call on Abdel Aziz bu Yunes whose tents were pitched five miles away in a dreary steep wadi of black shingle near Bir el Dei.' Familiarity with Arab customs and manners enabled him to make valuable and reliable contacts.

The force's work was complementary to that of the LRDG, which travelled vast distances, kept watch on German and Italian vehicles, and reported enemy movements and strength back to Cairo. The LRDG role was primarily intelligence-gathering by observation: on occasions it engaged in brisk action but preferred not to do anything which drew attention to its presence in an area. Peniakoff's Commando combined intelligence-gathering with sabotage. The SAS directed its efforts mainly towards destruction, but also contributed much valuable intelligence.

Peniakoff's headquarters was expert at evaluating information. Some sources were known to be more reliable than others. The importance of accurate, confirmed information could not be overstressed. The RAF would complain bitterly if asked to bomb an enemy target where no target existed. However, if the RAF could bomb a target, this was often better than blowing it up. Destruction by sabotage was usually followed by an Italian revenge raid on the surrounding Arab villages: suspects were liable to be hanged with an iron hook through the jaw: even if the suspects were not guilty, the Italians felt that this practice would discourage other would-be saboteurs.

Peniakoff's transport included his own Ford car, nine horses and four camels. The administrative problems of running his intelligence service were considerable. Contacts were paid a regular salary but were also liable to stoppages and fines for slackness or inaccuracy. An elaborate system of double-checking was established to discourage idle but inventive agents, who might wish to sit in their tents and draw up imaginary lists of enemy vehicles. The agents were also briefed to spread alarmist rumours: news of a vast unstoppable British attack was leaked to Italian ears already none too happy about the vulnerability of their position.

The Commando's most awkward moments occurred when the Axis forces suddenly surged forward, leaving them too far behind enemy lines for supplies to reach them. But these difficult periods did not last long. With their local knowledge and many contacts they could filter back through enemy positions to a more suitable base, often collecting stragglers and escaped British prisoners on the way.

In August 1942 Peniakoff was told to report to Cairo to be briefed

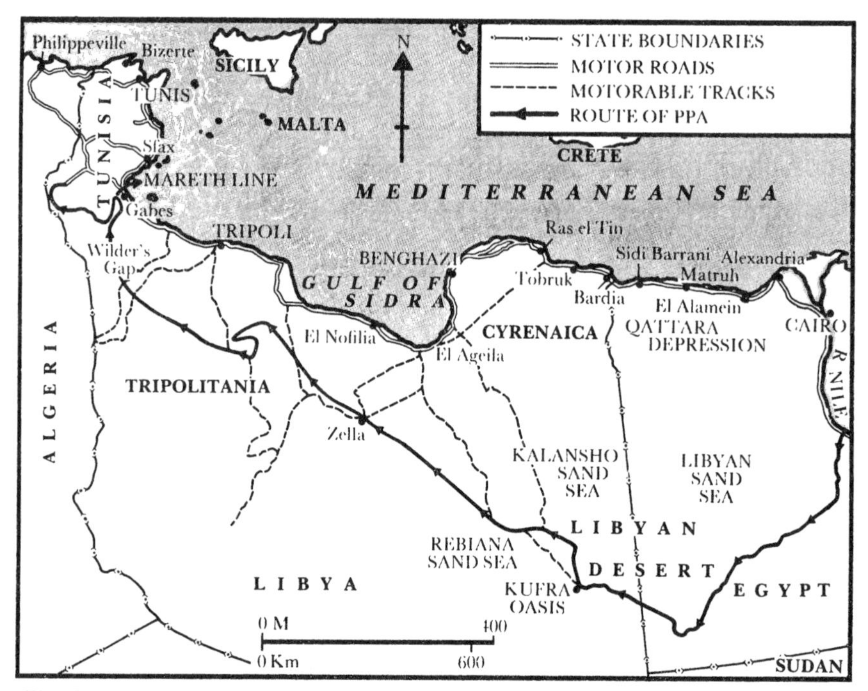

The Desert Journeys of Popski's Private Army

for further operations. To his amazement, on his arrival he found there had been so many recent changes that nobody knew anything about him. All records had been lost; he was even told that his unit had been officially disbanded months before. In the depths of despair, he ran into a young cavalry colonel who gave his name as Shan Hackett. Hackett was later to be General Sir John Hackett. Peniakoff poured out his troubles: after five months on operations he found himself back in Cairo with his unit disbanded and no other job, even his pay had been stopped. Hackett listened to the tale of woe, but pointed out that others might view it differently. 'Now, Popski,' he said, 'for your private reasons you fade out into the desert. You go and fight a private war with your private army for your private convenience, taking orders from no one, and when you choose to come back you expect HM Government to pay you for your fun!'

Always a realist, Peniakoff realized that that was no more than the truth. But he found Hackett more sympathetic to his aims, when properly organized and authorized, than he had expected. Hackett was all too familiar with wild-cat schemes dreamt up by young officers anxious to beat Rommel on their own. Many of these were inspired by the actions of the LRDG and the SAS but few had the drive, determination or organizational skill to make their own plans work, if in fact they were workable at all.

Peniakoff took part in the disastrous raid by a combined force of Commandos, SAS and navy to seize Tobruk. He was involved in the diversionary attack on Barce, not in the attempt to capture Tobruk itself. But his own party also ran into trouble. After much confusion, discomfort and two small wounds, Peniakoff was relieved to be rescued by a patrol from the LRDG led by David Lloyd-Owen.

After recovering from his wounds, Peniakoff was offered a job harassing the Germans behind their lines. He felt there were already too many independent units doing this type of work, so he asked if he could throw in his lot with the LRDG. This was approved. However, the LRDG establishment did not allow for an extra squadron, so after seven days he was required to leave. Instead, he was named as the commander of a new unit, consisting of five officers and eighteen soldiers. It was called No. 1 Demolition Unit. He was told to think of a shorter name which would give no indication of the purpose. Hackett told him, 'If you don't find a name quickly, we shall call you "Popski's Private Army".' The name seemed ideal. The Director of Military Operations gave his approval and the letters 'PPA' quickly appeared on the shoulder flashes. Peniakoff adopted an astrolabe as a badge and chose a black tank corps beret for the headgear. They were allotted four jeeps fitted with twin Vickers K machine-guns, two 3-ton lorries, each armed with a Vickers K. These latter would form their mobile base. Among those posted to the unit was a corporal named Locke. He had only one eye and his body was covered with scars. He spoke impeccable English and French: English soldiers accepted him as one of themselves and the French had no doubt that he was entirely French. He was said to have killed a number of the enemy personally in close-quarter fighting, but took very good care of his section and did not expose them to unnecessary risks.

Peniakoff realized that although they were not without experience, they were novices at desert navigation compared with the LRDG. Whenever they were in difficulties they turned to that friendly unit for help. They were not alone in this. The SAS relied heavily on the LRDG, whose navigational skills far surpassed their own; so also did various reconnaissance units such as Advance Force 'A' and G(R). Occasionally the PPA lost a truck through encountering a mine, of which there were many. And there was always a chance of a brush with the Germans or Italians: the unit soon had several casualties.

When they eventually linked up with the 1st Army and the Americans, they obtained lighter Brownings in place of their Vickers Ks. All this time they were collecting information, and identifying and destroying enemy supply dumps. They laid a number of mines on roads which the enemy was using.

When the North African war was over the future of PPA was once more in doubt. Fortunately for Peniakoff, he encountered Force 141, a planning group which had organized the St Nazaire raid and was now working on the invasion of Sicily. (It had also arranged the raid by Appleyard on Pantellaria, Jellicoe's SBS raid on Sardinia, and a number of other small adventures.) Peniakoff was not allowed to accompany any of these raids, for he knew too much to take the risk of falling into enemy hands, but he was taken into Force 141's confidence and could therefore suggest where his services might be used in the future.

For PPA was still in being, even though its Arab members now had to be discharged as being unsuitable for future tasks. They were replaced by British volunteers from other units, such as the LRDG which was also finding a new role now that the desert war was over. Peniakoff made friends with Major-General Hopkinson, Commander of 1st Airborne Division. Hopkinson was sympathetic to unorthodox and enterprising units: he himself had founded Phantom (of which more in Chapter 5). One proposed plan for the PPA was to land a force of five jeeps in gliders on the plain of Calabria. However, the disastrous experience of the gliders in the Sicily invasion caused the higher command to cancel the Calabrian plan and instead to send the PPA in by sea with the leading troops from Bizerta to an unknown destination, which in the event turned out to be Taranto. Italy was now endeavouring to make a separate peace (an action which the Germans were anxious to frustrate) and, after landing, PPA moved forwards quickly to Brindisi. Its task was to acquire information about the whereabouts of the Germans and their strength, about the siting of airfields, and the degree of cooperation to be obtained from the Italian officials. The local Italian army commanders were dismayed to find that they were now caught between two armies, both of which would be demanding their support. Peniakoff knew very well that the Allied forces in this area were very thin on the ground, and their presence was mostly due to the need to keep German reinforcements away from Salerno, which was the main point of attack. The PPA entered Bari unopposed on 11 September, and encouraged the Italian garrison to resist any German counter-attack. While he was at the Italian Corps headquarters a telephone message came through to the Italian commander urgently requiring him to send engineers to repair an aqueduct which the Germans had blown up by mistake; they had assumed it was the one supplying Bari but in fact it was that which carried water to Foggia, which the Germans still held. Peniakoff took the call himself and informed the German officer making the call that he was speaking to the commander of British armoured forces in Bari. (Peniakoff's German was fluent, though not always accurate.) It was somewhat of a shock for the German, who would, Peniakoff hoped, decide that any counter-attack on Bari would now need to be mounted by a substantial armoured force, if it was made at all. Substantial armoured forces take time to collect, and Peniakoff hoped that a larger British force might be there to meet the Germans if and when they came.

The PPA produced so much valuable information about German dispositions and strength that Allied tactical plans were considerably modified. There were, of course, other units working in the same field, notably Phantom and 2 SAS. These, however, had reserves and could give their troops a rest; the PPA was too small to have reserves and therefore had to treat its assignments as a way of life rather than a military task. There was no lack of variety. To their other problems was now added that of refugees. Peniakoff found he had an uphill task when he tried to impress on the Italian upper classes that they should take some responsibility for relieving the plight of their poorer fellow-countrymen: the richer Italians regarded the refugees as nothing but a nuisance.

In obtaining information Peniakoff found that cunning often paid greater dividends than force could have done. When he was asked to discover the number of Germans in the area of Gravina, he made the acquaintance of an Italian who had sold supplies to the German quartermaster in that district. Peniakoff learnt the German quartermaster's name, then rang him up (not without difficulty) and said he himself was an Italian quartermaster sergeant in a town recently occupied by the Germans. He (Peniakoff) said he had eight cases of cognac to sell. They haggled over the price. The German officer believed the cognac to be stolen, but needed it badly for the officers' mess. Peniakoff arranged to deliver it 'in a small captured American car', if the German would arrange for him to be let through the sentries. It was agreed that the cognac should be delivered at 11 P.M. Promptly the PPA arrived with cases full of stones, went into the office where the German was already in a drunken doze (it was clear why alcohol was always needed), and hit him on the head with a rubber truncheon. On the desk in front of the German quartermaster was a list of the entire ration strength and whereabouts of all German troops in the area; they included the German 1st Parachute Division. Peniakoff put it in his pocket, left the unconscious German a bottle of whisky – they felt he deserved a reward – and walked out. When he returned, he sent a message to the British 1st Airborne HQ giving the total number of German troops in the Gravina area as being 3,504.

The precise nature of this statement had the effect required. A message came back: 'Please confirm message re total strength.' Peniakoff said: 'I fell to the temptation of showing off and sent the entire information I had picked up from the German quartermaster's desk.' It was long and detailed, and clearly a revelation to 1st Airborne. Then, with a happy smile, Peniakoff went to bed.

As the war moved forwards to the north of Italy, the PPA became busier than ever. By now their value was fully recognized and the unit had been expanded to eighty. There was no shortage of volunteers. 'Popski' was a legendary figure, the DSO and MC he was awarded seemed to many small recognition for his versatility, courage and stamina. He established bases in the mountains and had their supplies sent in by air; jeeps, however, had to come in by sea with the help of the ever cooperative navy. The air supply came from No. 1 Special Force, an RAF unit which was closely linked to SOE and delivered supplies to partisans. 'A' Force, an organization for rescuing escaped British prisoners-of-war, was also active in this area; there was considerable mutual support.

PPA noted the roads and bridges the Germans used, blew up some of the bridges and mined some of the roads. Then when the Germans had decided which roads and bridges were safe, PPA set ambushes along those. They arranged that their attacks should be widely separated, making it impossible for the Germans to guess where the next one was coming from. But this work was not carried out without losses. It was also extremely uncomfortable and tiring. Few people realize how unpleasant steady rain can be, unless they are compelled to be exposed to it for days and nights on end. On one occasion, when events did not go PPA's way, Peniakoff was wounded again. In *Private Army* he wrote: 'The Germans came over the bridge once more in a pack. One of them leant against the parapet, stuck a rifle grenade into the muzzle of his rifle and took a slow aim at us. I tried to get him with careful bursts; three times he fired and missed and still I couldn't get him. I walked around the jeep to get a new belt of ammunition, when something that made no noticeable noise squashed and shattered my left wrist. The bones and the flesh of the wrist and forearm were in a pulp . . .

'I pushed my mangled hand into the breast of my battledress and asked Burrows to fit a new belt in my gun. He did so, and went back to his own gun. The Germans came over a third time, this time at a run. A few got across and dropped promptly behind the canal bank, the others either fell or crawled back across the bridge. After a while the German fire eased.' When reinforcements came up Peniakoff went to get his wound dressed. When he found a surgeon he discovered a bullet had gone through his right hand too, and his fourth finger was broken. 'That's why I had been so clumsy with my gun.' Three months later, with no left hand, he was back in action. When the war ended, PPA had taken 1,335 prisoners and sixteen field guns, including several 88mm.

In relation to its numbers, the PPA seems to have been one of the most valuable units in Allied service. Their intelligence, first by working with Arabs, and later by moving freely behind enemy lines in Italy, was greatly esteemed, being regular, accurate and detailed. The existence of PPA was soon well known, but its movements remained completely secret. The force was so completely British in style that it could only have been raised and commanded by a foreigner who appreciated the best British qualities, military and cultural.

A similar unit, though with a very different employment, was the Lovat Scouts. They had been raised forty years before by Lord Lovat, chief of the Fraser clan, to fight in the South African War where it was thought, rightly, that the background of its members would make them particularly suitable for guerrilla warfare against other experts in that art. Like all his family, Lovat was an expert at outdoor sports and adventurous trips in rugged country, but he was also intelligent and cultured. He was educated at the Oratory School, and at Oxford, where he took to English games such as cricket, rowing and Rugby football with enthusiasm. Subsequently he spent a year exploring north Somaliland and Abyssinia (now Somalia and Ethiopia).

When the South African War broke out, Lovat decided he could produce a force which would be a very useful addition to the British army. He obtained permission from the War Office to raise two companies to be attached to the Black Watch, to be used mainly for scouting. Although Lovat's ability to raise an efficient fighting force was questioned by some of his countrymen, he soon proved that their doubts were misplaced. The Scouts accepted volunteers from over thirty different clans as well as Borderers, Englishmen, Australians and New Zealanders.

In World War I, the Scouts began with two regiments; they fought at Gallipoli, Macedonia and in France. They were awarded numerous decorations, but also suffered many casualties. During the inter-war years they were an active Territorial Army unit and when World War II broke out were up to strength and well trained. Over one hundred of the members of the regiment were the sons of former soldiers in the Scouts.

Their first overseas assignment was the Faroe islands. The Faroes were of considerable strategic importance because they lie 200 miles north west of the Shetlands, and are approximately half-way between Norway and Iceland. A German presence in the Faroes would be an incalculable threat to the Atlantic shipping lanes.

Although there are seventeen inhabited islands, the total population is only 35,000. Those of the Scouts who thought they had known rough conditions in Scotland realized how temperate that had been compared with this saturated, misty, rocky country. As well as being important strategically, the Faroes were the centre of most of wartime fishing. The fish were not acquired without considerable risk; German submarines and aircraft sank every trawler they spotted. When the Scouts were posted to the Faroes their move was, like all wartime strategic moves, 'Top Secret'. No one was supposed to know their destination until they were actually at sea. However, when a dentist was added to the party before sailing, everyone could make a pretty reliable guess. His instructions informed him that if he required assistance there was a civilian dentist in Thorshavn. As Thorshavn is the capital of the Faroes, it was not difficult to guess the unit's destination.

Like Greenland, the Faroes are part of Denmark; very few of the Faroese spoke English but there was plenty of potential good will as Denmark was now occupied by the Germans.

The Faroes were often attacked, usually by Heinkels. A number of these were shot down; the most surprising success was when one was shot down by Bren guns and crashed in a fjord. The crew escaped but were promptly captured; the Heinkel was dragged up by means of a diver, a grappling iron and an Aberdeen trawler.

Patrolling over the rugged hills of the Faroes was good preparation for their next assignment, which was Italy. However, the Scouts had also been trained in mountain warfare (including skiing) in Canada before they arrived in Naples. There, in July, they had the interesting experience of unloading their ski-kit and mountain clothing. Nobody was unduly surprised: cynics say that if you are given tropical kit it is a sure sign that you are destined for the Arctic circle. In fairness it must be admitted that during the war troops who set off from the Clyde in winter could hardly be expected to embark wearing the sort of clothing they would require in the desert. Furthermore, even hot climates can have cold nights and serge battledress was often popular.

Once in the Apennines, the Scouts' particular skill in spying, fighting patrols, sniping and infiltrating paid handsome dividends. Here they became great friends with the Gurkhas and rather less friendly with the partisans. The partisans, they felt, tended to do more swaggering than fighting, but this opinion of the partisans was not widely held: the Scouts were probably unlucky in their contacts. They liked the Italian peasants, who were trying to make a living in spite of the war. Their commanding officer recorded: 'Another interesting unit we met in Italy was Popski's Private Army, an irregular unit that did a splendid job there.'

In the later stages the Scouts found themselves with a variety of unusual postings. At one time they were the link used between the 8th Army and the Americans, at another working with Polish troops commanded by General Anders, and at the end of the war brigaded with the Jewish Brigade.

The Scouts had fewer problems over security than most units. Their members tended to talk sparingly, and this was an advantage; the fact that when they did so it was as likely as not to be in Gaelic presented unexpected problems to would-be listeners.

Last but not least come the naval Commandos. Few people were aware of their existence at the time, and this useful unit has always been overshadowed by its brothers in the army and Marines. As we saw earlier, the navy played a vital part in the early commando raids. However, it was not until after Dieppe that Combined Operations HQ set up Force 'J' (October 1942), which was a permanent formation which included five gunboats, a motor torpedo boat and 130 landing craft of various types. This, it was thought, should be adequate to put a force of raiders ashore anywhere at almost any time. (It must not be confused with the 'J' Service, which was a listening unit employed in the Middle East.)

After the creation of Force 'J', a school for training beach parties was set up in Argyllshire. The task of beach parties was to ensure that in a major landing the beaches were organized to be able to handle the incoming traffic. The task of being traffic policemen on a bullet-swept shore, which was the beachmaster's job, was not necessarily to everyone's taste, but there was no lack of volunteers. Apart from courage, the job required enormous stamina and resourcefulness. The unit began by being called 'Naval Beach Commandos', but the title was soon changed to Royal Naval Commandos. The nature of their task required men of the highest quality, and the remainder of the navy was far from enthusiastic about the priority in obtaining recruits which Mountbatten acquired for the Commandos. Their skill was not limited to being able to organize the beaches: they also had to be as good as the army and Marine Commandos when there was fighting to be done. They were trained at Achnacarry under the redoubtable Colonel Vaughan. Their day began at six when they broke the ice in the nearby river for washing water (there was never hot water for shaving), they then dressed, which meant wearing trousers but never vests whatever the weather. They survived on rations of raw meat, potatoes and bread. Training went on all day, and often all night too. Some rare spirits actually enjoyed it; the majority regarded it as something which they would get through whatever happened.

The first beach task of the RN Commandos was in the 'Torch' landings, the Anglo-American invasion of North Africa. The Allied High Command had hoped that the landings would be a surprise and would also be unopposed. They were certainly a surprise – for the secret had been well kept, but there was much more opposition than had been expected. Nevertheless, the task was accomplished; the RN Commandos earned praise – and decorations – for their assistance to the Americans as well as others.

Subsequent landings in which the RN Commandos took part were Sicily, Italy (notably at Salerno and Anzio), in the Adriatic, in Burma and, of course, in Normandy on D-Day. Their value to the Allied war effort was shown by the fact that they were expanded rapidly until there were over thirty RN Commandos. Their standards of training never relaxed.

A lieutenant tells a story that on a training exercise he suddenly spotted a man walking about doing nothing. He yelled at him: 'Hey you, get hold of a spade and start digging a trench.' The man looked up somewhat surprised. 'What me?' he enquired. 'Yes, you. Get on with it.' The man did, and the lieutenant moved on. Only later did he discover the man was an admiral who had come ashore to see the unit in action.

But matters did not always go well for the RN Commandos. Elba was believed to be thinly held by German troops in June 1944 and it was felt that a force consisting of the French 9th Colonial Infantry Division, a battalion of French Commandos, and a battalion of Moroccan Goums, would be adequate. British and American Commandos would cover the landings. To divert the German attention from the main landings, a squadron of American PT (Patrol Torpedo) boats commanded by Lt-Com. Douglas Fairbanks Jr, better known for his film exploits on land, approached a different part of the coast, making as much noise as they could. However, the Germans were not entirely deceived and, when the main force came in, put up a spirited defence. Unfortunately, the intelligence reports on which the plans for the landing had been based now proved to have been inaccurate. The worst casualties occurred when the landing party was caught in a heavy barrage from inland. The cost, heroism and ferocity of the action was scarcely noticed at the time by a public which had its attention firmly occupied by events in Normandy, but this brief and bloody struggle for Elba was important for it removed a significant obstacle to the supply of Allied forces on the west coast of Italy.

It could be said of the RN Commandos that wherever there was a job of work to be done, they were there. Theirs was the task of creeping ashore quietly, clearing the way for those who came after and, when required, fighting off any counter-attacks. 'First in, last out' was truly their motto. Their expertise was not limited to sea landings: they learnt to be equally skilled at selecting suitable places for river crossings, as they showed on the Rhine and in northern Italy. In the latter stages of the Italian campaign, during the crossing of the river Reno, and the Lake Commachio water flats, the task was carried out by Commando forces using the amphibious carriers known as Buffaloes. It was a gathering of the clans for the Commandos, for 2 Commando, 9 Commando, 40 and 43 Marine Commandos were all engaged. In this action the RN Commandos proved they were as competent as their distinguished fellows and more than a match for the enemy.

Lieutenant W. G. Jenkins describes his experience with 43 Commando.

After Brigadier Fitzroy Maclean's mission to Tito's headquarters, Churchill had been persuaded to give full support to the partisans, who had acquired a good haul of weapons when the Italian occupation forces ceased to be engaged in the war. The Germans were quick to re-establish control of the Yugoslav coastal area, and were steadily garrisoning all the Dalmatian islands. In January 1944 2 Commando and 43 Royal Marine Commando, with some support units, were sent to assist the partisans in the defence of Vis, the last outlying island which the Germans had not yet occupied.

A Commando had five Fighting Troops, a Heavy Weapons Troop equipped with Vickers machine-guns and 3-inch mortars, and a Headquarters Troop, which included Signals. Seldom were they fully up to strength – in 'E' Troop, 43 Commando, there were fifty-five men instead of seventy, and I was the only subaltern, though there should have been two. Fortunately the Troop Commander, Capt Ralph Parkinson-Cumine, MC, was a regular officer of the highest calibre.

It was not long before the Commandos began offensive raiding from Vis, as there was good intelligence and support from partisans on the occupied islands. Two very successful operations were carried out on Solta, and other actions from troop to brigade level took place on all the other islands, and the peninsula.

Solta lies about eight miles off-shore from Split, and is ten miles long by two and three-quarters miles wide. Reconnaissance parties established that an enemy company was occupying the village of Grohote, which was linked to a small harbour on the north coast. On 17 March three troops from 2 Commando, supplemented by the Heavy Weapons Troop from 43 Commando and two units of the American Special Operations Force landed by night under the command of Lt-Col. Jack Churchill DSO, MC. After an exhausting approach march over the steep hills, they established themselves shortly before dawn on a hill overlooking Grohote. A bombing raid by thirty-six Kittihawks from Italy had been planned for 0600 hrs, which proved most effective. During a quick assault the Commandos managed to capture the German commander, a loud-hailer was thrust into his hand, and they got him to tell his men to surrender. Four Germans were killed and 104 prisoners taken for the loss of two men and fourteen lightly wounded.

Shortly afterwards a larger garrison was sent over, which established well-prepared positions protected by mines and wire, and added three fortified hill-top outposts. In May and July partisan battalions put in two more attacks, but they met with stiff resistance, and as they lacked adequate supporting fire they suffered heavier casualties.

On 17 September 43 Commando (about 420 men), just back on Vis after an operation on Brac, was ordered to attack the Solta garrison, now some 250 strong. With little time for preparation, stores were piled on to the landing craft in any order, and we landed in darkness, not long before

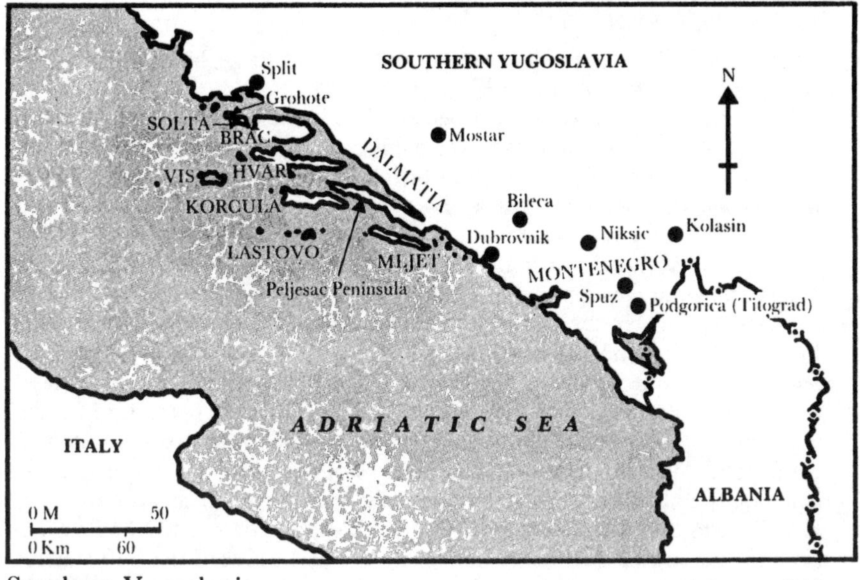

Southern Yugoslavia

Original map drawn by M. Fugmanna-Nicklinson

dawn. A stiff climb up some cliffs was followed by a long and arduous climb up the steep, stony and terraced hillsides. We had been told that we had to rely on our own resources, so in addition to our personal ammunition and grenades, each of us had to carry two 3-inch mortar bombs. How thankful we were finally to dump those damn bombs at a stock-pile within range of the German positions. We had to continue our advance down a forward slope, where we came under machine-gun fire, fortunately at long range. The cover was so sparse that it was decided that the attacks on the three hill-top outposts would be mounted at night.

As we in 'E' Troop got close to our objective several of us had the sickening shock of stumbling over a trip-wire, but there were no explosions. Neither were there the expected bursts of fire, and to our relief we found that the Germans had withdrawn to their main position. We snatched a couple of hours sleep, and I thought I'd done well to find an old mattress, until later: I learnt my lesson when I had to get rid of all the lice and fleas from my clothes. In the early morning light we saw the formidable array of stick-mines we'd come through. I crawled out to investigate, and discovered that the Germans had failed to cut the bits of safety string holding the pins in the detonators. The Gunners in the heavy batteries around Split were more professional, as they had ranged accurately on the positions during previous attacks, and we were pinned down by shell-fire. It was impossible to dig into the hard limestone, so we hurriedly built up loose rocks into sangar walls to protect ourselves from shrapnel. One could time the flight of the big boys after hearing the boom of the gun, but the snag was that the garrison on the island also had the range, so their mortar bombs came whistling down unpredictably as well. To add to our discomfort it began to rain heavily, and we had to go hungry, as it was impossible to re-supply us with rations.

Eventually the bombardment became less intense, and we continued to our next objective – the ridge overlooking the main position at Grohote, where we were able to do some mortaring. It was getting dark, and orders were issued for a dawn attack. The rain had stopped, and in the still atmosphere every sound came up to us clearly. The Germans were moving around, and we could hear their muted commands, though we could not determine what was going on. Then to my intense surprise I heard a calm English voice say in the most matter-of-fact way, 'I'm going in now, Spider. Prepare to give me covering fire.' There was a short silence and then pandemonium broke loose. The clatter of Oerlikons shattered the stillness; tracer rounds sped across the darkness below, and ricocheted up into the sky; cries and screams of anguish broke out, and there were sounds of utter confusion. After ten minutes the firing stopped, and the voice, still at conversational level, said, 'I reckon we've got them. Ease your way out slow astern, and I'll follow you.' Lt-Cdr Morgan Giles, DSO had turned up with his motor gun boats just when we had induced the unfortunate Germans to evacuate to the mainland – a perfectly timed combined operation. When dawn broke we saw that the hillside we were on was heavily mined, and we had a slow and tense time finding a way down when we were ordered to get to the harbour. There were some nasty leg injuries from the pernicious small wooden Schu-mines, which are almost impossible to detect. In Grohote many bodies were floating in the water, and the demoralized survivors all gave themselves up. The Commando had thirty-six casualties, but the island was liberated from German occupation.

During a previous operation on the much larger island of Brac inter-service communication had not been so good. Here too the Germans withdrew ahead of us, and we waved cheerfully at a couple of Spitfires as they flew over our heads. There was a swift change to astonishment and indignation as they wheeled and strafed us closely. It was incredible that no one was hit.

Apart from these spells of excitement the main memory is of the spartan life we had to lead. Throughout our stay on Vis we were under canvas on the hillsides, and lived on basic Compo rations. Hard tack biscuits day-in day-out for a year became a bit monotonous – I tasted bread only three times. Money was meaningless – exchange was by barter, and there was little to acquire. Relations with the 1st Dalmatian Brigade were very friendly for the first few months, when they really needed us. They loved to sing rollicking songs, which we learned too, so camaraderie developed between us, despite the language barrier. The partisans came from all walks of life, and there was no doubting their fighting spirit, their determination to get rid of the Germans, and their devotion to Tito. They maintained a stern puritanical code – those found guilty of looting or sexual misconduct were shot (women as well), and drunkenness was severely punished. During the whole time that we were in Yugoslavia not a single Marine became involved with a woman.

When the tide turned and the Germans began to retreat relationships became more strained. Saturnine unsmiling political commissars always appeared in the background, and formerly friendly field commanders became more guarded. At the end of October, 43 Commando landed at Dubrovnik just after the Germans had withdrawn, and the political atmosphere got worse still while we were in Montenegro. The partisans deliberately began to block operations on our part, much to our frustration. The reason was understandable – they wanted it to be absolutely clear that it was they who liberated their country. With the prospect of setting up a post-war government the internecine feuds became even more bitter. Cetniks (royalist supporters of Mihailovic) and Ustasi (Yugoslavs who helped the Germans in their reprisals against the partisans) were hunted down and shot out of hand. When we were first driving towards Niksic we saw two figures digging, watched by a group clad in greatcoats. Then the two men stood up; arms were pointed at their heads; the bodies gave convulsive jerks; and we realized with revulsion that we had witnessed an execution. Several weeks later I was in a farmhouse when four partisans came in and roughly questioned the woman. I couldn't understand the Serbo-Croat, but there was no mistaking the look of absolute terror on her face. She remained rooted to a chair while they carried out a thorough search. Fortunately they did not find what they were looking for and they left.

One began to develop some expertise in diplomacy. 'E' Troop was posted to a remote area near Bileca, and I discovered that the partisans were holding 300 Germans prisoner not far away. Knowing that they had never taken prisoners in the past I decided that I'd better go and see how they were being treated. One of the German officers spoke a little English and he told me that their main worry was about getting enough food. From a partisan who could just understand me I found out that they had been allocated some sheep, so I made sure that these were slaughtered. Then I stayed until I saw them all have a meal, and they seemed a shade less despondent about the situation. On my way back along a lonely part of the road a voice called out in broken English. Huddled in the ditch were two bearded and bedraggled figures who pleaded with me to smuggle them out of the country. I had to explain that the repercussions would be too serious if it emerged that we had helped Cetniks, but I warned them about the partisan dispositions that I knew, and wished them luck. By coincidence on that same day a party of former Italian soldiers also approached me to help them to get back to Italy. Again, with the partisans in control of the Dalmatian ports, I could do nothing. Unhappy times.

As a nineteen year-old subaltern I was faced with some unexpected responsibilities. One day my troop commander told me that he was off on a three-day recce, and he added that fifty mules would be arriving that afternoon, and that we had to re-supply a Long Range Desert Group detachment some forty miles away. I knew nothing whatever about such animals, so it was fortunate that they were accompanied by half a dozen former Mountain Troop Italians, one of whom was a vet. They gave us one day's instructions on loading, leading and feeding, and then we set off entirely on our own. There were numerous amusing incidents, and one Marine ended up carrying a Compo box behind his mule, but we got there and back. After that we learned how to break down 75mm Mountain guns into six loads, and we established quite a reputation for getting guns and supplies to difficult locations.

At the beginning of December I was sent to recce the high mountain road from Niksic to Spuz, along which the Germans had just retreated. They had blown six large gaps where it was embanked round the steep hillside, and after traversing across these missing sections I reckoned that it would take more than a week to repair the damage. Not a bit of it. The partisans rounded up every man, woman and child in the surrounding district; got them to the hillside; and with picks, shovels, bare hands and tremendous zeal they rebuilt the embankments in three days. Two batteries of 25-pdrs from 111 Field Regiment, a battery of 3.7s, and the Mountain guns from the Raid Support Regiment got through. They were in time to put down the most effective barrage the partisans had seen on German 21 Mountain Corps transport which was held up on the Podgorica-Kolasin road.

A few days later the retreating forces blew up a bridge across the river near Spuz. Bailey Bridge parts were transported there remarkably quickly; three Sappers were available; and 'E' Troop was nominated to provide the unskilled labour. The enemy shelled the area in the afternoon, so we had the added difficulty of having to do the job at night. There's nothing like necessity to help me get the hang of things, and we completed the construction. During the next day's shelling we were as anxious for the bridge as for our own skins. There were no hits, and the Germans had to pull back out of range.

Bivouacing out throughout the winter in the high barren interior Karst country was a real test of endurance, as we had no special clothing. On one occasion my section of the troop was in an outhouse which had no roof when it rained almost continuously day and night for a whole week. Time and again our ground-sheets couldn't hold the water, and collapsed. Wet through, the nights were bitterly cold, and it needed tremendous effort to get some form of fire going for cooking. I suppose it says something that none of us went down with exposure. The CO, Lt-Col. Ian Riches, realized our predicament, and somehow managed to get an issue of Navy rum up to us. Did it go down well!

So, what with one thing and another, we were by no means reluctant to leave Dubrovnik for Italy in January 1945. After spells in the front line, which had been static over the winter, we opened up the spring offensive with a Commando Brigade attack across the river Reno in the Lake Commachio area. The curtain of shells which shielded our advance was a dramatic change from the small-scale fire and movement that we'd been used to.

At Argenta Lt Jenkins was awarded a DSO. After the war he completed his academic education at the universities of Oxford and Yale.

Left: Brigadier-General W.C. (Billy) Mitchell, pioneer of parachute warfare, in Germany 1918.

Below: Major John Frost after his return from Bruneval 1942. Later he became a Major-General.

Above: Lieutenant-General Matthew B. Ridgway, photographed when he was commanding US 82nd Airborne Division in Sicily, 1943.

Right: General G.C. Kenney, 1947. He was a brilliant innovator in airborne strategy.

Left: General James Gavin fitting his T7 parachute prior to leading US 82nd Airborne Division into battle, 17 September 1944.

Below: Horsa and Hamilcar gliders after landing six miles west of Arnhem, September 1944.

Above: Corregidor, 16 February 1945. US 503rd Parachute Infantry Regiment landing on Topside.

Below: An American-manufactured Locust tank leaving a British Hamilcar glider, 1944.

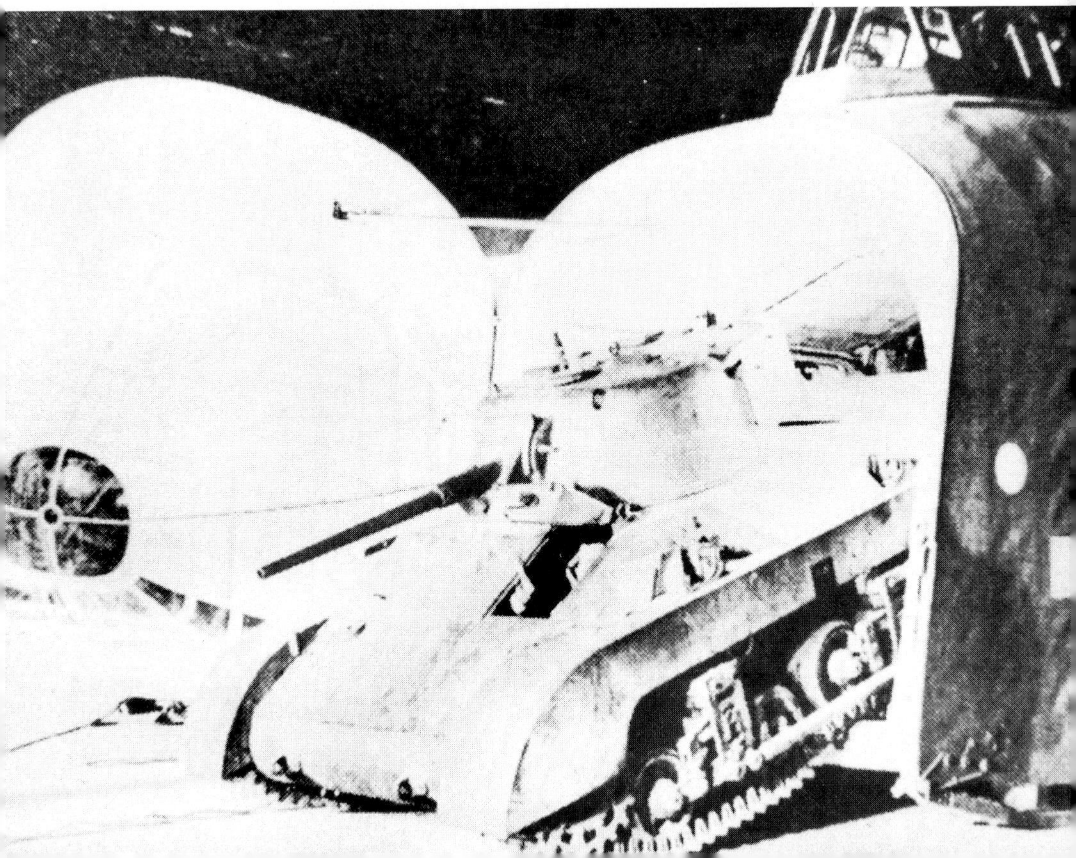

Above: A Russian demonstration of parachuting, 1935. Russians with manually operated parachutes leaving a TB3 Troop Carrier.

Below: German Fallschirmjäger jumping from a Junkers 52 (on static lines) in Germany in 1938.

Right: A glider being towed by a DC3 Dakota over the 8,000 feet high Assam hills.

Below: Mustang (P. 51) Fighter-bombers of No. 1 USAAF Air Commando. They were the Chindit Artillery and were used for deep penetration support, 1944.

Above: Chindit Sappers (Royal Engineers) preparing a bridge for demolition when an enemy troop train crossed it, 1944.

Left: Maskelyne Magic Mirrors for blinding raiding pilots.

Below: Major Maskelyne (left) with Douglas Fairbanks, Jnr, of US Navy Secret Section.

Above: Tank disguised as a truck opens up for action.

Right: Maskelyne's spinning search-light.

Below: Bofors gun disguised as a truck.

Right: 'Popski' (Lieutenant-Colonel Vladimir Peniakoff, DSO, MC).

Below: Popski's Private Army loads a jeep into a glider.

Above: Long-Range Desert Group lorries in the Sand Sea.

PPA in action in Italy.

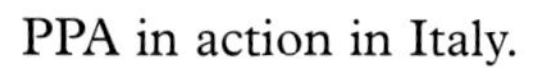

PPA returning enemy fire.

PPA making itself useful.

Above: Enigma machine, showing keyboard, plate and wheels.

Right: A Polish reconstruction of a German Enigma Machine.

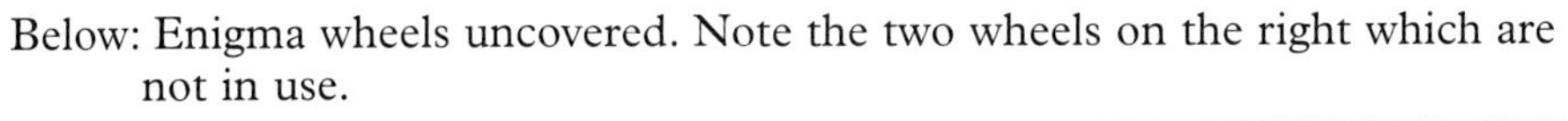

Below: Enigma wheels uncovered. Note the two wheels on the right which are not in use.

Right: A four-wheel Enigma machine. These were used by the German navy after March 1943.

Below: Drawing of an early 1920s American cyphering machine which was marketed at the time of the first commercial Enigma.

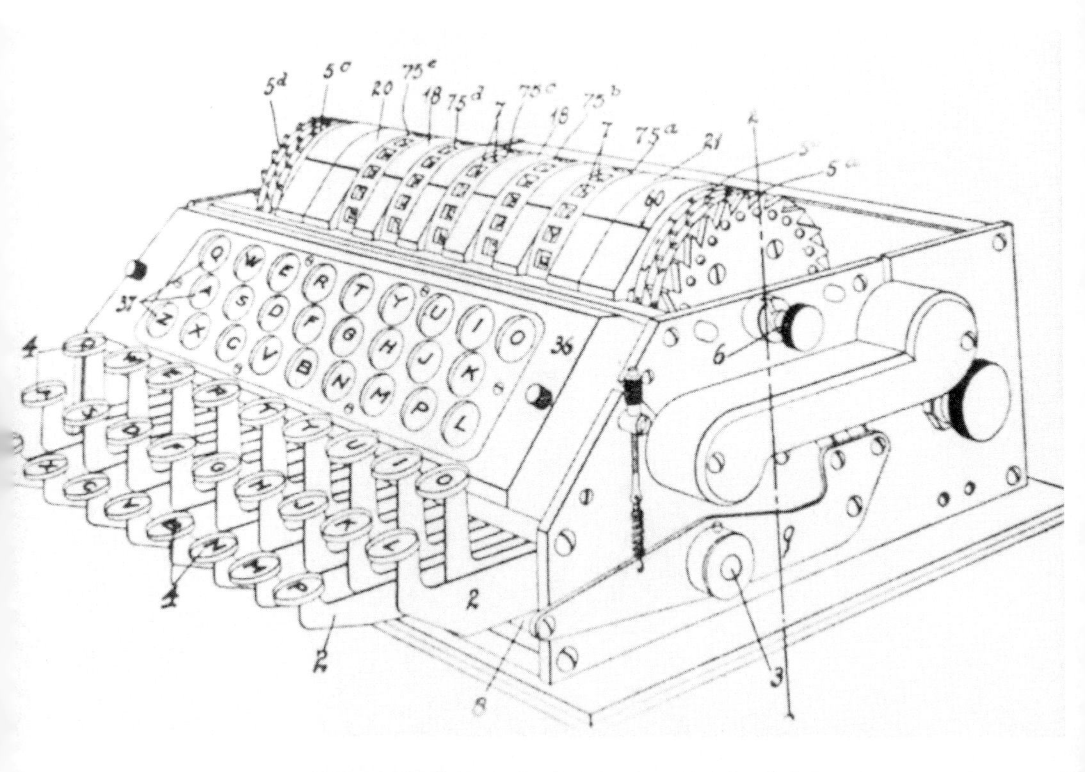

Above: American frogmen on an iceberg off Point Barrow, Alaska, during an operation.

Left: American frogmen placing mine detonator clips.

Right: An American underwater demolition team using a British X craft.

Left: American ‘naked warriors’ scuttling a Japanese midget submarine.

Below: A Limpet mine, front and rear view. On the left is the side which was fitted to the ship.

An aircraft hangar camouflaged to look like a house (from a distance) somewhere on the south coast of Britain.

A dummy target. The oil tanks on the left pour oil into the trough on the right. Enemy bombers assumed they had hit a vital area and continued to waste explosives on empty countryside.

An important stores dump (ammunition) camouflaged to look like a camouflaged lorry of little importance.

Dummy craft half-hidden to look like real ones badly concealed.

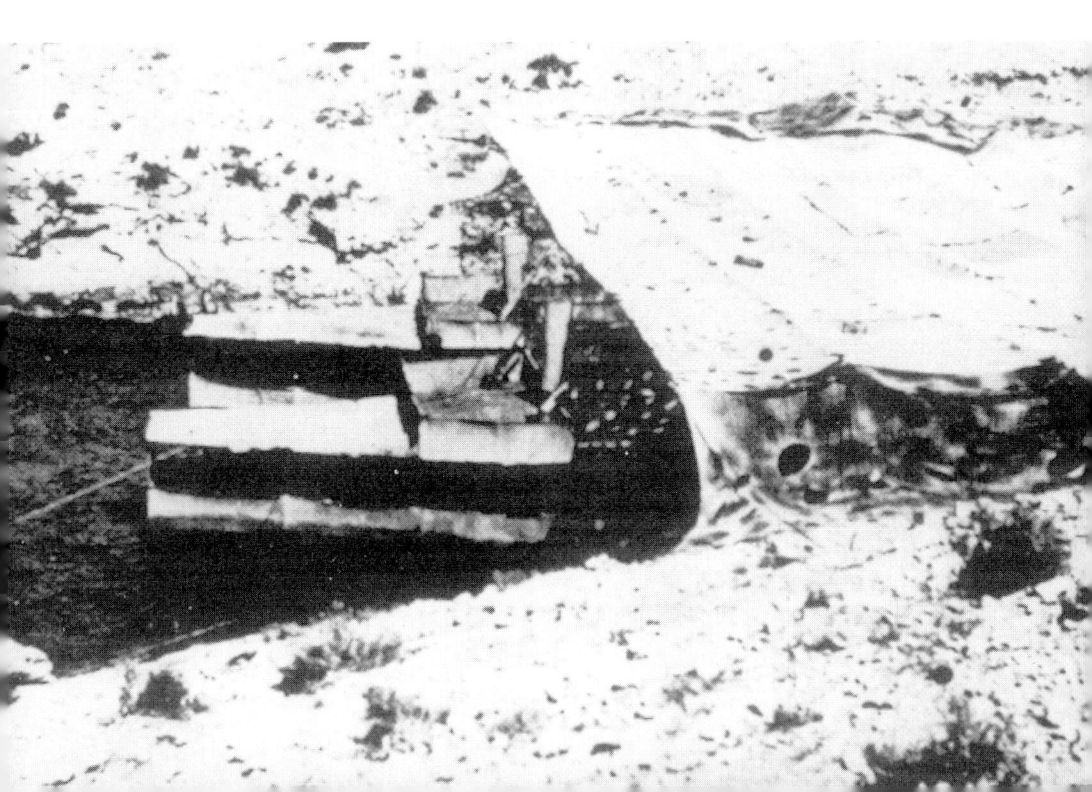

Padi fields from the air (flooded). Parachutists encountered many difficult landings, varying from dense jungle to swamp and mud.

Lysander landing on a jungle airstrip in Burma.

5: *The Seekers after Knowledge*

World War II saw an expansion of intelligence-gathering agencies on a scale that had never been dreamt of in previous wars. It also saw more secret operations. Undoubtedly this has set the standard for future conflicts. If there is ever another major war, it will begin because one side has obtained (or believes it has obtained) such a complete knowledge of the enemy's intentions and capabilities that it is sure that with its own resources victory is possible and easy.

At the beginning of World War II estimates of enemy capabilities were soon shown to be seriously awry. The British Ministry of Economic Warfare believed that Germany had not the resources to fight for more than ten months if blockaded, and the British Chiefs of Staff doubted whether Germany had the 'secret weapon' which Hitler constantly boasted that he possessed and which he said would soon end the war in his favour.

From the beginning of the war both sides made strenuous efforts to discover what the other was doing. In view of the size of the effort it is impressive how much was kept secret, and how much surprise was achieved. Perhaps the most astonishing aspect of World War II spying was that often when the higher command on each side was given clear, though perhaps circumstantial, evidence of some enemy plan, neither the story nor the evidence was believed. On the other hand, some quite flimsy deceptions often worked extremely well. In the former category, few people believed that the Germans would have such a rapid victory over Poland: yet in spite of this evidence of German capabilities the blitzkrieg through Norway, Denmark, Holland, Belgium and France came as a surprise, as if the campaign in Poland had never happened. German successes in the Balkans, Crete, and the Desert provided a further series of shocks for the Allies. Countering this, the Allies seem to have surprised the Germans at Mareth in North Africa, in the Sicily landings, and in the early part of the Italian campaign. The Russians were apparently completely taken aback by the German invasion of 1941; however, the Germans had underrated both Russian resistance and the Russian climate. Later in 1941, the early Japanese victories in the Pacific, particularly at Pearl Harbor, were a great shock to the Allies; it was the turn of the Japanese to be surprised when they were defeated in Burma and when the American Pacific fleet produced an apparently unlimited supply of aircraft carriers and assault craft. The atomic bombs on Hiroshima and Nagasaki undoubtedly shocked the Japanese into surrender, but it should be remembered that the conventional incendiary raids on Tokyo earlier in the year had produced greater casualties than the combined atomic bombs.

The best-kept secret of the war, combined with deception, was undoubtedly the D-Day landings of June 1944; however, it was almost equalled by the German offensive in the Ardennes in December 1944, which took the Allies completely by surprise. In addition to these major surprises, there were others less well known but still important: the method of U-boat warfare, the Allied fighter-bombers, and many of the technical developments made by both sides.

The process of information-gathering falls in two distinct categories: one is observation, such as that provided by aerial photography; the other is information provided by agents or spies.

The art of air reconnaissance was scarcely developed at the beginning of the war, but it soon made rapid strides. There had of course been much activity in this field before the war from commercial and 'amateur' aircraft; even so there were whole countries, such as Norway, about whose topography little was known accurately by the British. The Germans knew Norway and Denmark better than the Allies, for they had engaged in extensive, organised 'tourism' there.

In the second category comes the whole army of spies, agents, paid 'neutral' informers and listeners. I shall deal with this category first.

Listeners were of two main types. There were those who listened in to enemy broadcasts, and those who listened to their own. Listening to one's own radio might seem a somewhat unnecessary procedure, but in fact was extremely valuable. From the information thus gained aircraft were prevented from bombing their own troops, gunners avoided shooting down their own aircraft, raiders returning from missions were not fired on as they returned to base, units in the field did not collide with each other, and so on.

Listening to the enemy was practised at various levels by all the nations engaged in hostilities. Operators in forward areas knew their enemy opposition almost as well by their style as if they had known their first names. A morse key operator soon develops a style which is as distinctive as handwriting. A change of operator is immediately noticeable and often leads to polite enquiry from the other side as to why the change has occurred. 'Is the regular operator sick?' is the solicitous question. This front-line chit-chat happens in spite of official efforts to stamp it out. Often it is carefully exploited to gain valuable information.

A combination of joking, boasting and friendliness can sometimes exploit a regimental rivalry to give away useful military facts. In the Pacific the Americans became so irritated by Japanese operators who had once lived in America that they replaced a number of their forward operators by North American Navajo Indians who were told to talk in their own language. That completely baffled the Japanese. In the Western Desert the LRDG, knowing that the use of standard British radio procedure would immediately alert the Germans to the fact that there were British units working behind their lines (even though they could not read the codes), used French commercial procedure. Awareness of weakness of security in the front line was nothing new. In World War I a Scottish regiment had once crept up silently by night to relieve an English regiment. As soon as they arrived they were welcomed by the Germans playing the Scottish regimental march over the Tannoy system. It was no fault of the Scots, of course.

In World War II, chatter between Luftwaffe pilots supplied vital clues to British scientists who were trying to discover how the Germans were directing their bombers. Conversations between enemy prisoners of war were carefully monitored; even if the listeners did not learn much of vital military importance they learnt the *manner* in which the enemy chatted. This was very useful to interrogators who wished to assume a friendly, informal manner, while implying that there was nothing they did not know. Idioms were of great importance, and a great pitfall for foreigners. The German camp commandant who addressed a group and said 'You think I know nothing about your silly escape plans, but I can tell you I know damn all', really did use those words. Rather more serious was the case of the officer whose uniform, when searched, had a receipt for dinner at the Trocadero Restaurant (in Shaftesbury Avenue) in the pocket. One day, in an interrogation, the German interpreter said, 'Do you go often to the Trocadero?' The reply was, 'How do you know I go to the Troc then?'

The interrogator laughed and showed him the receipt. In future, the German noted carefully, he would never speak of the Trocadero, but only refer to 'the Troc'. It would help to establish the necessary informal rapport.

All these methods were important but the greatest listening project of World War II was undertaken by what was known as the Y Service. The Y Service was the name given to the monitoring of all enemy signals. It encompassed high-grade cipher, morse, speech and all levels of coded message. This was a vast undertaking which required many experts. The information thus gathered was delivered to the government Code and Cipher School at Bletchley Park in Buckinghamshire. Here low-grade ciphers often proved of great value in interpreting transcriptions from high-grade cipher. Fortunately for the Allies, the Germans believed that all their high-grade cipher was unbreakable. They placed their trust in an automatic coding device known as the Enigma machine.

The story of interception and code-breaking in World War II is, as might be expected, enormously detailed and complicated. A number of excellent books have been written on the subject, some by people who took part in the process themselves. The three published volumes of the official history of *British Intelligence in the Second World War* is full of references; its authors had the advantage of seeing secret papers which have not been released to the general public, and probably never will be. Some of the authors who wrote books on the subject interviewed key people who are now dead. It is, however, important to realize that there was not merely one, but several high-grade ciphers in use throughout the war.

Systems of sending messages in various forms of code are as old as warfare itself. The purpose was, of course, to send a message to a friend or ally in a form which, if it were intercepted by the enemy, would not be understood. A coded message uses a different form of letters from that of the original: thus 'Overlord' was the code word for the D-Day landings in 1944. Every child knows you can make a simple code by writing out the alphabet forwards and backwards and for every letter in the message substituting the one from the alphabet running backwards. However, the range of combinations produced by normal permutations of letters of the alphabet is necessarily limited, and even if the writer omits parts of words, or even inserts meaningless words into the text, the process of 'breaking' a code of this nature is the work of minutes rather than hours to a skilled decrypter. Figures, and combinations of letters and figures, introduce a new range of possibilities. The aim of cryptographers was ultimately to produce a code which could not be solved by a logical process. This meant introducing a form of random encoding. The Enigma machine did that perfectly. At first sight, an Enigma machine does not look particularly complicated (there are examples on view, such as the one in the Royal Signals Museum at Blandford in Dorset). The keyboard on the German version was the same as on an ordinary typewriter except that there were no numbers or punctuation marks. Behind this was another apparent keyboard, on which the alphabet was set out identically but here the letters appeared in small glass holes which lit up when a key on the other board was touched. However, when the letter lit up, it was not the same as the one which had been pressed. If the operator pressed A he might get B, but when he pressed A again he would not get B but another letter. This process does not sound very complicated but herein lay the whole secret of the machine. It was a battery-operated electric typewriter, and when the operator touched a letter the message was passed to plugs and drums. There were twenty-six plugs and they coupled any two letters. Thus, every time a plug coupling was changed a whole new range of codes came into being. But the main work was on the drum-like wheels. These were at first three in number but later were increased to five. The impetus triggered off when the operator touched a key (which did not, of course, depress a lever) went through the rotating wheels from left to right, in a highly involved manner, then having reached the end went back again, and through the plugs, until it lit up the chosen letter. The act of changing plugs is, of course, simple enough but what made the machine diabolically complicated was that the wheels, and their order, could be changed almost as easily. Each wheel was quite small, being three inches across. A message going through the system on the initial setting could come out on one of several hundred settings; when the plugs and wheels were changed this was multiplied by thousands.

The result was to change a straightforward statement into a random selection of letters which could not be worked out by any machinery existing at the time. (This, of course, was decades before sophisticated computers.) Each machine was supplied with an instruction book. The sender informed the receiver how to set his machine by prefixing his own message with a sequence of letters. It was all quite simple, if you had the machine and the right instruction book. Eventually the Germans had 100,000 of these machines in use.

The original machine had been invented by H. A. Koch, a Dutchman, in 1919. However, Koch did not have the knowledge or facilities to make a working model and it was not until 1923 that a German firm manufactured and put on the market a machine which they called Enigma. Selling it proved difficult. At that time nobody saw any use for the machine except for safeguarding business correspondence. However, it seemed an elaborate way of protecting something which could be kept secret more cheaply and easily in other ways, and although a few German firms and some other countries showed an interest in it, they did not show enough to make the manufacture of Enigma a paying proposition. Consequently, the firm went bankrupt. However, a few Enigma machines continued to be made and in 1926 they were adopted by the German navy, to be followed in 1928 by the German army.

At this time, the only European country showing a real interest in rearmament was Germany, and it was restricted by the Versailles Treaty to an army of 100,000 men, with no tanks and no military aircraft. However, with the help of Russia, Germany was able to train pilots (in Russia) and with the help of Sweden to manufacture tanks. Although Enigmas would eventually prove most useful to tanks and aircraft, it was not until Hitler seized power in 1933, and began flouting the provisions of the Versailles Treaty, that Enigma machines began to appear in that role. Meanwhile other countries, with the exception of Italy and Japan, adopted an attitude that if they did not think of, or prepare for, war, the danger would eventually go away. Britain, although possessing what was probably the most efficient secret service in the world, tended to regard espionage as an unnecessary, rather theatrical, activity, at best a joke, at the worst in rather bad taste. The expression 'cloak and dagger' encapsulates this attitude perfectly.

However, the commercial model of Enigma was available on the market till the early 1930s (though not produced by the original firm) and in 1927 the chief signals officer in Washington bought one for 144 dollars (about £30 at the current rate of exchange). America, at this time, was just building up a promising espionage organization known as the Black Chamber. This had developed an expertise at deciphering codes used by foreign governments. However, in 1929, President Hoover appointed a new secretary of state, Henry Stimson. As a product of the old school, Stimson stated firmly that 'gentlemen do not read each other's mail' and abolished the Black Chamber. With what now seems to have been undue optimism, he was under the impression that the world was entering upon a new era in which espionage, secret diplomacy and cryptography would be replaced by mutual trust and frankness. However, all was not lost, for the US Signal Intelligence Service simply took over the Black Chamber's records and work. The head of this unit was William Friedman. Friedman was an exceptionally talented cryptographer, but it appears that the commercial version of the Enigma machine which he studied was much less sophisticated than the military version which the Germans were now using and merely presented a tantalizing and frustrating challenge. In any event, Friedman did not consider that Germany offered any special threat to America; on the other hand, he thought that Japan did. Furthermore, Japan had also acquired an Enigma machine, developed it, and put it into use. It became known as the 'Purple' machine. Friedman's attention was therefore taken up with Purple rather than Enigma. Britain, to whom the German Enigma offered the most dangerous threat, remained loftily indifferent to this piece of German mechanical skullduggery.

The Poles, sandwiched as they were between Russia and Germany, did not regard their future with the bland optimism which characterized Britain and the United States. East Prussia, on the southern shore of the Baltic, was separated from the rest of Germany by the 'Polish Corridor', a tongue of Polish territory which gave Poland its only access to the sea. A glance at the pre-1939 map shows that the boundaries of Poland could only have been dreamed up by woolly-minded, war-weary delegates from countries with no proper knowledge of Poland's history or problems. Had there been good will on all sides, it *might* have lasted. As it was, with no good will from any side, Hitler was able to use the isolation of East Germany as a justification for every demand he wished to make on Poland.

The Poles, well aware that the Germans hoped to change the map of Poland in their own favour as soon as possible, showed a keen interest in all German military activities. They knew very well what was going on in Germany, and particularly in the German military mind, and realized that it boded no good for them. As they were expert cryptographers, they had had no difficulty in reading German codes and cyphers – until 1926. But in 1926 they hit a blank wall. The Germans were using the new Enigma, and the Poles were baffled. But not for long. They too acquired one of the original commercial Enigmas. What neither they, nor anyone else, had was the pattern of

German modifications and keys to settings. These raised the odds against deciphering even a short message to several million to one. Nevertheless, the Poles worked on it, and by a combination of espionage, stolen or bought papers and persistence, were able to build a version for themselves. Just when they had reached the point of reading most of the German messages, the Germans modified the machine once more.

By 1939 Britain had become well aware of the immediate danger of war, and was also pledged to help the Poles in the event of German aggression. But even the combined efforts of both countries' cryptographers could not unravel the mysteries of the German machine before Poland was invaded in September 1939. Poland was overrun, but its cryptographers escaped with their two machines and began working at Château Vignolles, forty miles north east of Paris. Here was assembled a team of seventy, which was made up of Poles, French and Spaniards. It maintained close liaison with the British Code and Cipher School, which had just moved from its headquarters in London to Bletchley Park, approximately mid-way between Oxford and Cambridge, where it was well situated to call on the talents of either university.

Most of the cryptographers recruited to work at Bletchley Park came from Cambridge. They were usually mathematicians, but to be a brilliant mathematician was not the whole answer. Cryptography was not merely juggling with figures: it required flashes of creative imagination mixed with the determination to persist in routine checking and cross-referencing. The factor which probably did more than anything to unravel the Enigma mysteries was the ability to make inspired guesses – one of the cryptographers was an international chess player.

As the war continued, BP (as Bletchley Park came to be known) expanded considerably. It maintained a twenty-four-hour watch. Its task was enormous. Each time the Germans sent a coded message they gave the receiver a clue by a prefix of a few letters, so that he could adjust his set to match it up with the machine of the sender. But as there were many thousands of these sets in use, mostly using different settings, a difficult message could take a week or more to decipher. Other messages could be handled much more quickly. People who learnt about BP some thirty years after the war gained the impression that as soon as a message was intercepted it was interpreted and acted on. This was a long way from the truth. When battles were taking place few Enigma intercepts were available in time to be of use to field commanders. There were, of course, exceptions. There was one occasion when a message sent to Rommel was intercepted by the Y Service, interpreted at BP and sent to Montgomery. However, Rommel's operator had not received the message accurately. He therefore had to ask for a repeat and by the time Rommel received the complete text, Montgomery was reading the same message.

But there were, of course, many messages which were not intercepted at all; this was inevitable in the vast volume of traffic. And some which were intercepted used codes which no Allied team was able to break.

The need to protect the security of Ultra (the name given to this high level of decoding) also delayed messages. At times it even meant that vital information could not be acted on. Thus, when the Allies were defending Crete, they learnt from Ultra that their troop dispositions were wrong. But to have altered them would have aroused German suspicions. So they were left as they were. Equally, if a German ship was known to be carrying vital stores to the Germans, it had to be spotted by an apparently random cruising aircraft before it could be intercepted and attacked by aircraft or submarine. Not even corps commanders were allowed to know of the existence of Ultra. Nor, fortunately, was the Foreign Office which at the time contained the traitors Philby, Burgess and Maclean.

The existence of Ultra was not made public until 1974. When this astonishing piece of information was disclosed, military historians rapidly began to revise their view of much that had happened between 1939 and 1945. Some versions of past events began to look distinctly suspect. Montgomery had been accustomed to say that he kept a photograph of Rommel in his caravan so that he could study it and from this physiognomical analysis predict what Rommel would think and do next. He could not have revealed that he had his German opponent's messages to and from his superiors lying on the table in front of him, of course, but the claim that he could deduce Rommel's intentions by studying his features was so dishonest that it threw doubt on many other versions of events which he had given. Not least was the conversation with Auchinleck, at which only the two were present, and in which he attributed a defeatist attitude to his predecessor, which was certainly no part of the Auchinleck philosophy. It seems sad that Montgomery, with a record of solid achievement which has rarely been surpassed, should have tried to enhance his reputation with such unnecessary and petty subterfuges.

Protecting the security of Ultra intelligence required a system of delivery (to approved recipients) which was efficient but did not draw attention to itself. At home this was no problem but abroad, to service commanders in remote areas, special arrangements were clearly necessary. The solution was the Special Liaison Units (SLUs). These were quite small, and usually consisted of an officer, a cipher sergeant and signallers to operate the sets. The Ultra messages, having been decoded, translated, evaluated and given the appropriate priority (whether requiring urgent action or merely containing useful information), were once more encoded and sent to the appropriate special liaison unit in the field. There they were decoded and passed to the named recipient. The SLUs performing this task needed to be close to various headquarters, but also secure from attention from outsiders. Their presence could not remain unnoticed and therefore a suitable cover story had to be devised. At British headquarters the presence of a signals unit occupying a couple of extra trucks excited little comment, and could be explained as a radar checking unit, or something equally nebulous. However, the presence of a small, secretive group of British soldiers near an American headquarters, completely surrounded by Americans, provoked more curiosity. In some cases this was best dealt with by having an American attached to the team. The SLU itself was a mixture. Usually the officer was from the RAF and rarely held a rank as high as wing-commander. This made difficult the task of ensuring that very senior officers abided by security regulations; however, this was not the only example of a unit where specialist junior officers had to prevent their superiors from breaching security, or otherwise behaving irresponsibly. The cipher sergeants also came from the RAF, but the signallers were from the army (Royal Signals).

The navy was not, at first, as welcoming to Ultra intelligence as had been expected. The admirals doubted whether it was as valuable as their own sources of intelligence which came from captured naval codes quite separate from Enigma. Even when the value of Ultra was appreciated, the navy retained a certain reluctance to have its actions influenced by intelligence which in its view did not always apply to naval conditions.

Since the existence of Ultra has been acknowledged, and its enormous contribution to Allied success recognized, there has been an impression that Allied victory was therefore inevitable: if you know what your opponent intends to do, it is easy to defeat him. This, alas, is far from true. If you are outnumbered and poorly armed, the fact that you know that the enemy is coming in your direction does not enable you to defeat him. Good intelligence is of value only if it can be put to use. Fortunately for the Allies in World War II, this did occur, but the process was not easy. One of the most useful aspects of Ultra was that it enabled the Allies to mislead the Axis through deception tactics. Ultra enabled Allied deception planners to know what the enemy thought their plans were: the deception tactic was to encourage that belief while doing something entirely different.

The dazzling success of the Ultra decrypting operation has unfortunately diverted some of the appreciation which should have been given to the Y Service. For, although the value of the skilled cryptographers has now been recognized, though not perhaps adequately rewarded, the achievements of the Y Service seem to have received less commendation than they deserve. The Y Service, working in arduous and often dangerous conditions, was the vital link without which none of the activities of BP would have been possible. However, those who are employed in listening and monitoring posts are well aware, even before they begin their tasks, that they are unlikely to receive public commendation for any of their services. The nature of their work means that even in peacetime it is not within the interests of the state to disclose details of their methods: monitoring of the signals traffic of potential enemies goes on in peacetime as it does in war, though not, of course, on the same scale.

Although some monitoring was and is done through high-powered receivers working from a secure base, much was also performed by small units working very close to the enemy, picking up low-powered transmissions. They also tapped telephone wires. These small field units covered a range which was often quite different from the high-level material. Commanders making an attack – such as the German break-through in the Ardennes in December 1944 – may order a wireless silence for a period before the attack. Only when the tanks begin to move will that silence be broken (if indeed then), and the defender may be taken unaware unless he has a local listening unit to alert him to the danger of being surprised. Then, if he has the resources, he will be able to take appropriate measures and will not be put at a disadvantage. Furthermore, any information which comes from high-level sources, such as Ultra, once the attack has begun, is likely to be out of date and useless in the fast-moving scene on the battlefield. There was not much Ultra information available at the time of the battle for France in 1940, but what there was made no difference to the Allies because it was out of date before it could reach the local commanders. Even if it had reached them in time, they did not have the resources to take appropriate action.

One of the few available personal accounts of life in the Y Service came from Aileen Clayton who joined the Women's Auxiliary Air Force in 1939 as an Aircraftswoman Second Class. Aileen Clayton (at that time Aileen Morris) had the advantage of speaking German fluently and therefore soon found herself employed in listening to German morse and radio telephone signals from the German air force. Her unit was at RAF Hawkinge, near Folkestone, although in the initial stages she spent some time at Fairlight perched on the cliff overlooking Hastings. This incidentally was the place at which the Germans were most likely to invade if they came, and if they did their arrival was likely to be preceded by some intensive bombing which would have made the survival of the Fairlight station highly unlikely. Working in six-hour shifts, with earphones clamped over their heads, members of the unit strained to hear every word from German aircraft above it and on the far side of the Channel. They picked up messages from reconnaissance planes, conversations from Junkers 88s strafing French roads packed with terrified refugees, and reports of the disasters which were being inflicted on British and French armies. Their work was made more difficult by atmospherics, by the pilots' use of code-words and slang, and variations in German accents. But, surprisingly quickly, they learnt to recognize the voices of individual pilots and commanders. Whatever they received was sent every day by despatch rider to Bletchley Park.

After the end of the battle for France, Aileen Clayton and her colleagues were listening to the orders for attack on targets in Britain, and on Allied shipping round the coasts. Most of the information they picked up was bad news, but all was a valuable contribution to the day when the tide would turn for the Allies. The Germans were well aware that their conversations were overheard (they operated a similar service themselves) and occasionally addressed remarks to their British audience. One interesting piece of information the unit picked up was that the Germans were using Red Cross markings on aircraft used for ordinary reconnaissance. The Germans were duly warned at high level that if this practice did not cease forthwith all Red Cross planes would be liable to be attacked.

Aileen Clayton was eventually sent on a course prior to commissioning, and by this time she was exhausted. But life was no easier after commissioning, perhaps worse. As the Battle of Britain became more intense, the unit was moved back to Kingsdown, in north Kent, but even there it was still at the centre of the battle. As their work continued, it became clear that the Germans were using a different method of aircraft control from that used in Britain. Both sides, of course, had radar, but this German method appeared to have certain specific characteristics. The Germans, at the same time, seemed angry and frustrated by the fact that the British were making better use of radar than the Luftwaffe did, especially in fighter control. The latter was good but, owing to lack of trained personnel, far from perfect. The shortage of trained, suitable people affected the Y Service too. Aileen Clayton recorded that often she and another WAAF officer would be on duty for thirty-six hours out of forty-eight; they were needed to make immediate appraisal of the value of intercepted German conversations.

The original Y Service had consisted of English women 'listeners', all of whom, at one time or another, had lived in Germany and were thus aware of German speech forms and slang. However, the number of women with this qualification was limited. This meant that soon their numbers had to be supplemented by nationals of other countries such as Austria, Poland and France. Although without exception these were outstandingly good at their job, they could not be commissioned under existing RAF regulations, because they were of foreign birth. (The RAF had numerous commissioned foreigners, but refused to extend this privilege to women in the Y Service.) In consequence there was a steady drain of these talented recruits to BP and the Air Ministry, where no objection was made to their being commissioned.

When the Battle of Britain was over, in 1940, the Germans switched their attack to night bombing. Mostly these aircraft proceeded in wireless silence but occasionally there was a transmission which confirmed the earlier impression that the bombers were being guided by some form of beam. Among the many brilliant scientists now working for Air Intelligence was a young man named R. V. Jones, who was greatly interested in this guided beam theory. Soon Jones had confirmation of his ideas about the beam from some papers found in a shot-down Heinkel. They referred to the *Knickebein* (Crooked leg). Soon other captured papers produced more, though tantalizingly small amounts of information. However, the knowledge that the Germans were using a directional beam was one thing; the apparatus and procedure to counter it was another. By persistence, though not without opposition from sceptics, Jones was able to set up an organization to study this new threat. The method of guidance was to send an aircraft along a beam towards its target, advising it if it were diverging by a string of dots on one side of the beam and a string of dashes on the other. The pilot merely needed an ordinary receiver to use this directional beam. When the pilot reached the point at which he should release his bombs, he received another directional signal from a cross-beam. Among other advantages, this method prevented a pilot, harassed by heavy anti-aircraft fire or night fighters, from releasing his bombs short of the target and scuttling for home. Later there were more sophisticated versions of the beam, the X Gerät and the Wotan, but Jones's team soon had the measure of them all. Among the methods used were the sending of a cross-beam short of the target, causing the pilot to release his bombs on open fields, and false beams which sent the pilots off-course. German pilots who followed the false beams instead of their own believed that the British had discovered some means of bending their original beams: this theory was wrong, but it had great vogue in both Germany and Britain after the war.

A further development in this rapidly growing beam warfare was the process known as 'meaconing'. Along the coast from Germany to France the Germans had set up stations transmitting direction beams to assist German pilots who were either on reconnaissance or returning from bombing raids. Luftwaffe pilots knew the necessary frequencies and would make periodic checks. A British unit, No. 80 Wing, soon learnt all the frequencies too and with a Post Office transmitter would retransmit on the same frequency. The Germans soon realized what was happening and altered their frequencies at prearranged but not regular times. It was of no avail. No. 80 Wing then added to the troubles of Luftwaffe pilots by jamming and misdirecting. One unhappy pilot landed in Dorset under the impression that he was in France. Not least of the pilots' concern was the fact that if they were flying along German guidance beams, and the British were well aware of the course of such beams, there was a more than likely chance that they would at some stage find a sizeable force of British fighters waiting to greet them.

All this knowledge of German transmissions, frequencies, call signs, codes and conventions was gathered in by the Y Service and forwarded to Bletchley for onward transmission. By now the Y Service stations were known as Home Defence Units (HDUs). It was chosen as a title because it sounded no more secret than the well-known Home Guard.

The choice illustrated a principle of secrecy: if you wish to divert attention from your real purpose adopt a title which sounds boring and inoffensive.

The strain on the Y operators was, of course, enormous. At the time nobody thought of long-term effects. But, like so many other wartime stresses, in desert, in jungle, in the air, above or under the sea, the effects might not appear until years later, affecting sight, movement or general health. The effect on Y operators was to give them an undue sensitivity to noise, of which, alas, the post-war world was over-full.

The main Enigma intercepts were made at Chicksands, Bedfordshire. Here, over one hundred sets were tuned in to German transmissions. Soon the Y Service became aware that there was an élite bombing force named K Gr 100, based on Vannes (France). This owed its existence to the fact that the German air force had lost faith in the old *Knickebein,* which was being so successfully mangled by the Allies. Instead, they were planning to employ X Gerät, in which a more sophisticated arrangement of beams would be used. However, X Gerät, although used successfully in the raid on Coventry, required more from the bomber crews, and thus a longer, more specialized training. Pending the introduction of X Gerät on a wider scale, the Luftwaffe used K Gr 100 as a Pathfinder force. It would go ahead and locate a target, drop incendiaries to mark it, then turn aside to let the heavy, really destructive, bombers move in. Once Air Intelligence realized what was happening it took precautionary measures which were, on the whole, effective. When intercepts informed them that the bomber force was on its way, local units ignited decoy targets away, but not too far away, from the intended target. This ruse, although crude, seems to have worked reasonably well.

In October 1940 the Y Service picked up a mysterious reference to 'Parlour' and 'Little Screw'. This baffled the experts for a long time but was eventually pinned down as being the method by which German night fighters were directed to their targets – which were RAF bombers. Frustrating 'Little Screw' was a difficult matter, for it was internally operated. Try as they would, the scientists could find no solution. But an answer finally arrived from the Bruneval raid, described in Chapter 3. From the pieces of radar equipment brought back by the commandos, Jones and his team learnt how 'Little Screw' worked and were able to devise an appropriate jamming method.

As soon as the Germans realized that one of their aircraft guidance systems was understood and frustrated, they moved quickly to introduce another. Somewhat romantically, they called their X Gerät beam stations 'Wotan I'. Wotan, Odin or Woden, as he was variously called, was a war god of Norse mythology, which had considerable appeal to Hitler in his more woolly-minded moments. (We use the word in our Wednesday – 'Woden's Day'.)

The advanced version of Wotan I was named Wotan II or Y Gerät. Thus the Allied Y Service was busy tracking down Y Gerät. Fortunately an aircraft using Y Gerät was shot down and its documents were captured intact. Owing to the sophistication of the new device, it was necessary for the German aircraft to carry operational instructions. These enabled Y Gerät to be jammed by a system specially devised for the purpose and named 'Domino'.

All this was at the higher end of the interception scale. Below, but none the less essential, was the routine RAF monitoring service A14, its counterpart in the army, M18, and the navy equivalent, NID9. All worked closely together. Although these interception-units were constantly expanded they were always fully stretched by the sheer volume of transmissions to be monitored. Various methods were tried to expand the range of the interceptor sets. They included the positioning of operators in gondolas suspended below observation balloons. A swaying gondola was probably the quickest way of making men and women airsick that has yet been devised. Fortunately for the operators it was soon decided to operate the interceptor sets in the gondolas by remote control.

The Y operators listened eagerly for frustrated Germans who, after sticking rigidly to their codes, suddenly lost patience and asked their controllers for their instructions in clear (uncoded). Almost as dangerous was to revert to using a code-word which was now well known to both sides. 'Angel' (height) and 'Bandit' (enemy aircraft) were early examples.

As the war progressed and the value of the Y Service became widely appreciated, the units found themselves with more masters than they would have wished. Enigma traffic went to BP (code-named Station X) but other traffic went to a variety of destinations, mainly intelligence units at headquarters. Overseas, the JDUs became FUs (Field units). These searched the wavebands for anything which might remotely concern them. There seemed to be no limit to the variety of traffic which the Y Service picked up, and which was put to use. Distress calls from either side meant that an air or sea battle had taken place and that survivors were hoping to be rescued. In some cases distress calls led to the capture of enemy aircrew before they could be rescued by their own side. The efficiency and thoroughness of the Germans often gave away much useful information. The Luftwaffe divided all areas which it overflew into districts, each with a headquarters responsible for the well-being of the aircraft in that district. The Y Service listened with interest to reports of all aircraft entering or leaving those districts; the Germans, of course, used codes for their messages, but would doubtless have been appalled if they had known how quickly and easily those codes were broken. In this way the range of German radar was learnt, and also the range of various types of German aircraft. So useful did some of these local services become to the interested parties that there were indignant but futile protests when the changing pattern of the war caused a Y field unit to be withdrawn and posted to a different area.

As the Allies drove forward through the desert, through Sicily, and through Italy, before making the decisive invasion of France, the 'radar' battle grew more intense and complicated. Both sides made strenuous efforts to knock out their opponent's radar stations. Meanwhile the Germans introduced a very effective long-range radar, known as the 'Wassermann', and also fitted 'Lichtensteingerät' (airborne radar) on some of their night fighters. Both sides used 'Window' which the Germans called 'Düppel', and the Americans 'Chaff'. This was the process of dropping strips of metal foil before and during a raid, in order to confuse the other side's radar. It was very effective, and worked better for the Allies than the Germans in spite of the latter's attempts to counter its effects by what became known as 'Würzlaus'. 'Meaconing' was used with increasing effect during the later campaigns and would have been used even more extensively if there had been sufficient transmitters to expand it to its optimum use. An example of the continuity of the challenge was 'Aphrodite', a sytem which baffled the analysts for a long time. It was eventually discovered to be a method used by U-boats to avoid being detected by radar. Among the most grateful recipients of Y Service intercepts were the intelligence officers of the United States air forces. One of them was Maj. Thornton Wilder, author of the best-seller *The Bridge of San Luis Rey*. The Americans were so enthusiastic that they volunteered to put German-speaking airborne monitors in their bombers. These had an appropriate cover story to mislead the Germans if they should be shot down and captured. The Americans, of course, had their own interceptor units too. There was no question of rivalry in this work:

liaison was perfect. Often a Y Service FU received information which it could not have obtained for itself because it lacked the numbers to give complete coverage.

Among the less well-known but nevertheless extremely important achievements of the Y Service was the jamming of communication between German dive-bombers at the time of Dunkirk. At the time this was happening the Y Service was picking up instructions to the Luftwaffe which, when passed to the Royal Navy, were invaluable for enabling the navy to control the movements of its shipping during the rescue. Y Service also provided the answer to one of the great controversies of the war: were the German panzers ordered to stop, or did they have to? In May 1940, when the German army had scythed its way through Belgium, Holland and France, leaving the Allied defence in ribbons, the defeated armies were forced back to the Channel ports. Over 300,000 fell back to Dunkirk, and the Allied High Command waited for a final onslaught by the relentless Panzer divisions. There seemed no way of stopping them if a final all-out assault was launched on the shattered army taking refuge in the beleagured town. But the final, crushing blow never came. It seems that Hitler was afraid that his Panzer divisions had overrun their resources and might now, at this moment of triumph, be caught at the end of their point of effectiveness and defeated. Neither he nor the German High Command had any idea how complete their victory was and how little material the remnants of the army in Dunkirk possessed with which to put up any further fight. Furthermore, it seems, he was afraid an unravaged French army might be coming up from the south to throw its weight into the battle. On 24 May at 11.42 A.M. an uncoded message was intercepted. It said, 'The attack on the Dunkirk–Hazebrouck–Merville line is to be discontinued for the present.' This was not an Enigma intercept: how the order had been given is not clear, but presumably it was by Hitler to Halder, his Chief of the General Staff, who passed it to von Runstedt. Although neither the originator nor intended recipient of the message was known, there is no doubt that it was genuine, and also that it represented a piece of carelessness. Its value to the Allies was enormous. It meant that they could now concentate on the evacuation without having to give thought to making a final bloodbath defence; thus over 300,000 troops were saved.

It was a bonus that the message was in clear, for many low-grade (as they were called) ciphers were extremely difficult to break. Often they received less immediate attention because it was thought that 'low-grade' implied that their contents were of no great importance. This was by no means the case. Even when a message was decoded, its significance might not at first be grasped; evaluation was all important. The American terms for interception were either 'Radio Interception' or 'Traffic Analysis', and the second of these is probably the best description of this work. However, the British services also used the term 'Traffic Analysis' for certain activities, but not for the whole interception service.

Although cooperation between the services and various interested departments improved steadily during the war (although there were internal rivalries) and relations with the United States were very harmonious, the same unfortunately could not be said of cooperation with Russia. On certain occasions the Russians supplied items of useful information: on others they produced nothing. The Russians had, in fact, ignored all warnings from Britain that a German invasion of their country had been planned for mid 1941. Although anxious to help the Russians defeat the mutual enemy, the British government had to be careful about anything it passed to them in the early stages. The Russians were well aware that the information supplied to them was of the highest quality and were extremely curious about its source. The Allies refused to enlighten them for a long time, for the simple reason that they were afraid that once the Russians knew of their possession of the Enigma secrets it would not be long before the Germans knew also. Russian security was, overall, poor. However, at Churchill's specific request, Enigma information was passed to the Russians at regular intervals, though suitably disguised. This procedure was followed without enthusiasm by British Intelligence, which knew that the Russians had captured a number of German air force codes on the Eastern Front but were keeping quiet about them. Most of what was known about the course of the fighting between Germany and Russia came from Enigma decrypts, not from the Russians themselves. However, in June 1943 the Russians captured a German code known as 'Auka', used by the German air force, and a German naval Enigma machine. Unaware of how to make the best use of these assets, they sought help from the British. This move looked a promising development and, in consequence, the British gave the Russians one of the Enigma machines they themselves had recently captured, with instructions on how to use it. (It must be remembered that the mere possession of the mechanical apparatus did not mean that it could immediately be put to use for code-breaking.) Sad to say, efforts in another field, that of cooperation between SOE and NKVD (now the KGB) against German targets, faded after a promising start.

It should not be assumed from the above account that the history of the Y Service was one of unbroken, glittering success. Success indeed there was, in many vital spheres, but there were long and wide gaps in the code-breaking service; the field was simply too large to be covered fully. One of the most disconcerting of the gaps was that in reading the German naval ciphers which were being used to direct U-boats. It took nine months, and would undoubtedly have taken longer if one of the German operators had not obligingly repeated a signal which had been originally transmitted on a four-wheel setting (which the Allies did not know) on a three-wheel setting (which they did). From this mistake the use of the fourth wheel was deduced. The process of decrypting difficult codes had been further held up by the slowness in delivering 'Bombe' machines. Bombe machines were mechanical decrypting machines which could be made to operate at high speed on random ciphers. But the term 'high speed' is relative. The official history of British Intelligence describes the slow and difficult progress which was made in breaking the German naval 'Shark' codes. 'It took six three-wheel Bombes seventeen days to break the settings for the day: a three-wheel Bombe had to work twenty-six times longer to test the text of a four-wheel signal than to test that of a three-wheel signal.'

Japanese diplomatic messages were encoded on a machine which was known as 'Purple'. Unfortunately for the Americans at Pearl Harbor on 7 December 1941, this traffic did not disclose any plans for a Japanese attack on that vital port, which was a military and naval matter. This meant that the attack caught the Americans completely by surprise. It has, however, been pointed out on more than one occasion that as American–Japanese relations had been deteriorating for some time, and war was thought inevitable by both sides, the Americans at Pearl Harbor were unduly casual about their security. However, if they had been lucky enough to pick up a Japanese naval message about the impending attack, the Americans would no doubt have taken precautionary measures. But the impression that the Americans should have learnt of the forthcoming attack from the diplomatic ciphers is nonsensical: military plans are never disclosed in diplomatic traffic except by accident.

One of the lessons of World War II was that tactical secrecy was vital and 'leaks' led to disaster, but *strategic* secrecy was often too tight and therefore many people whose tactical appreciation would have benefited from more strategic information were denied it. Thus in 1940, when the Germans cut the Allied armies into ribbons, they did so by a new tactical use of tanks (grouped in divisions), supported by dive-bombers which helped clear the path ahead. Had the Allied units known that this tactical approach was a possibility, they would have been better adapted to cope with it when it came. But the politicians and the higher command preferred to affect a disdain of the tactics the Germans were said to be practising, and thus field units were not supplied with information which might have helped them. Likewise, 'in order not to cause public alarm', the inevitability of a war with Japan was withheld from the American public. This 'non-alarmist' attitude was picked up by commanders in the armed forces. Thus, when the Japanese attacked Pearl Harbor, the American defence was caught napping: men were on leave, few of the guns were ready to fire, ammunition was locked up in stores (and much of it ineffective because it had peacetime settings). Fortunately, by pure luck, the American aircraft carriers were at sea and therefore survived the attack.

The diplomatic traffic passed on the Purple machines was code-named (by the Americans) 'Magic' – not to be confused with 'Magic', the code-name given to the deception and camouflage operations of Maj. Jasper Maskelyne (see p.157). The traffic between Japanese military and naval units was given the code name of 'Ultra'. Thus there were two Ultras: one was the European Ultra from Enigma machines and other decoding devices; the other was the material derived from Japanese military and naval codes. The latter was sometimes described as 'the other Ultra'.

Breaking the Japanese codes was the result of dedicated work by men and women whose dogged, meticulous intellectual thoroughness did as much, if not more, to win the Pacific war as did many more famous personalities. The cryptographers of Bletchley Park also received less than their due in terms of recognition (and that too late), though for very good reasons. At Bletchley Park there had been Gordon Welchman, Alastair Dennison, Dilly Knox, Alan Turing, Hugh Alexander and Dennis Babbage, to name but a few. The experts on Japanese code-breaking included the redoubtable William Friedman, Laurence Safford, Agnes Driscoll, Joseph Rochefort, Eddie

Pearce and Daniel McCallum. But it should never be forgotten that the code-breakers were members of a team, a team which at one point numbered thousands. It is no exaggeration to say that every member of the team was important and it should always be remembered that the attitude of responsibility over secrecy was absolute. A constant reminder of the necessity for meticulous secrecy on the Allied side was the fact that almost every code was broken because of stupid, careless mistakes by enemy operators. Long experience had taught the need for exact adherence to the rules of procedure when transmitting codes but this, fortunately for the Allies, was not universally applied. The Japanese were worse offenders than the Germans in this respect. It is thought that they became careless because of their exuberance over their initial victories. But there were other factors, too, which helped the Americans to break the Japanese codes. The early Japanese victories extended their forces over a huge area of land and sea. In order to read the messages received from Purple and other sources, each of the scattered headquarters needed an up-to-date code-book. But distributing code-books to far-flung units was a lengthy and laborious process. If therefore it was known that a distant unit had not received a new code-book, a message would be relayed in an earlier code based on a book which they were known to possess. As this was usually surmised to be the same message as the one to other units in possession of the new code, the fact that the Americans had the message in the old code, which had probably been broken, and the new one, which had not, was a giant step towards breaking the latter. There was also an additional factor which weighed down the balance in favour of the code-breakers. That was the suspicious hostility of senior officers to clever cryptography. There was a feeling that tried and known codes were probably the best. Everyone understood them. So, of course, did the code-breakers, as often as not.

The code-breakers' greatest triumph was probably their success in supplying Admiral Nimitz with the information which enabled him to win the critical battle of Midway, the turning-point in the Pacific War. Nimitz knew the Japanese plans and therefore was able to confront them when they least expected it. This, though a naval battle, was won by aircraft, though at very high cost in pilot casualties: the surface ships never came into conflict. At the end of it, the Japanese had lost four carriers and 1,000 aircraft; the Americans had lost the carrier *Yorktown* and 147 aircraft. The balance of naval power in the Pacific had now been tipped decisively in America's favour and there was no possibility that the position could ever be restored by the Japanese from an industrial base which was far inferior to that of America.

Sad to say, during World War II, the greatest danger to the security of American code-breaking came not from the Japanese but from ambitious American politicians and 'investigative' journalists. The latter, travelling as war correspondents, mingled freely with officers, with their ears tuned to picking up the vaguest hints of what might be a secret 'scoop'. The fact that disclosing the secret in a newspaper article would endanger countless American lives, appeared to have weighed little with them. Americans, of course, believe in frank and open administration, and feel that the public has a right to know what the government and armed forces are up to, but in time of national peril this otherwise admirable and healthy attitude can cause irretrievable damage. It has been said, unfairly, that there is no need for America's enemies to send spies into the country: if they buy the newspapers and journals all the information they want will be there. No doubt Purple would have made an excellent scoop for a technical journal.

A continuing problem with Enigma and Purple ciphers was that because their source could not be disclosed many senior commanders who were required to act on information thus given were distinctly sceptical. Who would not be? Astonishing inside information was being produced but no hint was given of its veracity. Suspicion was particularly strong when the intelligence information gave bad news.

The story of the successes which Magic brought Americans in the war against Japan are lucidly and vigorously described by the late Ronald Lewin in his book *The American Magic*. He concludes with an interesting observation on whether or not the atomic bomb should have been dropped on Japan, which was already at the brink of defeat. But, he points out, to be on the brink of defeat is not the same as saying you are ready to surrender, as has been shown by many other countries. Japan still had two million *soldiers* available to defend Japan, and these were backed up by a vast 'home guard' consisting of old men, young boys and women, all of whom had had military training. The Emperor certainly wished for peace and could see that a fight to the death would be a total disaster for his country. Unfortunately there were those who preferred total disaster to surrender and in the fight to the finish would have killed, it is estimated, over a million Allied troops. 'Magic' disclosed that without the demonstration of

American power in the shape of the atomic bomb, of which the Americans were thought to have an ample supply, the war would not have ended in 1945, and perhaps not in 1946 either.

In addition to the major interception and decoding operations of the two Ultras there were, in the field, smaller but extremely important intercept units. One of these was the J Service. The J Service was the creation of Major Mainwaring, of the Royal Signals, who in 1941 organized a listening service in the Western Desert which combined monitoring enemy radio traffic with recording its own. In the tactical conditions of the Western Desert a service such as that provided by Ultra was virtually useless. By the time an Engima intercept had been decoded the local situation would have changed so much that the original information would be out of date. What was needed was information, easily available from listening to tank commanders, of where units were, what they were, and, very often, what their intentions might be. Equally, it was important to know where one's own units were, whether they were moving in the right direction or straying off the line. J Service began in a modest way to check on the activity around Tobruk, where a break-out was intended in 1941, but it proved its worth so quickly that soon it had acquired eighteen receivers and three transmitters. It proved extremely useful at the third battle of Alamein, which began on 23 October 1942.

When a battle begins, it is usually extremely difficult to ascertain what is happening. There have been battles which both sides thought they had won and battles which both sides thought they had lost. Sometimes commanders never receive the orders which are intended for them; sometimes they act on orders intended for someone else. (In Europe Enigma machines usually overcame this problem by giving their coded messages a prefix which indicated clearly that unless the recipient had the correct code-book he would not be able to understand what he received from his Enigma machine.) J picked messages out of the air and very often relayed them to their own headquarters by a secure local line they themselves had laid.

For a unit which initially had no fixed establishment or organization and had to borrow or 'acquire' most of its equipment, J did outstandingly well. It was able to identify suitable bombing targets by listening to enemy formations withdrawing, it was able to log the number and movements of enemy tanks, all of which were talking to each other in clear, and give a very useful account of enemy morale. From this information the Allied headquarters was able to deduce any changes in the enemy's tactical planning.

The unit's work at Alamein was clearly of such value that its existence was recognized officially, and it was given an 'establishment'. Establishment, in military terms, means official permission for the employment of a certain number of troops, and the right to draw equipment, stores, rations, etc., for them to use. J's establishment was small, one officer and forty-nine signallers of lesser rank. J was always in demand. As the 8th Army pursued Rommel across the desert, J kept Montgomery informed when and where the enemy was likely to stand and make a counter-attack. In the critical Mareth battle of March 1943, J faithfully recorded the movements and traffic of the enemy forward troops.

When the 1st Army and the 8th Army joined up during the concluding stages of the North African campaign, J, which was now a much larger organization, continued to prove its usefulness. The value of its work had been noted by the 7th US Army, which decided it needed a similar service. In consequence, two officers from the British J were attached to the 7th US Army to provide details of the organization and experience of the service. By this time J had a comprehensive knowledge of how to interpret the signals it was intercepting, and how to ensure that nothing useful was missed.

J went with the army into Sicily. Owing to the hilly nature of that island, reception was bad and J therefore had to adopt a relay system of its own. However, in Sicily and later in Italy, the value of J declined when the campaign slowed down. When the armies were moving they used radio, which J and Signals Information and Monitoring (SIAM – J's American equivalent) could monitor. Once a front stabilized, land lines were used and were reasonably secure. However, as the principal use for J and SIAM was when the battle front was highly mobile, the fact that there was little opportunity for them when the front was stable was of no great importance. Ironically, during 1944 in Italy it became clear that J was receiving a taste of its own medicine. J was listening to enemy units and passing back information about them. But it transpired that the Germans and Italians were now monitoring J's own transmissions and finding them useful. The problem was overcome by J's use of cipher in conjunction with the one-time pad. (The one-time pad offered a reasonably secure means of passing messages. All that was required was that both sender and receiver had one. Each page of the pad contained enciphering information of the random type, and each enciphered letter belonged to a different system from the others. When a message had been enciphered, the page was torn off and destroyed. It could not be used twice. The receiver used his pad to decipher the message, then tore off his page and destroyed it.)

Although there was less and less use for J as the war drew to its close in Europe, the unit's experience was considered too valuable to be wasted: there was still the war in the Far East. Eventually, in 1945, J was amalgamated with Phantom.

Phantom was a much larger organization than J and had quickly attained the status of an official regiment. But even Phantom had had to win its spurs, and had done so in spite of many frustrations. It had originated in November 1939 as an RAF unit. Its name at that stage was No. 3 British Air Mission, and it was commanded by Wing Commander J. M. Fairweather, DFC. The task of the mission at that time was to liaise with the Belgian General Staff. Belgium, well aware of what had happened in World War I, hoped to avoid being involved in a second war by remaining neutral. But, as the Belgians realized sadly some six months later, when a belligerent psychopath sets out to dominate the world, the fact that one of the smaller countries in his path has optimistically declared itself neutral will not save it from being overrun, if to do so suits the psychopath. In 1939 there was a number of national leaders who preferred to ignore all the evidence for Hitler's ambitions, so Belgium's blindness was by no means unique. Belgium's neutrality did not stop it from maintaining a small though efficient army, but in its efforts to avoid upsetting and therefore provoking the Germans it was careful not to be too friendly to the British and French.

Fairweather's task was to ascertain where all British, French and Belgian troops were stationed and to pass that information direct to the commander of the British air forces in France. This would enable the RAF to construct a 'bomb' line – a line beyond which they would be bombing enemy troops. Even in the days of static trench warfare it was by no means impossible for shells and bombs to go astray and land on one's own troops instead of the enemy's. In modern warfare, where troops might be widely dispersed and not form a line at all, the chance of inflicting damage on one's own side was so great as to need special actions to prevent it. If the Germans came westward with the same determination as they had shown in Poland, the battle line would fluctuate so much that the RAF would be as likely to drop bombs on its own side as on the enemy, unless it received accurate and immediate reports of the fighting and dispositions.

Liaison with the Belgians required a special type of person: he had to be a fluent linguist but his knowledge of the language had to include a grasp of idiom, of technicalities and even of dialects. Because the Belgians were wary of being too friendly, the liaison officer needed to have the sort of personality which would be liked and trusted. In mid-November Fairweather was joined by Lieutenant-Colonel G. F. Hopkinson, MC, who had come to France as part of the Howard–Vyse mission, whose task it was to liaise with General Gamelin in Paris on behalf of the British forces. Liaising with General Gamelin was a considerable challenge, for he was unhelpful, appeared to know very little about the forces he was alleged to be commanding, and spoke French rapidly and almost inaudibly. It cannot have caused Hopkinson much distress to be separated from the Howard–Vyse mission.

'Hoppy' Hopkinson was a man with a genius for seeing what had to be done, then cutting through red-tape to do it. He and 'Fairy' Fairweather got on extremely well from the start; they understood each other's problems: Hoppy was a qualified pilot, and Fairy knew a lot about soldiering. There was nothing happy-go-lucky about their attitude to winning the war, but they knew that this one would be quite different from the last and would require a different approach. Fairweather died when the boat on which he was travelling was torpedoed off Ostend the following June, and Hoppy was shot by a sniper when he was doing some personal reconnaissance for the division he was commanding in Italy in 1943, but the unit they had created grew in strength and importance up till 1945, when one of its members (Hutton-Williams) was present when the American army met the Russian army at Torgau as the war reached its end.

Although the acquisition of important information was a vital part of the unit's task, the rapid transmission of it was no less essential. All armies have their communications system, and that in the British army is the province of the Royal Signals whose skill and reliability are universally acknowledged. However, the Royal Signals has the responsibility of handling *all* traffic from brigade to GHQ and back, which means that their networks are always busy. Urgent messages receive varying degrees of priority but when the lines are overloaded, as happens in busy times, even top priority messages take longer than they should. This new unit, officially named GHQ Liaison Unit, but soon better known as Phantom, transmitted its findings directly back to GHQ. Provided the quality of the information was good, the commander-in-chief could thus be aware what was happening, as it was happening. Long before he obtained official permission for the unit he wished to create, Hoppy was busy recruiting suitable members for it. They included wireless detachments acquired from the Royal Signals and manned by them, an armoured car squadron, a motor cycle troop and an intelligence section. If ever there was a mixed unit it was this one. The intelligence section included men who had lived for long periods in Belgium and France (not all were officers), the motor cyclists came from a territorial unit of the Greenjackets and reckoned to ride motor cycles where motor cycles could not normally go, and the armoured cars held a mixture of cavalry troops and members of the Royal Tank Regiment.

As soon as the Germans violated Belgian neutrality on 10 May, Phantom was in action, reporting on German advances, on bridges which should have been destroyed but which had not been, and in general reducing considerably the volume of the surprises the Germans had planned to produce. Phantom discovered that its motor cycles could move across country to gain information when roads were too clogged with refugees to be usable. Although the total strength of Phantom was not much above a hundred it proved that a unit of that size could cover the entire front and report on it each day.

In the confusion which followed the British withdrawal from France, Phantom might have been disbanded and its members sent back to their original units had Hoppy not been quick to plan otherwise. He realized that the losses in France would mean that commanding officers of regiments in England would immediately try to reclaim any men on detachment, even though they were employed in useful, official units like Phantom. Hoppy promptly went on the attack and applied for an establishment of 1,000. He knew very well that this would not be granted, but he hoped for a reasonable percentage; he got 500. Phantom was launched. The fact that the unit was 'secret' was thoroughly exploited by Hoppy. He had discovered that if your unit was branded with the magic word 'secret', scarce items of equipment became easier to obtain. However, Phantom did not find the 'secret' label invariably convenient. Later, when comparatively junior officers sought entry to operations rooms in order to question senior officers, they were sometimes greeted with the words, 'Who are you to ask me that sort of thing, and what the hell is Phantom anyway!' On such occasions, only the smoothest diplomacy achieved results.

Hoppy was a believer in relentless, though often unorthodox, training. He insisted that *all* members of Phantom should be efficient morse operators and kept them at constant practice until a satisfactory standard was obtained, and maintained. Sometimes he made the unit work all night and pick up what sleep they could during the day. He believed firmly in the virtues of mental concentration. Their main base in Richmond Park often received attention from hostile aircraft. Hoppy refused to let anyone take shelter in slit trenches even at the most uncomfortable moments. 'They make cowards,' he said. Discipline was relaxed, but none the less there: the regiment had to look smart as well as to be so. Being a member of Phantom was no easy assignment, but at least it was never boring. Hence it attracted an amazingly varied collection of personalities. By 1945 it had had among its members David Niven, and another well-known actor, Tam Williams, Robert Mark, future Commissioner of the Metropolitan Police, the Hon. Hugh Fraser, future Minister for Air, Maurice Macmillan, future MP, Norman Reddaway, future ambassador to Poland, Laurence Whistler, the engraver, the Hon. 'Jakie' Astor and his brother Michael, the future Lord Mayhew, E. E. Rich, Master of St Catharine's College, Cambridge, Peregrine Worsthorne, five hereditary peers, a Law Lord, many successful businessmen, athletes . . . It looks a very mixed bag but they had one thing in common: all were dedicated to enabling Phantom fulfil a vital need. Adaptability was taken for granted. When Hoppy decided to set up a pigeon loft, which soon had 500 pigeons, they were put in the charge of a distinguished future Professor of Political Science, Michael Oakeshott.

Phantom's first chance to show what it could do as a regiment came in Greece in 1941, although the opportunity led to heavy losses; its second came in the Western Desert when it was not only required to listen, but also to engage in deception operations; its third in Sicily and Italy; and its fourth, and largest, in the north-west Europe campaign.

Although Phantom spent much time listening to its own and enemy transmissions, its most useful function was to obtain situation reports from front line commanders and transmit these immediately to GHQ, where they would enable an invaluable up-to-date appraisal of the situation to be made. The Phantom service was not only front to rear but also lateral. In France, when divisions were moving forward, it was essential to know where every unit was. On one occasion, by logging exactly what point a division had reached, Phantom was able to call off an air-strike, which, under the impression it was clearing a path for the advancing troops would actually have annihilated them; the RAF was unaware how quickly the units had moved. Likewise, the artillery was notified when a supporting barrage was likely to fall on its own troops. In 1944 when Allied troops were closing on the Germans in the Falaise pocket, the fact that Phantom reported accurately on the whereabouts of each participating unit saved many Allied lives which would have been lost through misdirected fire.

Phantom was at first treated with great suspicion by the American and Canadian units to which it offered its services, but before long was regarded as absolutely essential. In fact, just as the American army had demanded the formation of its own J Service, so did it require its own Phantom.

As happens with units which are in constant touch with a variety of different formations, Phantom soon found itself expected to supply information on almost everything, from the number of casualties in their contacts to the condition of roads and bridges in the operational area. One squadron of Phantom was attached to the SAS and parachuted into France with them. Phantom was at Dieppe, at Arnhem, and operated right up to the final stages of the war in Europe. As soon as VE-Day had passed, it was organized to play its part in the war against Japan, but the surrender in August 1945 clearly put an end to that project. After the war, Phantom became a Territorial regiment, but finally ceased to exist in 1963. The official reason for the abolition of 'Army Phantom Signals', as it was then called, was that modern methods of signalling made it unnecessary.

Those who had seen Phantom operating in wartime expressed doubts whether machines would ever replace it, and suspected that the reasons given for its disbandment were related more to making economies than to maintaining efficiency. Estimates of what another major war might be like suggest that in those horrific circumstances Phantom would be even more essential than it was in World War II. One of the reasons for Phantom's success in maintaining communication in World War II had been what might be called 'the human factor'. Often senders wandered from their allotted frequency. They were eventually located by operators who displayed an almost creative persistence in tracking down a straying transmitter. The timing of transmissions could also be erratic, partly because even the most sophisticated watch can let down its user for various unexpected reasons; these, on occasion, were the result of such bizarre influences as sunspots. The ubiquitous computer will be relied on to replace the ingenious and patient signaller; perhaps the faith will be justified.

One aspect of warfare at which Phantom showed itself particularly skilled was deception. The regiment's first experience of this was in the 'Crusader' offensive in 1941. One of the squadrons in the desert was required to give Rommel the impression that the forthcoming 8th Army offensive, of which he was undoubtedly well aware, would be launched from the south rather than the north. Phantom therefore had to drive 300 miles across the desert to an oasis (Giarabub) which was 200 miles south of the coast. There it had to deploy patrols which would then call to each other as if they were an armoured car regiment. For this task they were so well camouflaged that enemy airmen never found them.

In spite of the long history of successful deception in war, ranging from the Trojan Horse, to dummy archers on the battlements of medieval castles, to disguised raiders in World War I, Britain began World War II with marked indifference to this adjunct to warfare. America was even less inspired by its possibilities. Yet by 1945 there had been more ingenious uses of deception than the most optimistic of its advocates could have expected in 1939. The scope of deception operations is, of course, enormous. At sea it involves disguising ships so that the harmless merchantman masks a warship, fireship or submarine supply ship. In wartime the sea becomes a vast chessboard, with the advantage of having some pieces concealed from view beneath the surface. In air warfare it involves deceiving the defenders so that the attacker may slip by, not perhaps unidentified but too rapidly to be intercepted. There is a constant effort to make the enemy believe you have more aircraft, more airfields, more firepower than you actually possess. However, on occasion you may wish him to think you are weaker than you are and be persuaded to attack you where he will be at a disadvantage; the attacker goes after his (supposed) weaker prey, only to find that he himself is attacked from behind by a superior force.

Likewise the enemy must be encouraged to waste bombs and shells on non-military targets. Simulated ships and dummy airfields are obvious examples, and these are made more realistic by the careful installation of dummy guns and dummy aircraft. But there can be nothing amateur or casual if this sort of deception is to be successful. A few aircraft beside a landing strip will deceive no one: if there is a dummy airfield there must be approach roads, living accommodation, fuel installations, signs of use in worn patches of ground.

Army deceptions involve many of the same techniques as those used by the other services, but here deception is even more difficult; the passage of large numbers of troops – which is what the deceivers usually wish to depict – has a multitude of side effects which are very difficult to simulate. The essence of successful deception is to create a scene which resembles what the enemy in more despondent moments would expect to see; this may not always be what the man on the ground has simulated. The deception planner must be fully aware of the latest developments in the technique of interpreting aerial photographs. Usually a dummy target was camouflaged very well, but not quite well enough to prevent it being spotted.

The presence of a military unit has often been revealed to aerial observers by someone's careless mistake. Soldiers who cross dew-covered ground during darkness imagine they leave no trace: on an aerial photograph taken at dawn their movements are clear. There can be no mistake about such signs. Unlike painted shadows, they vary every day and through the day.

Finally, there is the range of intelligence deception, of which much of the previous manoeuvring may be a part. Hitler deceived the Allies into thinking that he had limited objectives, and that when the Polish campaign was over he had no further military ventures in prospect. That view was rudely shattered when he invaded Norway and Denmark, to be followed by Belgium, Holland and France. The success of his deception lay largely in the wish of his enemies that his lying statements were, in fact, the truth. Perhaps his greatest triumph in deception was his making a pact with Soviet Russia in 1939 (a pact which nobody in the West could possibly have foreseen), using it to keep the Russians happy while he conquered Poland, and then, under the guise of friendship with the Soviet Union, preparing to invade Russia, as he did less than two years after the pact.

Britain, having been badly deceived in 1940, made every effort to turn the scales. The bluff that Britain could help the Poles if they were invaded was exposed for the futile gesture it was. But when Britain itself seemed likely to be invaded, deception plans worked very well. We have seen how the adroit use of the Y Service and radar enabled the Luftwaffe to be frustrated. At the same time Hitler was persuaded to believe that there were twenty-four well-equipped divisions waiting in southern Britain, ready to repel invaders. (The actual figure was nearer two, and their state of readiness was far from satisfactory.) Information of this type (now known as disinformation, as it is designed to mislead) is usually spread through the press of neutral countries. The process of deceiving neutral journalists is not, however, simple. In wartime, press releases from belligerents are treated with reserve and scepticism. If a country wishes to mislead a foreign journalist he must be given the impression that he is making important discoveries himself. A very simple way of doing this is to arrange that the journalist has access to a certain area then suddenly to cancel that permission without notice or warning. The journalist, who previously had no intention of visiting the area, is now filled with a burning curiosity about it. As he becomes more persistent, he is given a series of unsatisfactory answers. For good measure, an appeal to his better nature may be thrown in; when that fails, a hint is dropped that he will be declared *persona non grata* if he makes a nuisance of himself. At best he may try to see for himself and be arrested on the way. He then writes his despatch, which is almost entirely speculation. Other neutral journalists, not to be outdone in the eyes of their editors, produce slightly embellished versions. In consequence, an uninhabited tract of land might receive a heavy air attack, or better still an enemy's operational plan might be delayed and disrupted while the new hypothetical threat is being investigated.

Deception was of two types: one was the local variety which involved simulating installations or equipment on the ground; the other was concerned with persuading the enemy that your intentions were different from your real ones. At the same time, the enemy must be made to believe that whatever your intentions, you have the means of carrying them out.

One of the most ingenious deception excercises of World War II was 'The Man who Never Was'. The full story has been told by Ewen Montagu, who was working in naval intelligence at the time and was directly involved. It also became a successful film.

At the end of the North African campaign it was clear that the Allied armies would soon make a landing on the Continent. But where? There were several possible areas. The south of France was one, Corsica was another, Sicily yet another and Greece was a fourth. Of these, Sicily was the most likely and would be well prepared. It was therefore desirable that the enemy should decide that the Allies were too subtle to attack in the obvious place; thus, Sicily should be only one of a number of areas to be defended. For every German soldier not sent to Sicily there would be a considerable advantage to the Allies. The best deception would be one which sent as many German troops and aircraft as far from Sicily as possible, as this would delay their return when the real objective of the attack became known.

The Allies realized that the Germans would know that Sicily must be invaded sooner or later, but hoped they might be persuaded that it was only one of several objectives, and a minor one too; the others would be Sardinia and Greece. In fact the Allies had insufficient shipping for a diversified attack of this nature, but the Germans were not aware of it; for many months Allied agents had been supplying the Germans with false information about the number of ships which were available.

Useful though 'turned' spies and Allied agents were, there was a limit – it was thought – to what they could do. That limit stopped short of convincing the Germans that Sicily was not a prime objective of top priority. The only way to deceive the German High Command seemed to be to allow them to see the contents of a personal, confidential, semi-official letter. It would be the sort of letter one general might send to another 'for your eyes only', putting him in the picture about what might otherwise seem a rather puzzling course of action.

The letter was one written from the British Deputy Chief of the General Staff (Nye) to the British general (Alexander) commanding the British forces in North Africa. It implied that Eisenhower had wished to have a mock operation staged on the Greek islands as a diversion from his planned invasion of Sardinia. This, said Nye, was not possible because the Greek islands had been allotted already as a diversion for an attack on the Greek mainland, which would take place at the same time as Eisenhower's invasion of Sardinia. Eisenhower was therefore being required to *pretend* he was attacking Sicily. The beauty of this letter was that if the Germans now heard information about a serious attack on Sicily, they would think it was a 'plant' to disguise the real Allied objective. Normally such information could only have been sent in a top-secret *official* letter. Some reason had to be found for making this semi-official and person-to-person. The solution was to enclose information about a difference of opinion about decorations when British and American troops were engaged in the same actions. Alexander's deputy was an American, and until the eventual decision had been explained to him by an American (Eisenhower) it was better for him not to know about it.

So much for the letter. The problem was how to get it into the right (that is, the wrong) hands.

The letter was put in the pocket of a drowned Royal Marine major, William Martin. There were several William Martins in the Marines at the time, but this was not one of them. It was the body of a man who had died of pneumonia, and therefore would be indistinguishable – except to an expert pathologist – from that of a man who had died by drowning. 'Martin's' body was frozen, then taken by submarine to a point off the Spanish coast whence it would float ashore. Martin carried other papers which gave him a genuine identity so, when he arrived on the coast off Huelva, wearing a Mae West life-jacket, it was obvious that the aircraft in which he had been travelling had come down in the sea, taking the rest of its occupants with it. Martin had been the only one to get out, but it had done him no good.

The Spanish authorities at the time were anxious to be on good terms with the Germans and, having abstracted the contents of the envelope (with great skill and without showing it), gave copies to the Germans who reacted as had been hoped. The original despatch was, very properly, handed over to the British consul, apparently intact, by the Spaniards. The Germans were completely deceived, and deployed their forces in the way the Allies had hoped.

With each large deception plan there were usually a number of smaller ones confirming the larger ploy. In this one there was a minor, but important, arrangement over headquarters. It was obvious that the commander-in-chief of an invasion force would wish to site his headquarters conveniently near the invasion point. But if this were done before the Sicily invasion, the sheer volume of traffic might well give the game away. In consequence, Eisenhower had a simulated headquarters at Oran and the signals traffic between this headquarters and Washington was made extensive. Meanwhile, his real headquarters at Algiers was given a very low profile: there were no conspicuous comings and goings of senior officers, and signals traffic was kept to a minimum.

It has been stated that during World War II every German spy sent to Britain was captured, and either 'turned' or executed. The number of spies executed is given as twelve; it seems possible that the number may have been larger. Some German spies did not wait to be captured; they gave themselves up on arrival and offered to work for the Allies. They were joined by spies from neutral countries whom the Germans had approached as likely prospects. These last had decided they could act for both sides, if they were clever. On arrival, they settled for being honest with the Allies and dishonest with the Germans.

The army of genuine agents, whether 'turned' spies or volunteers, was considerable, but it was far exceeded by another category. This last group was believed to have been recruited in Britain by the agents the Germans had sent over. They existed only on paper. It was, of course, much more convenient for the Germans if agents to work for them could be recruited in Britain. They therefore avoided the problem of smuggling them in, though, of course, they had to supply them with equipment and funds. The methods which were chosen for importing spying equipment and money into Britain usually involved 'neutrals'. The fact that the 'neutrals' were unaware that the British knew all about their duplicity was an added bonus.

A major problem with 'turned' agents was supplying them with sufficient 'good' information to maintain credibility. It was no use their sending off a series of untrue stories: the Germans had ways of confirming the truth of much of what their agents sent in. Whether they always exercised their ability to do this seems a debatable point.

The Abwehr was the official German intelligence service, and contained departments which in Britain came under separate organizations (e.g. counter-intelligence, MI5; overseas espionage, MI6; sabotage, SOE). Since 1935 the head of the Abwehr had been Admiral Wilhelm Canaris, but he, like a number of other leading Germans, had become convinced during his time in office that Hitler would destroy everything which he and his friends valued in Germany. He therefore set himself the task of frustrating the Nazis, and to do so enlisted a number of like-minded friends into the Abwehr. Suspicion fell on him in early 1944. After the unsuccessful attempt on Hitler's life on 20 July, Canaris was arrested and executed with extreme brutality and humiliation.

However, the fact that the head of the Abwehr was opposed to the government he was serving did not mean that the Abwehr itself was totally ineffective. It contained many fanatical Nazis, and was carefully watched by the Gestapo. Anything which Canaris did to help the Allied cause needed to be extremely subtle. In 1945 the fact that the head of the German secret service for nine years had been working for the enemy seemed incredible. Subsequently, when Blunt, Burgess, Philby, Maclean, all working in intelligence, were discovered to have been busy passing British secrets to potential enemies, the story of Canaris is less sensational.

Canaris's hand may now perhaps be seen (long after the event) in the alarming reports which the Italian generals in the Middle East received about the strength of the British. These, totally unfounded, certainly affected Italian morale. In addition, the equipment of German spies sent to Britain suggests that they were meant to be tracked down easily. (Britain already knew from intercepts that they were coming.) Most of them had identity cards which were obvious forgeries, out-of-date ration cards, and totally inadequate briefing. For the first four years none of their radios was suitable for making contact with their home controllers: had they been able to do so they might have managed to get off quick messages before being captured and those messages might have torn the Canaris conspiracy open. In order for the sets to be used for the purpose intended they all needed a spell in British signals workshops. But, of course, some of the mistakes made by the Germans may well have been genuine. As SOE discovered, the number of citizens who have lived long enough in a foreign country to pass themselves off as native is very limited: idiom, mannerisms, bearing and attitude of mind are not easily taught, even in the most professional spy schools.

Ewen Montagu quoted an interesting example of how a turned spy could be used to pass information which might act as a deterrent. The aim of this particular exercise was to give the false news that a battleship was being fitted with torpedo tubes. This would influence German ships to avoid it if possible rather than engage it in close combat. The 'spy' was made to overhear a conversation between two naval ratings in a dockyard town. They were speculating on how much leave they would get while their ship was being fitted with torpedo tubes. Another agent then reported that he had seen a battleship in dry dock as he went through the same town in a train.

The turning of spies, and their subsequent use, was the province of the Twenty (XX – i.e. Double Cross) Committee, which had originally been named the 'W' Section. The XX Committee worked under the chairmanship of J. C. Masterman, an Oxford don (Christ Church) who had been interned in Germany during the whole of World War I. He learnt a lot about German thought processes during his long, enforced stay in that country. Masterman later wrote a book about his experiences in the XX Committee, but was forbidden to publish it in Britain. He felt that the achievements of those who had done much to assist the war effort could be revealed, and that publication of his book could do no damage to security, so many years later he sent it to America where restrictions on secret information are considerably less; it was published there, and subsequently printed in Britain. Not surprisingly he was much criticized for this rather uncharacteristic action.

The XX Committee's most successful spy was 'Garbo'. He was largely responsible for the Germans' belief that the Allied invasion of France, when it came, would be in the Pas de Calais. The Germans did not discount the possibility that a landing might be made in Normandy, but believed that this was only a diversion for the main operation near Calais. One might have thought that the Germans, after being deceived over Sicily, would have been extra-cautious over the Normandy deception, but spies traded on the fact that people believe what they want to believe, even if it is against their best interests to do so.

The Allied D-Day deception plan took into account the fact that if a diversionary raid was staged on Calais the Germans would soon assess its strength and realize that the main thrust must be going elsewhere. They would quickly realign their forces to meet the larger threat. To prevent them doing this involved two separate projects: one was that all the preparations for the Normandy landings, the assault craft, Mulberry harbour, the troop dispositions, must be kept secret. No German aircraft must be allowed to penetrate the area in the south and west of England where huge preparations were being made. Added to this, they should be given every reason to believe that a large concentration of force was being built up elsewhere. In south-east England, and particularly in Kent and Essex, a completely fictitious invasion force was created. It simulated everything the real force would have; the area was covered with dummy installations and the volume of signals traffic was exactly what one would expect for a main invasion thrust. Furthermore it was ringed by tight security: the security had to be genuine because the slightest breach of it would give the game away completely. In fact the area was included in the top security strip which involved everything up to ten miles inland all the way from the Wash to Land's End. Strict security extended to refusing the entry or exit of foreign diplomats and put an end, for the time being, to their privilege of sending uncensored mail. Meanwhile, agents sent back to Germany a series of reports which were so carefully presented that they confirmed every opinion that the Germans were beginning to form themselves. They trusted 'Garbo' implicitly. He was a Spaniard whose brother had been taken into custody by the

Gestapo when the Germans entered Paris in 1940. Garbo offered his services as a spy to the British embassy in Madrid, but his qualifications were considered to be too slender and he was rejected. Unabashed, Garbo decided to be a spy in England for the Germans without going any nearer to it than Lisbon. He hoped that if he built up sufficient credibility he could present himself again to the British and work for them as a double agent. He invented credible information about what was happening in Britain, and even appointed fictitious sub-agents (who were put on the German pay roll). Even so, he began to run out of ideas and money and pleaded once more to be taken on as a real English agent. Reluctantly he was accepted, though not as quickly as he had hoped. Garbo's particular genius was his understanding of what the Germans wished to hear, which, in view of the fact that his early reports, when he was working on his own, were merely intelligent guesswork, seems astonishing. Nevertheless Garbo went from strength to strength, and before the end of the war had been awarded the MBE by the British and the Iron Cross by the Germans.

A considerable part of the bogus signals traffic, to which the Germans listened intently, was produced by one squadron of Phantom, which was so accustomed to handling real signals traffic that the task presented no difficulty. The deception proved so effective that, even after the Normandy landings had taken place and the Allies were pushing inland, the German High Command refused to move important divisions from the vicinity of Calais. Calais was where the attack would eventually come, they were certain, and they must be ready to meet it there.

The devices used on the ground in deception operations were, as we saw earlier, mostly the brain children of Dudley Clarke. One of the most skilled practitioners of the art was Maj. Jasper Maskelyne. The Maskelyne family, famous for its brilliant conjuring and illusion tricks on the stage, had a history of assisting the country in time of crisis. Jasper Maskelyne's grandfather had helped the government to use balloons successfully in the South African War, his father Nevil Maskelyne provided useful information for the services in World War I, notably in the avoidance of 'flashback' burns to gunners. At the beginning of World War II, Jasper Maskelyne tried several times to persuade the services to make use of his knowledge and skills but at the point when he had given up in despair was commissioned as a second lieutenant in the Royal Engineers. He was then sent to Farnham on a course to learn about camouflage, which was rather like sending William Tell on a course to learn archery. Fortunately for everyone, on an exercise he managed to impress Lord Gort, the commander-in-chief in 1939, and was given authority to organize a deception unit.

Maskelyne set to work to create the impression that Britain was full of guns, defences and men. In the course of his experiments he even invented a usable mine. The Germans heard that Maskelyne was working for the British Services, but considered this was no more than a joke. (They themselves never showed great interest in deception devices through the entire war; they preferred to spring their surprises with real weapons and men.)

In addition to creating the illusion that there were guns and men where these did not exist, was the task of camouflaging those which did.

Maskelyne was then despatched to the Middle East to play his part in the war there. At first his problems seemed to have begun all over again. The Allies were on the point of losing Greece and nobody had the time to bother with an apparently mad conjuror with absurd ideas. But persistence won at last. Maskelyne was given permission to form a Camouflage Experimental Section. Its first success was to build a mock harbour at Mariut Bay to draw attention from Alexandria, a mile away. Everything was there, 'warships', buildings, roads, even dumps of explosives which would go up convincingly when 'hit'. It worked. On a night when there was a large concentration of warships in Alexandria itself, Mariut received the raid destined for them. The enemy airmen must have thought their bombs were particularly successful, so many violent explosions took place. Everyone was satisfied, not least those in Alexandria harbour itself, which was untouched.

From then on Maskelyne was given every encouragement. He was given workshops and the authority to manufacture models in complete secrecy. Intruders to his camp were kept out by genuine minefields (well inside warning notices). These caused many casualties, though whether these were of genuine spies or merely of the insatiably curious was never known. The range of inventions was astonishing, some simple, some not. Genuine tank tracks were erased by a device that removed all trace: bogus tank tracks were made where it was thought suitable to put them. Thirty-six dummy tanks could be carried in a 5-cwt truck. Once one of his dummy submarines was mistaken for an intruder (German or Italian) and was nearly bombed by Allied aircraft. Searchlights ceased to be a purely defensive means of observing enemy raiders; they were adapted to produce a dazzling succession of beams to blind incoming pilots. Experiments led to success in making camouflage materials fireproof. There were ventures into the science of using intensified light as a weapon (as is now possible with laser beams) and ultrasonic noise which could damage human cells without actually being heard.

But it was not all tricks and success. Once Maskelyne was lost in the desert for four days, with his truck stuck in soft sand. He was rescued by a stray tank; one more day would have been too late.

Maskelyne became part of Dudley Clarke's 'A' Force, whose purpose was to deceive the enemy about everything everywhere. His colleagues appreciated the fact that Maskelyne was no mere conjuror; he had a genius for creating devices which could be photographed by enemy observers a short distance away and appear perfectly genuine. His cheerful self-confidence does not seem to have made him universally popular outside his 'Magic Circle', but there is no doubt that his contribution to winning the war was immense. He received no British award for his services but felt some satisfaction that Hitler, who had begun the war deriding him, later had him put on the Gestapo list of people to be eliminated at any price.

The successes enjoyed by Maskelyne and his colleagues may perhaps give the impression that deceiving the interpreters of aerial photographs was comparatively easy. Such a view would be far from the truth. Both the pilots who flew the observer aircraft and the interpreters who inspected the photographs were highly skilled in their exacting work. And although camouflage worked on numerous occasions, there were times when it did not; and photo-reconnaissance supplied invaluable information about troop and shipping movements, suitable targets, defences, and new weapon systems (e.g. developments at the German rocket station at Peenemunde).

It is not generally realized that all but a minute fraction of maps are out of date by the time they are printed, and most are based on surveys made many years before. Sometimes attempts are made to up-date maps by overprinting, but while these tend to record new installations they give little indication of those which have disappeared. Aerial photographs are completely up to date: they show the state of crops, vegetation, woodland, even the time of the year, from prevailing shadows. In wartime a landscape may change daily, or at even lesser intervals. The battle between the deception unit and the photographic interpreter is one between very resourceful and intelligent equals.

Although this section is mainly concerned with the gathering of intelligence, it is obvious that no activity by a wartime secret force could be self-contained. Just as radar relied on the Bruneval raid to take a step forward, so did Phantom's work bring it into direct contact with the enemy; the Y Service was linked with Bletchley Park and the discoveries of the cryptographers led to the XX Committee, which, knowing what the Germans required in the way of intelligence, sent falsified reports via 'double' agents. (A double agent sometimes works independently and supplies, for money, correct information to two or more belligerents. In Britain 'double' agents were men whom the Germans believed to be working for them but who had been 'turned' and were working for the Allies.)

Allied spies in Europe undoubtedly supplied much valuable information, but except when they were members of organizations such as SOE cannot be described as 'forces' and therefore are not discussed here.

Although the Germans never showed much expertise in the concept of deception, except in very local operations, they had a valuable organization which the British imitated later. This was the Abwehr-Truppen – intelligence commandos. They accompanied the front-line troops in invasions or major attacks. Their task was to collect all relevant plans, codes or documentary material which could be of use in the future. The next move in an offensive operation would presumably be planned with the same data, and it was therefore of the greatest importance that this should be captured before it could be destroyed. Often it compromised 'neutrals' who had been considered to be friendly.

The fact that the Allies learnt what the Abwehr-Truppen were doing in the middle of the war meant that plans could be made to create something similar before there was an urgent need for it. The results will be shown in the following chapter.

6: *The Range of SOE*

The Special Operations Executive (SOE) came into being in a strange, somewhat haphazard manner in July 1940. By the end of the war it was employing thousands of agents – no one seems to know the exact number, but it was probably well over 10,000. A figure of over 20,000 has been mentioned, but this doubtless includes people who were very loosely associated with it.

Churchill's dictum 'Set Europe Ablaze' applied not only to commandos, whose raids, though secret, were hardly likely to be subtle, but also to two other organizations. One was SO1, which was formed to coordinate security, and the other SO2, for 'black' propaganda. 'Black' propaganda was the process of disseminating information to an enemy country in a form which made it seem to have originated within its own boundaries. Eventually it proved easier to pretend that the source of such information lay in occupied countries rather than in Germany itself. Sometimes this made the information even more convincing; everyone knew that subversion information was extremely difficult to collect in Nazi Germany, but it was believed that until the Gestapo and Abwehr tightened their grip there was a good chance of interesting leaks from the newly occupied countries. 'White' propaganda was BBC broadcasting (a form of propaganda whose effectiveness was the greater for being in the main true, unlike German and Italian broadcasting), and RAF leaflet raids, which took place in the first six months of the war in the optimistic hope that the Germans would depose Hitler and make peace on the strength of a leaflet dropped by the RAF, each containing a friendly message and the less friendly statement, 'This could have been a bomb'.

'Black' propaganda included leaflets and newssheets which looked as if they had been printed under conditions of some difficulty, such as would be experienced by 'underground' presses. Likewise, broadcasts had to simulate the problems to be experienced by a clandestine station: this might involve sudden breaks in transmission as if the Gestapo was prowling nearby.

After July 1940, SO1, SO2 and Section D all came under the general cover of SOE. Section D was a branch of the Secret Intelligence Service which specialized in sabotage. Also under the same umbrella came Military Intelligence Research (MIR). MIR's research was into the possibilities of raising, training and supplying guerrilla forces in enemy-occupied areas.

The coordination of all these departments was obviously a sensible move. The executive heads were successful businessmen, such as Sir Frank Nelson, and Sir Charles Hambro. These were followed by Colin Gubbins (later knighted), a regular army officer whose career had included first-hand experience of guerrilla warfare. SOE was made part of the Ministry of Economic Warfare which ministry busied itself with studying the enemy's raw materials and other resources, with a view to recommending the best methods of interfering with them, e.g. blockade, or pressure on neutrals not to trade with the enemy. For obvious reasons, the very existence of SOE was kept out of the public view.

The Minister of Economic Warfare was Hugh Dalton, an enthusiastic, intellectual socialist, a product of Eton and King's College, Cambridge, and a man whose aggressive enthusiasms tended to make him less than popular. His confident assumption of what SOE might accomplish produced more criticism than admiration, for most of those he addressed took a more realistic view. Their more conservative estimates were confirmed when, after a year, the main accomplishments of SOE were in organization and training. There were, indeed, a few agents in enemy-held territories, but most were still situated in neutral countries. SOE, it was obvious, would need time. By the end of 1941 it was becoming equally clear that the heads of SOE would need considerable tact. If the Secret Intelligence Service was operating unobtrusively in an area with a view to collecting information, it would be infuriated if an SOE agent blew up the local telephone exchange and brought a herd of Gestapo investigators into the district.

SOE had enough problems of its own without needing to worry too much about the difficulties of its fellow-conspirators. First there was the problem of finding sufficient qualified agents. There were plenty of volunteers, once the word got around that there were opportunities for adventurous, reliable, fit men in a new secret service venture. Unfortunately, when it came to assessing the language skills and other qualifications which could not be learnt quickly, the numbers were greatly reduced. SOE has been criticized for recruiting on what is known as 'the old boy network', but this often proved the most effective method. The upper middle class, the products of the better-known public schools, the smarter regiments, and Oxford and Cambridge, were more likely to have spent long periods abroad and be familiar with mountaineering, small boat sailing, and the customs of foreign countries than their less privileged contemporaries.

SOE training was extremely thorough, and the strong element of military discipline irked some of the participants. Agents brought in from abroad, who were unfamiliar with the British military belief that smartness in drill, as well as on and off parade, are the most valuable military qualities, were baffled but had to conform. SOE training was designed to strengthen the ability to survive on one's own, even if ill or wounded, to resist interrogation mixed with torture if caught, and to remain alert even when exhausted. There was no prestige or recognition in being a member of SOE. If you were unlucky you were liable to die very unpleasantly; if you survived and served your country well, nobody would know about it till years afterwards and then everybody would have lost interest.

In August 1941 the black propaganda element of SOE was separated to continue as the Political Warfare Executive (PWE). This too, of course, was top secret, although to disguise its existence it functioned inside a non-secret department of the Foreign Office, named the Political Intelligence Department (PID). It was unnecessary for a department whose stated purpose was to record information about the political state of the enemy government to be secret, and PID remained such a good cover that PWE's name, as well as its actitivies, were unknown except to those working in or for it. When its name and activities were eventually disclosed, there were plenty of critics who denounced it as a scandalous waste of time, money and talent.

The most successful member of PWE was Sefton Delmer, later known to many as a trenchant journalist on the *Daily Express*. His early life had given him exactly the sort of experience PWE required. His parents were both Australian, but at the time of his birth in 1904 his father was employed by the University of Berlin, and so Sefton Delmer was registered as a British citizen by the British Consul General in that city. When war broke out ten years later, Delmer's father was interned; however, his family was left at liberty so Delmer continued at the local German school as usual. The family was repatriated in 1917 and he continued his education at St Paul's School. From there he went to Oxford. His life in Berlin, as an observant schoolboy, had given him an invaluable knowledge of German ways, which was increased when his parents returned to Germany after the war and he visited them frequently. He became a successful journalist and interviewed many leading Nazis. During the first nine months of the war he reported on crises in various parts of Europe, but when the Germans entered France he came back to England (not without difficulty). His attempts to become an infantryman, as a thirty-six-year-old weighing seventeen stone, were smilingly rejected, but when he applied for an intelligence post he received another rebuff, this time with less courtesy. His knowledge and experience of Germany made him suspect in the eyes of MI5, and the fact of having been born in Berlin was an added disqualification. He was eventually accepted through the influence of Leonard Ingrams, at that time an Assistant Secretary at the MEW.

Another highly talented member of the PWE team was R. H. S. Crossman. Crossman was not everyone's idea of a congenial colleague but nobody questioned his ability. He had already had an academic career of glittering success, at Winchester and Oxford, and had given popular radio talks on classical themes. In *Who's Who* he gave his recreation as 'Broadcasting'. Undoubtedly he was very good at it. After the war he became a Minister in the Labour government. In spite of his skilful war-work, his efforts to further the socialist cause in Britain when national unity was the order of the day had not contributed to his popularity, and there was some relief in PWE when he moved to Supreme Headquarters Allied Expeditionary Force (SHAEF).

Among other talented people who worked for PWE were Dr Leslie Beck, who thoroughly understood the French process of thought, Harold Robin, who ran the 'Aspidistra' transmitter and Reginald Leeper. But one of the most effective members of PWE did not actually exist. This was Gustav Siegfried Eins, a personality created by Sefton Delmer, who gave regular broadcasts. Eins was a moderate, patriotic citizen who voiced the fears of many like him. 'Der Chef', as this quintessential middle-class German was known, gave details of military events and local scandals. He became very indignant about corrupt practices, black-market deals and sexual perversion, and undoubtedly encouraged – as he was meant to do – a number of Germans to indulge in dishonest practices which seemed to be making so much money for other people. Eins broadcast coded messages to imaginary agents. German counter-intelligence soon broke the codes, but had no success at tracking down their intended recipients. Eins was no respecter of persons. Hitler was not criticized, but all his entourage were. Hess had branded himself a fool by trusting in the good will of the evil Churchill. The person chosen to broadcast these diatribes was Peter Seckelmann, a German-born journalist who had settled in Britain and at the outbreak of war had joined the British army. When PWE took him on, he was a corporal working in a bomb-disposal squad. His accent and manner were absolutely right for his task, and he even wrote some of the best scripts himself. Delmer knew that the denunciation of vice had a widespread, if titillating, appeal but was careful not to overdo the pornographic content of the broadcasts. But PWE even created a young woman whose deplorable life-style was one which many Germans envied. As many of the listeners were men in the armed forces, using their short-wave sets illegally, she may have had a wider following than anyone realized. Periodically Eins read out lists of people who were avoiding military service for no proper reason. 'Der Chef' was righteously indignant that the German war effort should be undermined by unpatriotic, corrupt, depraved people.

There were various theories in Germany and neutral countries about the way this clandestine station continued to operate without being discovered by the Gestapo. It must of course be very mobile, and probably used recorded material. Reading such speculations gave great pleasure to Delmer and his friends, as they worked happily on in Woburn Abbey, Bedfordshire.

As time went on other talented performers joined PWE, and so more stations seemed to be broadcasting in Germany. 'Der Chef's' opinions were shared by others.

Not least of PWE's achievements were those involving printed matter. Forged ration cards were an obvious opportunity and were dropped from aircraft in large quantities. They were excellent imitations and very popular with German citizens who apparently had no scruples about upsetting the German rationing system by using them. Stamps were also forged; one carried Himmler's head instead of Hitler's and was used to support the rumour that Himmler (head of the SS) had planned to take over the Führer's authority.

German workers who wanted a few days off work, but doubted their ability to convince their doctors that they were ill, were given useful advice about symptoms suitable for malingerers to claim they were experiencing. The widespread faith in astrology was used to discourage the departure of U-boats on 'bad' days. Much of this radio advice was clearly given with the best of intentions. Sometimes it was repeated in the neutral press, which added to its authenticity.

There is, of course, a fascination in listening to clandestine broadcasts. They give the impression that the listener is receiving inside information. Illegal newssheets have always been able to trade on this belief. The Germans made good use of 'black' broadcasting themselves. William Joyce ('Lord Haw-Haw'), whose rasping voice was familiar to millions, produced easily discredited material (he sank one aircraft carrier five times), but many people had a sneaking feeling that there was an element of truth in what he said. Joyce, though of American birth and a naturalized German, had in 1938 claimed to be a British subject, and obtained a British passport. He had lived much of his life in England and had once tried for a commission in the British army. His German naturalization was invalid because it is not possible to discard one's citizenship and become a national of a foreign country if that country is at war with your own. His post-war trial was an intricate one legally, but the outcome of it was that Joyce was condemned to death as a traitor and executed.

The fact that the Germans were by no means inexpert at using the radio to make propaganda points is shown by their handling of P. G. Wodehouse. Wodehouse was living in tax exile in France when the Germans marched in; they interned him but left his wife free. He had an uncomfortable time in the early days of internment. As he was approaching sixty in mid 1941, he was released (as were others of the same age). Rather surprisingly he was taken to Berlin and put in the Hotel Adlon; his wife, who had been living in Hesdin, France, was brought to join him. He gave a few interviews and then was approached by an American journalist, Harry Flannery, to make a broadcast about his experiences. He did so. The German Foreign Office then asked him if he would care to do some more broadcasts to America, which was not yet in the war. He was allowed to write his own scripts and he gave five talks about his experiences in internment. They were humorous and did nothing to assist the German war effort. The Americans thought they were anti-Nazi. However, the fact that one of the most popular and successful British humourists (he had been earning £100,000 a year in the 1930s) had been broadcasting from a luxury hotel in the enemy capital, while millions were experiencing rather different treatment, caused some excitement in Britain. At the end of the war there were demands that Wodehouse should be put on trial. However, he was ably championed by various friends and went off to live in America, from where he never returned. His books continued to sell in huge numbers, and he kept up a steady output. At the age of ninety-three he was created a Knight, largely at the instigation of Harold Wilson, the British Prime Minister.

There is no doubt that the Germans were clever to use Wodehouse. His books, which made a pleasant antidote to rationing, air raids and general discomfort, seemed somewhat less funny to wartime readers after he had made his broadcasts. The explanation given for his cooperation with the German Foreign Office was that he was naïve. However, whatever other characteristics his writing possessed, näivety does not seem to have been among them. Nor perhaps does patriotism. At the beginning of World War I he is said to have volunteered for the Royal Navy, but been rejected on grounds of poor eyesight. He stayed in America for the whole of World War I, writing very successful stories, lyrics, articles, novels and scripts. He returned to England in 1918. There is no hint of his ever contemplating assisting the British war effort by using his talents in some capacity where bad eyesight was less of a handicap than it would have been in the navy. He might be described as 'a flawed genius'. The Germans seem to have shown considerable astuteness in the use they made of him; there are more ways of breaking an egg than hitting it with a sledgehammer.

The Japanese had a counterpart to William Joyce, a young lady named 'Tokyo Rose', who broadcast bad news to American forces in the Pacific theatre. Her baleful predictions gave more pleasure than pain to her listeners.

There was, of course, no means of measuring the effect of black propaganda, whether by leaflet, broadcast or disinformation rumours. But the fact that France had collapsed so dramatically in 1940 after a decade of morale undermined by a largely foreign-owned press suggests the effects can be greater than is generally appreciated. In Britain, largely through Churchill's broadcasts, morale remained high even in the darkest days; German armies fought to a finish, not because the cause was right but because ten years of incessant propaganda had trained them to do so. The Germans, it should be remembered, did not merely fight until they were beaten; they took punishment which would have made other forces disintegrate, fell back, then rallied to put up a further spirited fight. 'Morale is to manpower as ten is to one.'

The achievements of SOE are also far from easy to measure, though isolated incidents, such as 'Operation Rubble' in March 1941, stand out. In that month SOE agents went into Gothenburg harbour, Sweden, where several British freighters loaded with special steel had been immobilized since the outbreak of war. Although the Germans were exporting huge quantities of Swedish iron products to Germany via Norway, the fact that Gothenburg lay within the territorial waters of a neutral country meant that the freighters could not be moved. But in March 1941, teams of SOE agents went aboard, put to sea and brought the freighters back to Britain.

Successes were mixed with frustration.Two of the most desirable objectives were the Iron Gates (gorge) on the Danube, which was an ideal demolition target, and the Ploesti oilfields in Romania. Unfortunately both areas were too well defended for SOE to get near them.

From the outset it was clear that SOE was a link service. It could not run a resistance unit on its own; its function was to assist and foster local movements, arrange for them to be supplied with arms and other equipment, and to coordinate the effects of different groups. The last was a major task requiring great diplomacy and tact: a depressing feature of many groups which resist tyranny is that they are often as hostile to fellow resisters as they are to the common enemy. There were other alarming features of resistance groups which SOE agents working with them had to overcome: one was their casual attitude to security, another their impetuousness, another their ignorance of modern methods of warfare. Members of SOE had to be masters of the skills they were trying to teach; there was no scope for theory without performance. As the task of agents was virtually unlimited, they had to learn to be burglars, lock-pickers, safe-blowers and, in case they were arrested, expert escapers. Some knowledge of medicine was essential; if there was no doctor available an SOE agent needed to understand the uses of the medical supplies he carried. At a pinch he might have to engage in a little temporary dentistry or even a minor operation. He also needed to be honest: large sums of money were despatched to groups abroad, and these often included gold coin.

SOE agents were liable to find themselves anywhere from the depths of the jungle to the middle of an important town. It did not do to be fussy. Sleazy brothels in neutral ports usually contained girls in the pay of Abwehr or the British secret service. These showed an almost motherly interest in their clients' voyages, where danger was greatest, what routes they took, and so on. Many sailors were delighted to find a woman so clearly interested in their welfare; it was all very understandable. Lisbon could perhaps be correctly described as the 'spying' capital of the war. Other neutral cities had good claims – Geneva, Madrid and Ankara, for example – but Lisbon outshone them.

Although SOE was expanding rapidly, it conducted its affairs so discreetly from its Baker Street headquarters that very few members of the armed forces, even at very high levels, were aware that it existed. When they were officially informed the first reaction was not so much of admiration but doubt about the advisability of granting facilities, such as scarce aircraft, to such a nebulous concept. Fortunately for SOE, Churchill stepped in and said that SOE should be given priority over aircraft.

The story of SOE is in many ways the story of the Lysander. This small aircraft, whose ability to fly at low speeds made it ideal for army cooperation, could land and take off in a very small space. Many SOE agents were deposited in France by Lysanders. Other workhorse aircraft for SOE were Hudsons and Dakotas (C.47s).

SOE in Western Europe (France, Belgium, Holland and the Scandinavian countries) was organized from Baker Street, SOE in the Mediterranean from Cairo, SOE in the Far East from Ceylon (now Sri Lanka).

Groups of agents organized by SOE were designated by numbers: 133 (from Cairo) was concerned with Greece, the Aegean islands and Bulgaria; 266 (from Bari) operated in Albania; and 399 (Bari) in Yugoslavia. The numbering of these units appears to have followed the normal army practice of using multiples. However there was also a No. 6 in Algiers whose purpose was to arrange sabotage in France prior to the landing which would be made there later. There was also a Force 139 for Poland and Czechoslovakia, and 136 operated in Burma, Siam, Indo-China (Vietnam), Malaya and Indonesia.

There was no liaison with PWE, although Dalton was the head of both organizations. There was, however, liaison with the Office of Strategic Services (OSS) which was the name the Americans gave to their equivalent service.

The story of OSS began in 1940 when Roosevelt appointed Colonel William J. Donovan as Co-ordinator of Strategic Information. Donovan was a prosperous lawyer of Irish descent, but unlike some Americans with Irish ancestry he was well disposed towards Britain. He was also a republican, which made him a somewhat unorthodox friend for a democrat president. Donovan spent several months visiting Britain and the Middle East with a view to assessing the strategic problems of the various areas. At the end of it he wrote a report describing the problems and dangers of the areas he visited, and recommended that some provision should be made by the US for psychological warfare. As a result the Office of Coordination of Strategic Information (OCSI) was set up. Its establishment was far from popular with the services and because of their opposition to it it was made directly responsible to the president and to no one else.

Five months after the establishment of the OCSI, America was drawn into the war by the Japanese attack on Pearl Harbor, and six months later OCSI was given the more manageable title of the Office of Strategic Services (OSS). Donovan, who had close links with SOE, now organized a department within the OSS to be called SO (Sabotage Operation). However, unlike its British counterpart, SO activities came under the theatre commanders of the areas in which it planned to operate. In theory this was sensible, in that SO moves could be coordinated with the military back-up; in practice it was often less than happy because the theatre commander would almost certainly be a general with no knowledge of the possibilities and limitations of sabotage activities, would know next to nothing of the terrain in which OSS was functioning, and was likely to ask too much or too little of SO.

Donovan was able to establish a very competent corps of operators at a very early stage. Not least of his assets was the large numbers of Americans who were children of recent immigrants and were bilingual. The fact that their countries of origin were now under the Nazi heel made them very determined in their attempts to attain a high standard of operational skill. Additionally, not only did they speak the language of another country but they were already versed in the domestic background. Once Donovan got into his stride, he organized groups by the hundred.The exact number is not known but overall was probably not less than one thousand. And these were only a part of OSS.

OSS work also included propaganda of the type which PWE operated and which has already been described. It worked separately from PWE, by mutual agreement. It included a secret weapon and equipment development section; when a need was expressed, OSS tried to design the answer to it. It also looked into the development of larger weapons with more than local use. There was a special boat section on much the same lines as the British SBS, and an extensive communications section for codes and radio equipment. Clearly there would be some overlapping with SOE and duplication, if not dislocation, unless suitable arrangements were made, and these were agreed in June 1942. However, as may be imagined, this did not mean that complete harmony would invariably exist, but in view of the different approaches, and the fact that SOE had already been functioning some two years before OSS had come into being, the relationship was remarkably cordial.

It got off to a very good start in North Africa, where, as we saw, the British were *persona non grata* after they had shelled French naval units which had preferred to cooperate with the Nazis rather than join the Allies. Long before the 'Torch' invasion of 1943, the OSS had set up combat teams in the main ports, had armed resistance groups and contacted reliable guides who knew the area well. The OSS also circulated a number of deception rumours which diverted Nazi attention from matters in which it was undesirable that they should be interested. A combined operation with the British was mounted when, on 22 October 1942, General Mark Clark was taken from England by submarine, landed on the North African coast by the British Special Boat Section, and met General Mast, commander of the Vichy French XIX Corps in a well-guarded villa. The arrangements for the arrival of General Mast had been carefully coordinated by the OSS. The object of the meeting was to reassure the French that the landing was an American venture, not a British one, and to ensure that there would not be bitter fighting when it took place. Mast had been recommended by General Giraud as being the French commander most likely to help avoid bloodshed.

Although the 'Torch' invasion was comparatively painless, the rest of North Africa did not fall without a protracted struggle. During the ensuing six months harmony prevailed between SOE and OSS, largely due to the diplomatic skills of Col. Douglas Dodds-Parker, who would later become a Member of Parliament and Under Secretary of State in the Foreign and Commonwealth Offices from 1953 to 1957.

As was expected, with so many Americans of Italian descent, the OSS was at the peak of its efficiency in Sicily and Italy. It was particularly effective in preparing the way for the Salerno landings. The official report states that there were sixty-three OSS agents operating in northern Italy in 1944. At that time the OSS headquarters in Italy was known as 'Company O'. Both OSS and SOE maintained close links with the Italian partisans and arranged for their supplies.

In the Balkans the political situation made the activities of both OSS and SOE more sensitive. As we remarked earlier, resistance groups are often as hostile to other resistance groups as they are to the common enemy, so aiding resistance groups, or freedom fighters, may involve delicate political questions. In Yugoslavia, where there was a long history of bitter conflict, it seemed at first appropriate to assist Mihailovich and his right-wing supporters. Soon, however, it became apparent that Mihailovich was more interested in defeating his rival Tito, a Moscow-trained communist, than the German invader. Tito knew that his Russian helpers would expect adequate efforts to be made against the Nazis but at the same time hoped to have something to spare to crush his rival Mihailovich. As the war progressed, Mihailovich (who was subsequently executed by his rivals) actively collaborated with the Nazis in order to defeat Tito's partisans. And, as we saw in relation to the LRDG and SBS in the Adriatic, political considerations (which involved allowing Tito to appear to be the liberator of Istria) meant that anything the two British regiments wished to do was inhibited by the need to let Tito have his way. In Yugoslavia SOE was first on the scene, and when OSS came in the Americans used British communications, including ciphers. In late 1943 OSS began using its own communications system. In the same year the US government, against British advice, sent a team of liaison officers to Mihailovich, partly to reclaim US airmen who had been shot down and partly to collect intelligence. Tito's anger and suspicion were aroused; they were only partly quenched when the US sent a military mission to him in September 1944.

Greece was another area where the OSS was particularly active, but whose local politics were much more complicated and vicious than had been previously understood. Here ELAS (the military wing of the National Liberation Front – EAM) wished to establish a communist government, while EDES preferred a right-wing rule. EDES wanted a republic, but not a communist one.

The British had been first on the scene in Greece when Brigadier E. C. W. Myers and Colonel the Hon. C. M. Woodhouse had arrived in October 1942. They had been surprised at the strength of feeling against a return to the pre-war pattern of government, which, of course, implied the return of the monarchy. Myers and Woodhouse made strenuous efforts to make the rival partisan groups work together; they succeeded rarely but one occasion was a brilliant success. Eighty per cent of the supplies to Rommel's army in North Africa travelled on the railway line between Salonika and Athens. Just before the critical battle of Alamein in October 1942, a team of British sappers, helped by a combined force of ELAS and EDES, blew up an important viaduct on the Gorgopotomos river. The effect on Rommel's supplies was considerable. Further sabotage attacks took place just before the invasion of Italy but it soon became clear that ELAS was cooperating only in order to obtain arms with which to attack its rival EDES. As EDES was cooperating with the British, Britain stopped supplying arms to ELAS. This brought ELAS to heel temporarily.

In October 1944, British troops landed near Patras. The remainder of Greece was soon liberated but the political situation remained as intractable as ever. In the latter stages EDES assisted the Allies; ELAS, bribed with arms from the Germans, did nothing. At the end of 1944 ELAS, using those arms, captured parts of Athens and Piraeus; dislodging them required two British divisions withdrawn from the Italian front. In January 1945 ELAS agreed a truce, and all but a few hard-core members who went to fight in the mountains settled under the restored monarchy.

The political situation in Greece and Yugoslavia has been described briefly here to show the special difficulties of SOE and OSS agents. They were required not merely to harass the Germans but also to reconcile warring factions. In Yugoslavia the royalists had been prepared to cooperate with the Germans to achieve the one aim; in Greece the communists had been prepared to do exactly the same. Another conflict of interests was between the natural desire of SOE and OSS to blow up railway tracks and bridges to hasten the inevitable end of the war, and the wish of the returning government not to find a country in ruins, without communications, when it tried to restore pre-war conditions. The major achievement of OSS was to demolish two bridges (at Svilengrad and Alexandropolis) on the Greek–Bulgarian border in May 1944. The loss of these bridges temporarily stopped the transport of chrome from Turkey to Germany.

The OSS did not involve itself in Albania, though SOE did. In addition, Albania saw the SBS and the LRDG. One SOE agent sent to Albania was Dare Newell. Newell had joined the army in 1942 after some difficulties, for the temporary job he had taken in forestry was apparently a reserved occupation. In the Royal Tank Regiment he soon became bored with routine soldiering and volunteered for SOE. Newell was taught how to blow up transformers and heavy machinery but, having been deposited in Albania by submarine and canoe, he found there were no transformers there and very little heavy machinery. SOE activities had to be restricted to blowing up bridges and ambushing enemy convoys. (The full story of Albania is given in Col. David Smiley's *Albanian Assignment.*)

An equally difficult area was Bulgaria. The OSS dropped two small groups but did little except arrange for the evacuation of captured American airmen. They had been there only a month when the Russians arrived and ordered them (and SOE) out of the country.

The Bulgarian government had been firmly in the Axis pocket since the beginning of the war. It cooperated fully with the Nazis when the latter were invading Yugoslavia and Greece and was, as a reward, allowed to annex the Greek and Serbian provinces of Macedonia. However, when the King of Bulgaria died suddenly and mysteriously in 1943, many Bulgarians suspected that he had been helped on his way by the Nazis. In consequence a resistance movement came into existence. It was predominantly communist and grew rapidly. Soon it became known as the Fatherland Front. When the Russians crossed the Bulgarian frontier the Fatherland Front set off a general uprising and captured Sofia. Soon, however, the Bulgarian partisans and army were under Russian control. The Fatherland Front was abolished and all but trusted communists were executed. In 1946 Bulgaria became a 'Democratic People's Republic' under the Moscow-trained Georgi Dimitrov.

One SOE agent who was unaware of the political undercurrents in Bulgaria was Paul Pike. In 1943 Pike was a young Gunner officer who had shown himself to be both courageous and reliable in desert fighting. When asked if he would care to volunteer for a dangerous but important job he had no hesitation. He was told it was for SOE, which he had not, at the time, heard of. He was given a brief training as a parachutist and informed that he would be dropped in Bulgaria to assist the partisans. Pike never claimed to be an intellectual (though he was full of sound sense and judgement) and he had only the vaguest idea of where Bulgaria was. 'Bulgaria,' he said. 'I don't speak any Bulgarian or whatever language they speak.' 'Never mind, old boy,' he was assured, 'they'll all speak English. You won't even need a dictionary.'

Shortly afterwards Pike and another SOE man were dropped into the wilds of Macedonia. No one there spoke a word of English. Macedonia had been invaded by Bulgarians who, with the aid of Germans, were busy 'bulgarizing' the country, but there were several bands of partisans making life difficult for the invaders. Pike's task was to coordinate the groups and arrange for drops of arms and equipment. The area was vital to the Germans for it was on their supply route to Greece.

For eleven months Pike and his companion (Lt-Col. Kitcat) harassed the Bulgarian army, disrupted its supply lines, and organized resistance. Because of this they soon had a large price on their heads. Avoiding capture meant continually moving and often living in bitter weather among the mountains. Eventually Pike was caught in an ambush and shot through the thigh. He was taken prisoner but two weeks later the Russians invaded the country, the Bulgarian army changed sides, and Pike was released. He was awarded a Military Cross.

On discharge from hospital Pike went to Baker Street to be debriefed by Maj.-Gen. Sir Colin Gubbins, head of SOE. 'Well,' said Gubbins. 'What would you like to do now?' He assumed Pike might like to complete his convalescence in some quiet backwater. 'I'd like to go somewhere where there's plenty of action,' said Pike. 'What about the Far East?'

In spite of having to walk with a stick, he was soon operating behind the Japanese lines in Burma. And at the end of the war he was sent to Indo-China to cope with the guerrillas who, having failed to do much against the Japanese, were now a threat to the re-establishment of law and order. After Indo-China he qualified as a pilot and commanded a squadron in the Army Air Corps.

This intrepid, cheerful and modest man died in 1984.

Another SOE man who tried his luck in Bulgaria was Frank Thompson, formerly of the Royal Artillery and Phantom. Thompson was an intellectual, a product of Winchester and New College, Oxford. He was already a communist when he joined the army but his military qualities and courage were so distinctive that his political views were regarded as mere flights of fancy. In July 1944 he was dropped in south Serbia where the Bulgarian resistance was trying to establish dropping zones, prior to finding them in Bulgaria itself. After some brisk battles with the Bulgarian army (which was working with the Nazis) Thompson was captured. On a previous occasion he had escaped after capture, but this time was more carefully guarded. He was put on trial and with some thirty other partisans was condemned to death, and shot. Before his execution he spoke to his fellow-partisans, calmly and bravely, assuring them their sacrifice would not be in vain.

The story of Romania is too long and complicated to receive more than an outline here. Nearly a million Romanians were dragooned into fighting against Russia, although badly clothed and ill-equipped for the task; they incurred tremendous losses. The only advantage that Romania had over the other satellite countries was that Antonescu, the German-backed dictator, was able to protect the Romanians, including many Jews, from the worst excesses of Nazism. However, the importance of the Ploesti oilfield made Romania too valuable an asset for risks to be taken, and the number of German troops stationed in the country exceeded those elsewhere. Although law-abiding Romanians were left unscathed, the way of the intending saboteur was made as difficult as possible. This fact did not prevent sabotage taking place on a huge scale. Some of it was unobtrusive, being in the form of defects in goods, such as tanks, shells and vehicles; other examples were more obvious, such as the damage done in the Ploesti refineries, and fires in the Tirgoviste arsenal, and at the Mirsa warehouse. Much of this resistance was aided by Soviet agents but SOE was also active from 1941 onwards. The chief value of SOE agents was to obtain information about bombing targets, notably at Ploesti. Subsequent bombing raids by the USAF reduced the output of the Ploesti oilfields by as much as eighty-five per cent. In August 1944 Romanian guerrillas rose and captured Bucharest, and many other strategic areas, including the Ploesti oilfields. The Romanian army changed sides, the Germans were forced to withdraw (the Russians were closing up) and Romania joined the Allies and declared war on Germany. However, those who hoped for an independent existence were soon to be disillusioned, for by 1947 all political parties except the communists had been suppressed. In December of that year King Michael abdicated and the People's Republic of Romania came into being.

Force 133 had been responsible for SOE activity in Romania and its task had not been easy. The head of the Romanian peasant party was Juliu Maniu, but he proved a broken reed. SOE agents were murdered by bandits, or captured soon after arrival. However, an OSS team which landed at Popesti airport with B17s was able to evacuate 1,300 American airmen.

Most of the backing for resistance in Romania seems to have come from the Russians, who did not subsequently provide details of their operations.

Both Czechoslovakia and Hungary proved unfruitful for SOE and OSS activities. In Czechoslovakia the Nazis were too numerous and strong for the resistance movement to take effective military action. The Czechs were advised to confine their activities to information-gathering. When they tried to do more than this the Nazis inflicted an appalling vengeance. The most notorious example was when Heydrich, head of the Nazi Secret Police and deputy head of the SS, was ambushed and killed in May 1942. In retaliation the Nazis totally destroyed two villages, Lidice and Lezaky, killed all the male inhabitants, shot thousands of hostages, and sent thousands of men and women to concentration camps. Needless to say, all but a handful of these victims were totally unconnected with the ambush. Two years later, in July 1944, revolt broke out in Slovakia and quickly spread. Sporadic fighting went on during the following months, and large numbers of German troops were involved to crush the resistance. They failed, and when the Russians arrived, the Czech partisans made their task of liberating Prague much easier. Sadly, the Czechs and Slovaks paid a high price for their resistance activities: over 350,000 died in battle, by execution, or in concentration camps.

Although Czechoslovakian resistance had been encouraged and assisted by Russian agents, few Czechoslovakians realized that after the war they would not be independent but become part of the Russian empire. OSS and Force 139 had made considerable efforts to assist the Czechs, but had had little success until the final stages of the war. A number of the OSS were captured and executed; the remainder died of exposure.

When the Germans had been defeated at Stalingrad and in the African battles in 1943, Admiral Horthy, the Hungarian dictator, decided that the Germans might not be going to win the war. So far he had cooperated with German demands, though from necessity rather than will; now he deemed it advisable to offer limited cooperation to the Allies. He therefore sent an emissary to the OSS. In consequence the OSS despatched a party of three officers to examine the internal situation. At the moment they arrived the Nazis decided to impose full control over Hungary, and the OSS men fell into their hands. At the end of a gruelling interrogation they were interned, but survived the war.

However, SOE continued the liaison with Horthy, who by 1944 was more apprehensive of the Russians than he was of the Germans. The latter realized what Horthy was planning and in October 1944 removed him, just when he was on the point of signing an armistice with the Russians. The Nazis then imposed a reign of terror on the Hungarians, deporting many to concentration camps. Finally in February 1945 Russian troops entered Budapest, and the country passed into the Soviet sphere of influence. Like the other Balkan countries, Hungary was forced by the Germans to send troops to fight on the Russian front. They were badly armed and clothed and suffered appalling hardships during the Russian winter.

Italy, as we saw earlier, had many different groups operating behind the German lines. They included SAS, LRDG, MI9, PPA (Popski's Private Army), among others. In the north of the country, in particular, there was a strong undercurrent of anti-fascist feeling. The task of SOE and OSS was to persuade groups with different political ambitions to submerge their private feelings for the time being and cooperate to defeat the common enemy. Some of the more militant and effective of the partisans made no secret of the fact that their aim immediately after liberation was to establish a communist government, closely linked with Russia. However, SOE and OSS made Italian resistance into a great success story. They supplied leadership where required, they organized supply drops on a huge scale (and did their not unsuccessful best to prevent the communists hiding away weapons for future use), and they fought side by side with partisans in pitched battles with the Germans.

The tasks of the special forces were enormous and varied. There were large numbers of deserters from the Italian army who saw no future in fighting for the Germans, there were escaped Allied prisoners-of-war who needed assistance to find their way through the German lines so that they could rejoin their own forces, and there were refugees who had fled from the Nazis or from areas in which heavy fighting was taking place. In view of what had happened in Greece after liberation, it was important to see that the communists did not stage a similar coup in Italy.

Over 100,000 Germans were killed or captured, dozens of towns were liberated, and the war in Italy was brought to an end much more rapidly than had been expected. The Germans could not take to the mountains and fight on from there, as the partisans were already in possession. But the cost was not less than 100,000 partisans killed in action, and many innocent people deported or executed in reprisal for partisan sabotage. At the end, Italy was spared the bitterness and chaos of Greece and Yugoslavia: instead the country settled quickly to democratic government. As the country had been under fascist rule since 1922, its harmonious return to democracy was one of the more heartening aspects of the war.

A somewhat unusual task fell to Maj. Philip Worrall of Force 133. Worrall had come to SOE from the South Wales Borderers and after various adventures elsewhere was parachuted into the Pindus mountains in Greece on 14 September 1943. In this area (Thessaly) were the Italian Pinorolo Division and the Aosta Lanciere. When the Italian government had surrendered eight days previously, these formations gave themselves up to the Greeks. They assumed that the war in those parts was now over and that they would be granted honourable terms. However, as we know, the war was by no means over; the Germans occupied Rome on 10 September and the war in Italy was to continue for another eighteen months. The Greeks, who had no love for the Italians, disarmed their prisoners, robbed them of most of their clothing, and made no effort to feed them.

Worrall was informed by SOE that he was in charge of 7,000 Italians and 1,600 horses. They had no food, and many were dying. He arranged for the purchase of food, and established hospitals for the sick. He also organized a defence against the Andartes (Greek guerrillas) who were intent on revenging themselves on these Italians for the injuries their country had experienced from their Italian overlords. The Germans also tried to reach them, not in order to aid them but to force the able-bodied back into service with Mussolini, and their own army. For a time they lived in a small village in the mountains. Periodically the Germans made raids into the district and burnt whatever buildings they came across. At one point ninety sick Italians had been left behind in a makeshift hospital, on the assumption that the Red Cross convention would ensure their being unharmed. However, the Germans took them all out and shot them through the head. As Worrall led the remainder to a safer area, they were reduced to living on chestnuts (for about four months). They died at the rate of twenty a day. Worrall himself contracted appendicitis. An aircraft was sent for him. Although it was delayed, it eventually took him to Bari when he had an immediate operation – just in time.

After a brief convalescence he returned to the Italians. Gradually, conditions improved, but when Worrall led them down from the mountains so that they might be evacuated from Greece and return to Italy, they found themselves caught in the middle of the Greek Civil War. At last they reached Volos, and a troopship which took them to Taranto. Worrall continued his journey to Cairo. Soon after his arrival, he was writing his report on his experiences, when someone walked into the room. 'Would anyone like to volunteer to be dropped into Germany?' the newcomer asked. Two people put up their hands: Worrall was one of them. He was on an aircraft to England the same night, destined to become a member of T Force (see page 226).

On Crete SOE staged an ingenious and daring kidnap. In 1943 and 1944 the German Commandant in Crete was one General Müller, whose policy of ferocious reprisals on the innocent after any sabotage had made him feared and hated. Crete contained some enterprising SOE agents, among them Patrick Leigh-Fermor, Xan Fielding and Tom Dunbabin. They were joined in April by W. S. Moss, by which time Müller had been replaced by General Kreipe, who was less objectionable than his predecessor but by no means benevolent. Moss and Leigh-Fermor, assisted by Cretan partisans, stopped the general's car as he was driving home from his headquarters to his villa, and then, with the German sitting in the back with a pistol at his ribs, drove through twenty-four checkpoints. At each one they received a salute which Leigh-Fermor returned, for he was wearing the general's hat. The party was then taken out of Crete by a ship from the Raiding Support Regiment.

It was a stupendous achievement, as daring and enterprising, though not as important, as Skorzeny's capture of Mussolini earlier in the war. There was, however, a dark side to it, for the Germans shot 200 Cretans as a reprisal. In the circumstances, it can hardly have served as a warning to the Germans to be less brutal. There were misgivings in SOE about the wisdom of allowing agents to practise this sort of enterprise. Collecting information did not attract reprisals; kidnapping, sabotage, guerrilla action, did. Although the Germans behaved reasonably well to their prisoners-of-war, and regarded their escape attempts – for the most part – as legitimate activities, their policy to others, whether irregular forces or even harmless civilians, was savage by any standards.

As the war progressed, SOE gave more and more thought to the long-term effect of operations.

7: *Gains – and Losses*

Inevitably, the most suitable area for SOE and OSS activity was northern Europe, particularly France, Belgium, Holland, Norway and Denmark. French resistance groups began their various activities as soon as the Germans completed their conquest of that country. Intelligence networks were soon established; the first was organized by the Polish army and was given the code-names F1 and F2. There was also a well-organized British network, and each local resistance group had its own intelligence service, as it needed to have if it were to survive. There were wide differences of political and regional opinion between the members of the various groups. One complication was that many French people felt that de Gaulle could not be a loyal Frenchman as he had not stayed and supported Marshal Pétain, who represented the government of France, even though it had surrendered to the Germans. De Gaulle, of course, became a symbol of French resistance later, but his antipathy to the British and the Americans, who were trying to help him, and his inability to keep a confidence to himself, made him a difficult comrade-in-arms.

The French section of SOE was organized in 1940 under the headship of H. R. Marriot. In 1941 Marriot was succeeded by Col. Maurice Buckmaster. In its ranks were British citizens who spoke fluent French, and French citizens who wished to work for the resistance but who would have nothing to do with de Gaulle. De Gaulle and the Free French regarded F Section of SOE as having no business to be in France without their agreement. F Section had a highly organized intelligence system by which each circuit – and they eventually numbered fifty-two – had no contact with any other circuit but only with London. Thus, when individual circuits were penetrated, as was inevitable, the damage was limited. Sometimes circuits were closed abruptly by SOE on the suspicion that they had been infiltrated; this happened to at least ten.

Although de Gaulle regarded the French section of SOE as quite illegal, he had no objection to SIS (MI6) working in France, nor for that matter MI9, which specialized in helping prisoners-of-war or shot-down airmen to escape. He had his own Bureau Central de Renseignements et d'Action (BCRA). In 1943 BCRA went to Algiers, leaving the London function to BRAL (Bureau de Renseignements d'Action Londres). These two were intended to collect intelligence and to organize sabotage. De Gaulle saw them as the basis of the post-war government he planned to set up in France after the liberation; in the event, matters did not work to the timetable he expected.

Although de Gaulle strongly disapproved of F Section, he requested assistance from SOE for BCRA. An RF (Resistance France) Section was therefore formed. De Gaulle wished it to build up a secret army with formations in various parts of France, which eventually it did. One of the heads of RF was Bickham Sweet-Escott, who subsequently wrote a book entitled *Baker Street Irregular*. Sweet-Escott was a wise and shrewd planner and had considerable operational experience himself. His book, which is packed with detail, gives a lively but not uncritical account of SOE.

The official account of SOE operations in France is M. R. D. Foot's *SOE in France*, which covers the subject as part of the official history of the Second World War, and is therefore published by Her Majesty's Stationery Office. It is a full and detailed account, and has the merit of being easily digestible. Not least of the virtues of this book is the selection of photographs of various agents. Professor Foot is the author of a number of other works on resistance, all of which are highly instructive and eminently readable. The same, alas, cannot be said of accounts of SOE by many of the participants.

No account of French resistance would be complete without mention of Jean Moulin, code named 'Rex'. Moulin had been Préfet (Chief Administrative Officer) at Chartres, but had escaped through Spain in late 1941 with information about the resistance groups already organized in France. He was then parachuted back into France with the mission of contacting these groups and linking them all under de Gaulle. He accomplished this task superbly and laid the foundations for a coordinated, powerful, resistance movement, rather than a series of disconnected, relatively ineffective units. Unfortunately for him, and everyone else, he was arrested by the Gestapo and tortured to death while on a train en route to Germany. This disaster was attributed to a weakness in security, for Moulin was not the only one to be caught by the Germans at that time.

Although there were numerous resistance groups working in France, and they had some notable successes, agents, whether SOE or others, were in constant danger. German counter-intelligence, which was extremely efficient, was helped by French collaborators. Many clandestine radio operators were caught before they realized that the secret of evading German detector vans was to keep their messages short and be off the air except for very brief transmissions. A particularly bad year was 1943; many operators were arrested and some sets stayed in use, operated by the Germans. In theory this should not have been possible, for operators were drilled in a procedure for indicating that their transmissions were from genuine agents. The technique involved making certain mistakes. In Lorraine in 1944, the Germans captured a radio operator's entire equipment, including instructions about codes and security checks. This enabled them to pretend the operator was still functioning and arrange for SOE agents and stores to be dropped directly into German hands. Buckmaster subsequently said: 'Of the 480 service members of F Section 130 were caught in five years.' All but a handful met death in various unpleasant ways.

J. G. Beevor, who was deputy head of SOE, mentions that in February 1944 SOE mounted an operation known as 'Ratweek'. The objective was to kill as many senior German Secret Service officers as possible in Western Europe. 'Ratweek' had its greatest success in south-eastern France where Francis Cammaerts was in command. He was the son of Emile Cammaerts, a well-known Belgian writer and poet, who had settled in England and become a professor at London University. Francis Cammaerts had regarded the outbreak of war without enthusiasm, as he held pacifist views. None of his contemporaries at St Catharine's College, Cambridge, shared his opinion, and when they joined the services he eventually went into farming. In August 1942 he changed his views, offered his services to SOE, and became one of its most daring, skilled and successful leaders. His particular virtue was the ability to sense whether an operation was viable or not: too many people lacked this vital quality. His code-name was 'Roger'.

There were, of course, innumerable small acts of sabotage throughout France during the occupation. Usually these were undetected, and all the more effective for that. Resistance men and women who worked on railways or other forms of transport were particularly valuable.

One of the most useful activities was to change either the destination or description labels on German goods. Thus 37mm ammunition could be sent to batteries requiring 88mm shells: it would then have to be returned, blocking already heavily congested transport routes. With luck, an engineer unit in the field would receive crates of agricultural machinery instead of the technical spares they urgently needed. There was little chance of the saboteur being detected: as often as not the error was attributed to some bureaucratic inefficiency.

Sabotage on a larger scale included the destruction of the power supply at the Le Creusot armaments works, the demolition of the Gigny barrage on the river Saône, the derailment of oil supply trains en route to submarine bases, and the destruction of a huge aircraft component factory at Toulouse. Perhaps the most important sabotage was that which delayed the arrival of German reinforcements in Normandy after the D-Day landings. D-Day was preceded by a number of BBC coded warnings, of which the most famous was the passage from Verlaine deliberately broadcast with two errors:

Les sanglots longs
Des violons
D'automne
Blessent mon coeur
D'une langueur
Monotone.

The first part of the message, up to '*automne*', was a general alert; the second that the D-Day invasion would begin that same night. What is less well known about this famous message is that the Germans heard it and knew what it signified. They had captured codes some months before which gave the secret away. However, the Germans failed to realize that the message referred to the invasion itself, but assumed it merely meant a general sabotage alert. Perhaps their perception had been dulled by the fact that for some time previously the BBC had been broadcasting a series of totally meaningless messages, and the German Secret Service knew this.

Two classic examples of delaying actions were those which hindered 2 SS Panzer Division and 11 Panzer Division. When the D-Day invasion occurred on 6 June in Normandy, the German High Command, as was mentioned earlier, was reluctant to believe that this was the Allies' main effort; instead they preferred to think that it was a diversion and that the main Allied attack would quickly follow in the

Calais area. In consequence there were retained in the Pas de Calais area, troops which could have had a decisive effect in counter-attacking the invasion force in Normandy. 2 and 11 Panzers were therefore urgently needed in the Normandy area to compensate for this. 2 Panzer was stationed at Toulouse and, on the day after D-Day, was instructed to move to Normandy. The journey, which should have taken two or three days, actually took sixteen. 11 Panzer was withdrawn from the Russian front, and took a week to reach the Rhone; it needed another three weeks to reach Normandy. These delays were effected by blowing up tunnels, track, bridges, signalling systems – in fact, everything which normally makes a railway function.

But the story of the resistance also contains many disasters. Brave men and women were trapped, tortured, executed or sent to die in concentration camps. Four women were burnt alive in furnaces by the Gestapo. And at the Vercors there was a massacre which the French recall with bitterness as being an unnecessary sacrifice. The Vercors, a plateau due south of Grenoble and due east of Valence, was the headquarters of a resistance group which had a good collection of light arms, such as stens and grenades, but lacked artillery and anti-tank guns. Its function was seen as one of harassing the enemy and fading away, not engaging in heavy fighting. However, on 28 June 1944, SOE sent in two English officers, in uniform. Neither spoke French, although both had been in SOE for three years. They were accompanied by a French-speaking American officer, and two Frenchmen. An OG (American Operational Group), numbering fifteen, followed them the next day. Cammaerts, who was head of SOE in south-eastern France, had not been told of the impending arrival of these teams, neither had they been informed who he was. The newcomers cleared any Germans they found off the plateau. A fortnight later there were 3,000 Maquis on the Vercors plateau and they had received an American drop of more stens, ammunition and clothes, but no heavier artillery. On the 18th, the Germans attacked the plateau with 10,000 men and air support. Heroic resistance held them off; in one action the OG performed brilliantly. However, the Germans landed gliders full of SS troops on the Vercors' one landing strip, and these could not be disposed of with the weapons the Maquis had available. As it was obvious that the Germans would now win this particular battle, the orders was given to disperse. The Germans then murdered all the men and raped all the women they could lay their hands on. The verdict of the Allies was that the Vercors rising had come too soon and tried to do too much; the French, who suffered appalling cruelties, saw it as an Allied betrayal.

Delays inflicted on the 2nd Panzer (Das Reich) Division as it made its way to Normandy made German behaviour worse than usual. When a company commander had been shot by a sniper in Oradour-sur-Vayres, the SS descended on Oradour-sur-Glane, which was fifteen miles away. But the SS would probably not have cared, even if they had known of their mistake. The population of the village was herded into the square, and the women and children were sent into the church. The men were then all shot, and the church was set on fire, with SS men standing around to see that nobody got away. In the event a few escaped under cover of the smoke, but nearly 700 died. However, even savagery on this scale did not stop the efforts of the resistance.

The greatest disaster to SOE took place in Holland. At best, Holland was a difficult country to work in, for it has no mountains and a very small percentage of woodland; there was therefore no safe place to lie up. SOE began its Dutch campaign in 1941. The Dutch were passively hostile to the conquerors, and deeply resentful of the deportation of their Jews to concentration camps. One of the early agents to be parachuted in was Hubertus Lauwers. Lauwers's transmission was located by a German detector van and he was caught with his set. He had been instructed by SOE to begin by refusing to collaborate with the Germans, but to give in after a short period and to start to transmit the messages they gave him. This process would enable him to communicate, by the previously agreed code, that he had been caught and that everything he would send in future was suspect. The code for this purpose was a simple one: he must make a mistake on every sixteenth word he sent.

To his dismay he realized that his initial warning had passed unnoticed. In desperation he inserted the word 'caught' into messages he was required to transmit by his captors. No more notice was taken of this than of the earlier warning.

The result of the failure to take note of the warning was that Hermann Giskes, chief of the Abwehr in Holland, was able to use the captured set and material for over two years. During that period, fifty-eight other would-be agents were dropped, all straight into the hands of the Germans. In addition the Germans were given a present of large quantities of secret radio equipment, of guns and of ammunition. With this, Giskes set up fourteen other links from Holland to SOE.

Agent after agent was parachuted to imprisonment and subsequent death. The agents were, of course, unaware of the horrible fate awaiting them and set off full of optimism. The RAF, which had the task of dropping them but found its return journeys unusually well attended by German fighters and flak, had increasing suspicions of the purity of the Netherlands link. But it was only when two agents escaped from captivity and worked their way home via Switzerland, France and Spain, that the truth came out. Once Giskes realized they had escaped, he took the wise precaution of warning SOE that two collaborators had staged a mock escape and would in fact be working for the Germans. As SOE in London was at first inclined to believe this version of events, the two men, Dourlein and Ubbink, were received with suspicious hostility, even being imprisoned in Brixton jail for a while. Eventually their incredible story was believed and the game which Giskes had named 'Englandspiel' came to an end. Giskes, who had a curious sense of humour, sent a message to SOE regretting that such a pleasant interlude had now terminated. Fortunately other resistance groups in Holland had not been affected and in the following two years a further 100 agents and 35,000 weapons were supplied to them.

When, in the autumn of 1984, the BBC transmitted a series about SOE during World War II, the account of 'Englandspiel' inevitably attracted much attention and comment. Some of this found expression in letters to *The Times*. In view of the treachery which was occurring in other areas, there seemed some reason to believe that the failure to detect 'Englandspiel' was deliberate. All the records of this particular event were unavailable; most were said to have been destroyed. One correspondent who interviewed Giskes on this subject some ten years after the war said he could not believe that British intelligence had been deceived so easily and so completely over such a long period. Apparently when Giskes was engaged in Englandspiel he would say to himself, 'They pretend to me they are deceived by me for some deep, deep reason that escapes me . . .'

The question remains unanswered. It has been suggested that poor atmospheric conditions caused portions of the messages to be lost; it seems unusually unfortunate that these lost portions must have included the missing checks, and also Lauwers's insertions of the word 'caught'. The most disturbing feature of the episode is that there were no *external* checks. Instructions from Holland were followed meticulously; the RAF alone seems to have had suspicions. It was suggested that there might have been a muddle over the security checks owing to incompetence or poor liaison between departments. But it is virtually impossible to imagine that experienced operators, or the addressees, could have failed to note discrepancies. And why only Holland? In Belgium and northern France, where Giskes was also in overall command, there were no similar occurrences. The Belgian section was an unbroken success story. That section was commanded by Claude Knight, from the regular army; his deputy was Hardy Amies, the future royal dress-designer, who performed his duties with skill and verve and managed to find time for a little dress-designing too.

Before leaving this area we shall take a look at Jedburgh teams and OG. Jedburgh teams were made up of an Englishman, an American and a Frenchman; two of these were officers and the third a sergeant wireless operator. All three were trained in sabotage, leadership of guerrilla units and tactics. Unlike most SOE forces, they wore uniform. When they were parachuted into France in 1944 their task was to be a link between local guerrilla units and the Allied command. Once on the ground they assessed the local situation and potential, and requested more supplies if these were needed. Ninety-three Jedburgh teams were dropped in France in the summer of 1944. They provided an immediate rapid link between the local units and Eisenhower's GHQ, and therefore ensured that the efforts of the Maquis would be used to the best possible advantage. They used suitcase radios (Jedburgh sets) for communicating with their home bases. Like all radios used in World War II, these were heavy (thirty pounds was an average weight) and bulky, being about two feet long. Their biggest disadvantage was that they required approximately seventy feet of aerial if they were to perform efficiently. This was manageable for work in remote areas but very risky elsewhere. Nevertheless, the sets gave sterling service. Suitcase sets had been designed by a lance corporal in the Royal Corps of Signals early in the war, and no one came up with a better design before it ended. Nowadays, when technological advances have made miniature receivers and transmitters easily available, the difficulties of wartime agents in concealing, maintaining, carrying, and operating their cumbersome radios are not normally realized.

Although the Jedburgh teams had twenty-one casualties, all, except for one or two in the initial parachuting, were incurred in action against enemy forces. No one was captured; if any had been, it is unlikely that their uniforms would have saved them from being shot as saboteurs.

The Jedburgh teams included approximately a hundred Americans, and there were other Americans at work in larger units, known as Operational Groups (OGs). These had a high proportion of French speakers, a lesser proportion of officers, and more equipment than the Jedburgh teams. Their brief was the same as Jedburgh's: to coordinate resistance, arrange for further supplies if necessary, and to engage in any form of military activity in rear areas which would help take pressure off the advancing Allied forces. Like Jedburghs, and for that matter the SAS which had over two thousand men operating behind the German lines, OGs were not allowed into France until D-Day itself. To have let them go in earlier would have lost surprise, and probably allowed them to be hounded by the Germans. Once D-Day had begun, the Germans had too much on their hands in Normandy to be able to spare many resources for chasing resistance and saboteurs in their rear areas. On the few occasions when they did, such as at Oradour and the Vercors, they behaved with the utmost brutality.

Among the special forces used by the Allies were units based on a German idea. From radio intercepts the Allies learnt that in 1941 a German 'Intelligence Commando' had been with the leading troops when the Nazis entered Athens. Its target was the British army's headquarters in that town. It was more than probable that this would have been evacuated before the town capitulated, and highly likely that in the hurried retreat valuable documents would have been left behind. This indeed proved to be so; the Germans not only acquired information about the British forces they would be opposed to in Greece and Crete but also in other areas too, such as North Africa. Naval intelligence promptly suggested that Britain should form a unit briefed for a similar purpose; in consequence, No. 30 Commando was formed and went into action at Dieppe, North Africa, Sicily and Italy. It proved extremely valuable, particularly in the acquisition of coding encipherment material. A major success was the capture in Sicily of the Italian air force ciphers for homing beacons. These were then used to enable the Allied air forces to fly to selected targets in Italy guided by Italian beacons. Details of mining and minesweeping were also obtained.

A similar unit was X Troop. This was officially No. 3 Troop No. 10 (Inter-Allied) Commando. Its sixty-four members all spoke colloquial German fluently; many of them were Jewish refugees. They were given totally new identities in case they should fall into German hands. The future of a commando in German hands was not likely to be promising; the fate of a commando who was also a Jew would not take more than seconds to decide. X Troop (disguised as fishermen) made expeditions across the Channel immediately before D-Day to report on German defences and interrogated German prisoners as soon as these surrendered or were captured. Many of the unit's activities still remain secret.

SOE operations in Norway posed a difficult problem. In spite of Quisling, the collaborator who proclaimed himself prime minister, Norway never made peace with Germany. Air operations over Norway were very difficult in the early stages of the war; there were few aircraft which could manage the distance, and safe dropping zones were difficult to find. The shortness of the Arctic night added to the problems. As we saw earlier, the first Commando raids proved a mixed success.

Most of the saboteurs who were to work in Norway did so by means of what became known as the 'Shetland Bus'. The 'bus' was in fact a fleet of fishing boats and submarine chasers, manned by Anglo-Norwegian crews. They were credited with over 150 successful trips, and with landing 220 agents and 300 tons of stores. They also took out sixty agents and 350 refugees. Later in the war the work of the Shetland Bus was supplemented by massive air drops. By that time Norway was on the point of national uprising; had that occurred, the arms and ammunition would have been invaluable.

Denmark had a somewhat uneven record. The initial overrunning of the country had been so swift, and the subsequent occupation so mild that most Danes saw no necessity to indulge in what seemed to be a futile resistance which could only result in reprisals on the innocent. However, as the Nazis began to turn the screw, SOE found much support. But even in the early stages one group of Danes, who used the code name 'The Princes', had supplied valuable information about German organization and weapons. Better still, they had sent a photograph of a prototype V1 which had come down on Bornholm.

By 1943 the honeymoon was over, and the Danes set to work on a massive programme of sabotage which involved ships and shipyards, railways, rolling stock, communications and factories. They also suggested many targets, which the RAF made full use of. The comings and goings of German shipping were noted and reported, and so, unsuspected by the Germans, were U-boat trials with new equipment.

Belgium's part in anti-Nazi activities fell into two sections. One was concerned with intelligence and sabotage, and inflicted enormous damage on the electrical industry and the waterways; the other was the complete opposite in that it mounted a coordinated and successful operation to prevent the Germans demolishing bridges, ports, railways and roads when they were retreating through the country in 1944. But, as with other countries, Belgian resistance proved costly in lives. Fifteen thousand died, by execution, in concentration camps, or in gun battles. Of all the countries which resisted Nazi tyranny, Belgium probably faced the greatest difficulties, achieved the greatest success and paid the highest price.

8: *The Far Eastern Scene*

The Far East had become a neglected zone long before the Japanese swept across it in late 1941 and early 1942. There were already large Japanese armies occupying parts of China and, if that was not enough for the government of Chiang Kai-shek to contend with, there was also a sizeable communist revolutionary movement growing progressively stronger under the leadership of Mao Tse-tung. Indo-China had been a relatively stable French colony before the war, but now it was subject to the Vichy government in France, and through that to the Germans. There was a strong communist movement in the country led by Ho Chi Minh, but the clearest sign to the inhabitants of Indo-China that life would never be the same again was the fact that the Vichy government had already agreed to the use of Indo-Chinese ports and airfields by the Japanese. This gave the Japanese a forward base deep in the heart of the region they planned to conquer.

The Netherlands East Indies (NEI) comprised most of the Dutch empire. When the Germans overran Holland in 1940, a Dutch government was set up in London, but it was in a weak position to control such huge, varied and wealthy territories as Java, Sumatra, Borneo, the Celebes and a host of smaller islands. The NEI was rich in rubber, oil and contained most of the world's sources of quinine, a vital anti-malarial drug. Burma had considerable resources of useful raw materials, as did the Philippines (an American colony), but Malaya was undoubtedly the jewel in the crown, producing over half the world supply of tin and a third of its supply of natural rubber. To the north of Malaya, Thailand contained thick jungle but also managed to produce so much rice that it was known as 'the rice bowl of Asia'.

In 1941, with France and Holland controlled by Germany, and with Britain fully stretched to hold its own shores intact while maintaining a precarious hold in North Africa, it was clear to Japan that the oriental fruit was ripe for the plucking. Japan had made no secret of its military ambitions since the failure of the League of Nations to stop aggressive action in Manchuria in 1931. Japan had a well-balanced navy, an efficient air force which was completely underrated by all its potential opponents, and millions of soldiers who had been firmly indoctrinated with the belief that the greatest fortune they could wish for was to die in battle. This credo, and the ability to cope with the jungle better than their European opponents, gave them a temporary reputation for being almost invincible. Fortunately for Britain, they decided that if they were going to attack British and Dutch colonies, they must knock out America at the same time. Relations between the two countries had deteriorated rapidly over the previous year, and the Japanese felt that an unprovoked attack on Malaya and the NEI would be the last straw. The only threat posed by the Americans as far as Japan could see was a naval one: it was therefore essential to remove that threat by a surprise attack on the naval base at Pearl Harbor, in the Hawaiian Islands. The surprise strike was made, without the preliminary step of declaring war, but, unfortunately for the Japanese, some of the American ships were at sea and survived. This was a bitter blow for the Japanese, whose efficient espionage had given them every other essential detail of Pearl Harbor, as it had also done for Hong Kong and Malaya.

Japanese espionage was meticulously efficient. Every town in territories coveted by the Japanese had a contingent of photographers and dance-hall partners who knew their job perfectly. Their photographers took pictures of interesting buildings and supplied valuable details to military surveyors. Soldiers, sailors and airmen were photographed very cheaply and a battle order built up from their cap badges and shoulder titles. 'Taxi-dancers', as the girls in the dance-halls were called, were keenly interested in anything servicemen could be persuaded to tell them about their life, grievances, units and work. It was all quite painless. Some Japanese people had jobs in the telephone exchanges too . . .

When the fighting began, British units were often surprised by the speed at which Japanese aircraft identified targets. On more than one occasion an obliging local laundryman had arranged washing lines in the form of an arrow. There were also German spies, masquerading as Swiss, but these were hardly necessary.

Not least of the inconveniences caused by the brisk succession of Japanese victories in the Far East in 1942 was the fact that, when Burma was overrun, the overland route to China from India was cut.

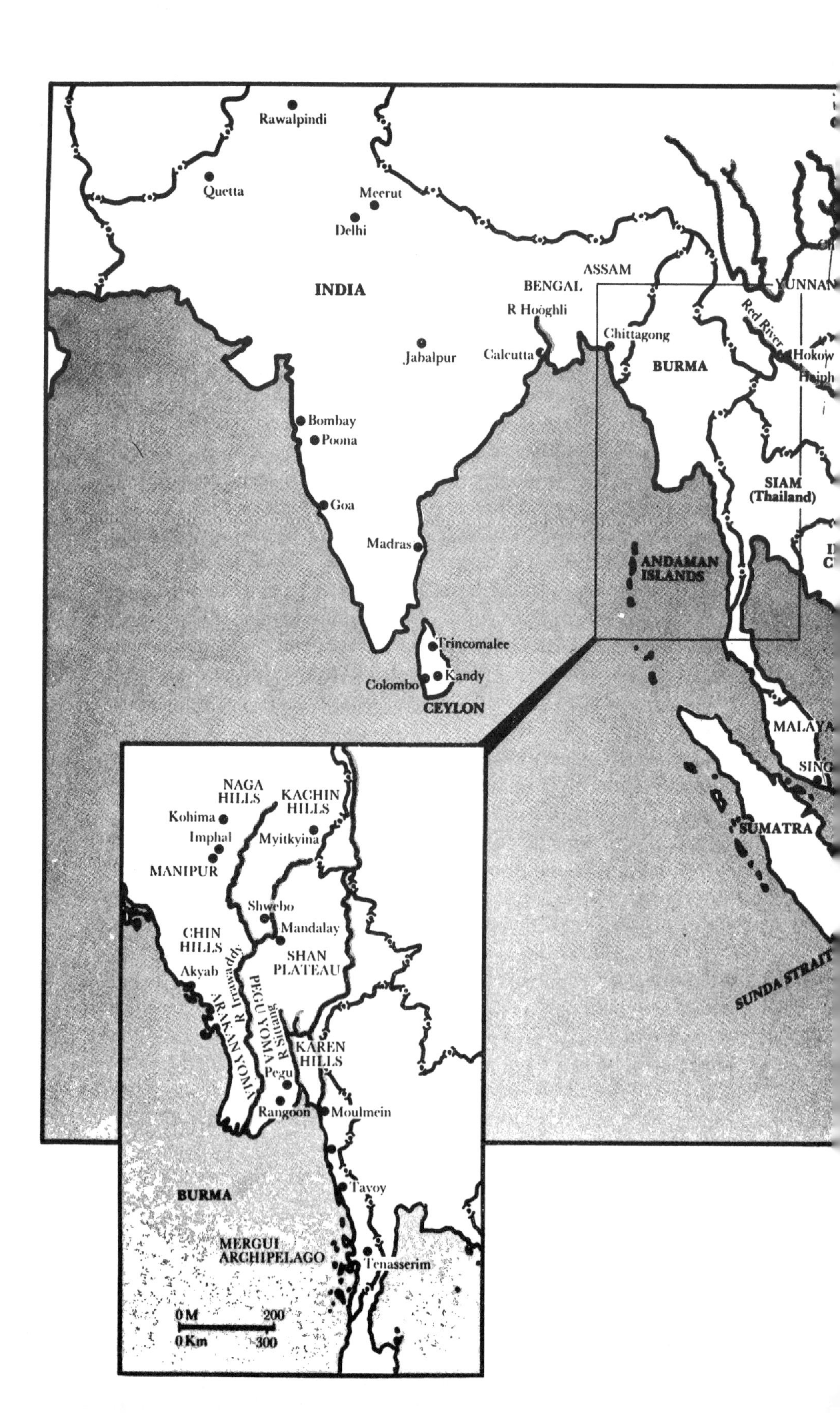

Rawalpindi
Quetta
Meerut
Delhi
INDIA
ASSAM
BENGAL
R Hooghli
Chittagong
Calcutta
Jabalpur
BURMA
Red River
Hokow
YUNNAN
Bombay
Poona
Goa
Madras
SIAM
(Thailand)
ANDAMAN
ISLANDS
Trincomalee
Kandy
Colombo
CEYLON
MALAYA
SUMATRA
SUNDA STRAIT
NAGA
HILLS
KACHIN
HILLS
Kohima
Imphal
Myitkyina
MANIPUR
Shwebo
Mandalay
CHIN
HILLS
SHAN
PLATEAU
Akyab
R Irrawaddy
PEGU YOMA
ARAKAN YOMA
R Sittang
KAREN
HILLS
Pegu
Rangoon
Moulmein
BURMA
Tavoy
MERGUI
ARCHIPELAGO
Tenasserim
0 M
200
0 Km
300

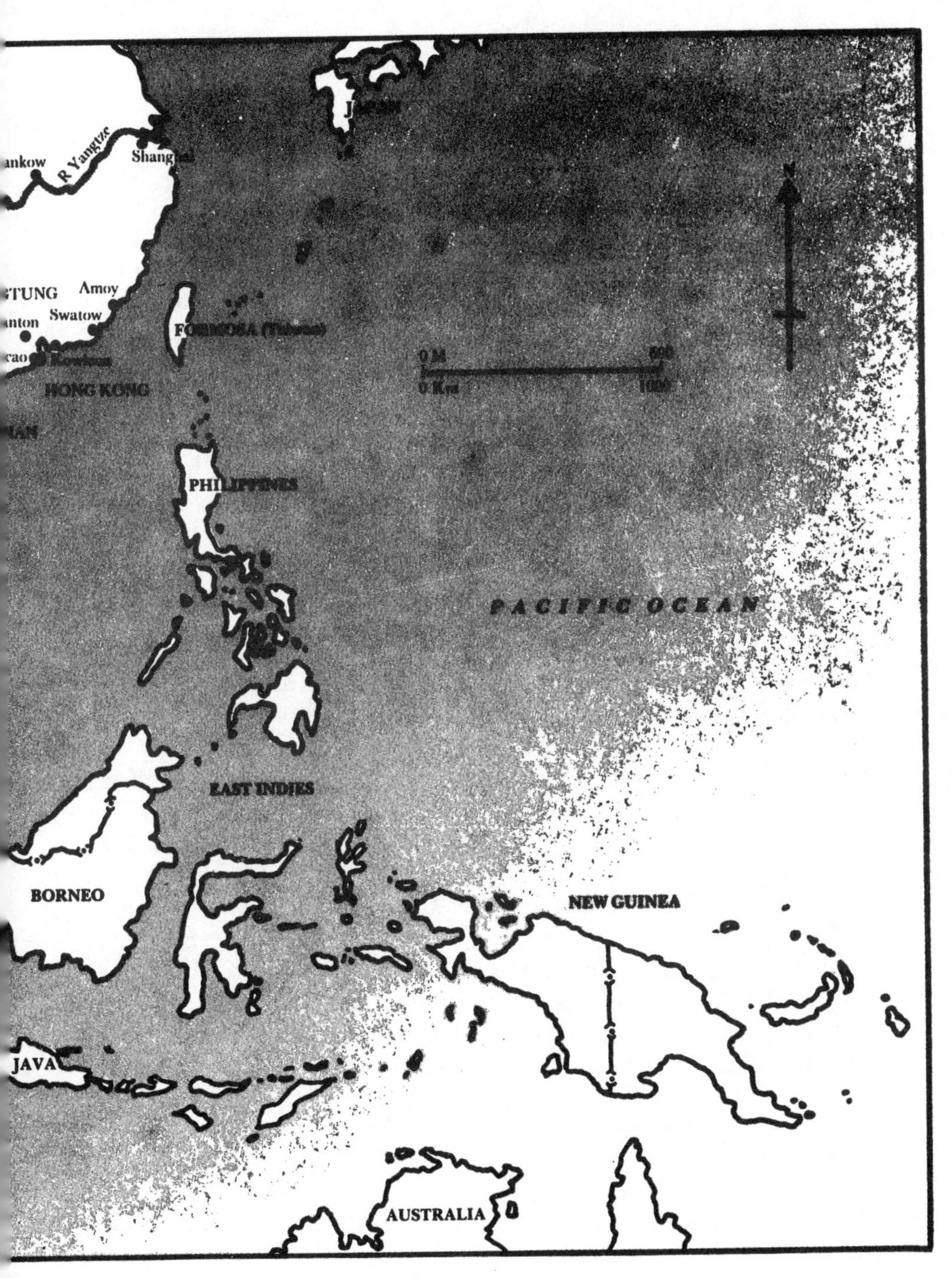

South-east Asia

This meant that American supplies to China where, as we saw earlier, Gen. 'Vinegar Joe' Stilwell was a formidable deputy to Chiang Kai-shek, had to be flown over the difficult range of mountains known as 'the Hump'. The Americans were anxious that Britain should take the offensive in northern Burma and enable a 500-mile road to be built from Assam to Chungking. The British were equally anxious to recover territory in Burma, and therefore remove the threat to India, but were rather more aware than their allies of the problems of the terrain. As we saw, Merrill's Marauders made a not very successful attempt from the north, and Wingate's Long Range Penetration Group came from the south and west. Wingate and Merrill were both anxious to dispel the Japanese reputation for invincibility, but in fact it was a platoon of the Northamptonshire Regiment which first inflicted a defeat on a Japanese force, in a toe-to-toe battle, and sent them fleeing.

The fact that the Japanese had overrun vast territories meant that, even with their quantity of manpower, they could not possibly police them all successfully. There was therefore considerable scope for subversive operations in the years which followed 1942.

From Admiral Lord Louis Mountbatten's headquarters in South-East Asia Command (SEAC) a unit with the simple code name of 'P' began its planning. Its aim was to organize amphibious landings in Burma, Malaya and the Andaman Islands (which occupied a convenient position in the Indian Ocean due south of Burma and due west of Thailand). This planning involved most of the other secret forces, notably MI6, MI9 and the PWE.

There was already in existence a branch of SOE, known as Force 136. It had begun its life at Meerut, but then moved to Kandy in Ceylon. Its director through the entire war was Colin Mackenzie, of J. & P. Coats textile firm. However, Mackenzie was rather more than a successful businessman; he had all the connections needed to obtain backing and continued support for the organization. He was a product of Eton and Cambridge, a classical scholar and a man of great diplomatic skill.

In Force 136, Group A was to be responsible for operations in Burma, Indo-China, China and Thailand. As OSS was already established in the latter three countries, close liaison with the Americans was essential so that there should be no overlapping or clashes of interest. Group A had its headquarters in Calcutta. Group B operated in Malaya and the NEI and had its headquarters in Colombo. Parachute training was to take place at Rawalpindi, and jungle training in Ceylon (Sri Lanka). Airfields were made available in India and Ceylon and in addition submarines from Colombo could be (and were) used to transport agents. There was a plentiful administrative staff.

It all looked very cosy on paper. However, it is a long way from Sri Lanka to China, Malaya or Borneo, long not merely in physical distance but also in the psychological sense too. There was nothing in Europe to compare with the variety of hazards likely to be encountered by an agent in the Far East. The first hazard came from the colour of his skin. If an agent in Europe ran short of food or medicine he could, by taking a calculated risk, go into the nearest town and buy what was needed. He would probably pass unnoticed. But anywhere in the East his colour and general appearance would give him away immediately. Even if he stained his face brown and dressed like a coolie he would be starkly obvious for what he was to all the local people. Secondly there was the climate. During the monsoons, rivers could rise twenty feet in a day, tracks be obliterated, movement made impossible. Thirdly, insects, leeches and disease, particularly malaria and its offshoots, could reduce a fit man to an emaciated wreck within months. (Leeches could penetrate the laceholes in boots or clothing. In Malaya in the 1950s one crawled into the penis of a soldier on jungle patrol, where neither a lighted cigarette nor salt could reach. Prompt evacuation and an emergency operation saved his life.) Climatic conditions could quickly make radios useless. Thus, before the agent could begin to take the fight to the Japanese he had to win his own particular battle to survive and remain militarily useful in a hostile environment. It was possible, but it was not easy. Not least of the frustrations of the agents in the field was the conviction that headquarters had no conception of these problems, and would not care if it had. When Stanley Moss, one of the kidnappers of General Kreipe in Crete in 1944, was in Thailand in 1945, his party received an urgently needed air drop. When they opened the containers they found the desperately needed radio had not been sent, the generator had a bent shaft, the ammunition was the wrong calibre for their pistols, and the jungle boots were all for right feet only. (In 1855 during the Crimean War a consignment of boots was sent to the long-suffering troops there. These were also for right feet only.) The story of the boots appeared in Moss's account of his SOE adventures, *A War of Shadows*, and was quoted in Charles Cruickshank's *SOE in the Far East*. When I reviewed Cruickshank's book for the *Daily Telegraph* and mentioned the boots, I received a delighted response from a former

SOE agent who had been in Burma at that time – it had solved the mystery of where the right-foot boots had gone. His party had received a consignment of left-foot boots and on sending a fairly sharp radio message to their headquarters in Calcutta had received the answer, 'That sort of language will get you nowhere.' It was an opportunity not to be missed. 'Neither will trying to walk in left-foot boots,' went the immediate reply.

Humorous though some of these mishaps may seem some forty years later, they were far from so at the time. Radios were sent with flat batteries, and some watches did not merely keep time badly: they often did not go at all. Had this muddle occurred in Europe it would probably have been as the result of sabotage. In the Far East these factors were recognized for what they were: the result of hastily expanded staffs trying to cope with problems which were well beyond their imagination or conception. In Italy and India, in order to prevent pilferage, boots left factories before being paired off, and with no size marked on the cases. But this is no excuse.

The most spectacular success of SOE became the subject of a book (*Boarding Party* by James Leasor) and a film (*The Sea Wolves*). Nevertheless, the operation code-named 'Longshanks' was not quite the unblemished success it appeared to be. On the outbreak of war in 1939, three German merchant ships and one Italian had taken refuge in neutral Goa (then a Portuguese colony but now a part of India). Their presence there was far from welcome to the Goans, and even less to the British who suspected that they were using their favoured position to transmit details of Allied shipping movements in the area to enemy submarines. SOE began its operation by kidnapping a Nazi agent who lived in Goa. This made future planning a little more secure. An attempt was made to bribe the captain of one of the German ships to take his ship outside territorial waters and surrender it to the Allies. However, by 1941 the ship (the *Ehrenfels*) had been at anchor too long to be able to move without assistance. A plan was therefore devised to take her out with a tug, but when the tug approached the *Ehrenfels* the German crew opened fire. None of the boarding party was hit but before the ship was overrun the Germans set off various demolition charges and also opened the sea-cocks. The other ships, including the Italian, did likewise. There were no British casualties, but five Germans were killed.

Although this action disposed of the 'radio spy' in the Indian Ocean, it had considerable political repercussions. The Foreign Office, which had the task of maintaining friendly relations with neutral Portugal, had insisted that no violence should be used in a neutral port. The fact that SOE had never hesitated about using violence caused grave misgivings.

The day was saved by the British consul who had been unaware of what was planned but who gave a very satisfactory explanation of events subsequently. He exonerated SOE from blame by reporting that he had discovered that the crews of the ships had mutinied and opened fire on the British tug: they were too scared of the Gestapo to do otherwise, although there were no Gestapo present on the harbour. The Portuguese governor-general accepted the explanation. The four surviving captains – one had been killed – were found guilty by the Goan port authorities of disturbing the peace. It seemed to prove that the man on the spot knows best.

Burma, being close to India and a long way from Japan, was obviously a suitable area for SOE work. There were numerous SOE missions. One of the most successful was with the Karens. The Karens were very friendly towards the British and had the advantage of being skilled guerrilla fighters. In his book, *SOE – Recollections and Reflections, 1940–1945*, J. G. Beevor, senior staff officer in SOE, quotes Hugh Seagrim as the outstanding British figure in Burma. He organized a guerrilla army of 200 Karens and used it to harass the Japanese outposts and lines of communication for over two years. The Japanese retaliated with draconian measures against the Karen tribes, so much so that Seagrim felt that the only way to call a halt to the Japanese reprisals was to surrrender himself. The Japanese executed him, and continued the reprisals. But within a year the Karens were more active than ever.

The OSS was also extremely active in Burma but here, as in other parts of the Far East, cracks in Anglo-American unity began to show. America, having broken away from Britain in 1783 and built a thriving nation subsequently from immigrants, many of whom had fled from oppressive regimes, believed firmly that all colonial regimes were inherently bad. The fact that the Philippines were an American colony, and that some American territories such as Florida and Alaska had been acquired by purchase was an embarrassment but did not seriously undermine the strongly-held view that one thing this war must not do was to restore the Asiatic colonies to their former European overlords. The initials SEAC were said to stand for 'Save Europe's Asiatic Colonies'. Some Americans went so far as to say they would rather fight the British than the Japanese. Yet, in spite of this, the cooperation between SOE and OSS in Burma was perhaps the most successful joint secret venture of the war. Where the British and Americans got to know each other and had to rely on each other neither side was ever disappointed.

This is not to say that there were no creakings in the structure, and occasions when one team acted without the knowledge of the other. But in view of the basic difference of view over the colonial question it was a triumph beyond all expectation. Unfortunately, the harmony did not always reach the highest levels. Stilwell had detested all British officers except Auchinleck, and MacArthur refused to allow the British back into Malaya immediately after the Japanese surrender. The result of the latter decision was that the communists were able to hoist the Red Flag in the principal cities of Malaya and claim they had liberated them. In the circumstances the achievements of the OSS, who operated effectively in many parts of the Far East, seem underrated. They had to contend with the hostility of Stilwell, who despised irregular and clandestine forces, and with MacArthur, who refused to allow them into the areas he controlled. One OSS man did succeed in getting into the Philippines, but he did not manage to stay long: he was captured and sent back by MacArthur's troops.

Malaya seemed to offer a promising field for guerrilla and sabotage activities because three-quarters of the country was covered by jungle and forest in which the saboteurs would be able to lie up unseen. In addition there was a strong, disciplined communist party with marked military potential. There were innumerable places where small parties could be set ashore by a combination of submarine and canoe.

The story of Malaya and Singapore, both before and after the Japanese occupation, may be outlined here. There was a naïve belief that if SOE had been allowed to establish stay-behind parties before the Japanese attack the course of the subsequent campaign would have been different. The reason they had not been permitted to do so was that the higher command in Malaya refused to do anything which might suggest that the Japanese could ever succeed in successfully invading the peninsula. It was also true that normal sensible precautions against an invasion had not been taken because that same higher comand believed that to take such measures would be bad for Asiatic morale. But that need not have prevented *secret* groups of SOE parties establishing themselves in jungle hide-outs. The only reason why they were not worth establishing was that they could not have been effective. They could not be supplied by air once the main airfields had been captured, and the chances of support for them from the sea may best be judged by the fate which overtook the *Prince of Wales* and the *Repulse* within four days of the Japanese attack; both were sunk by Japanese aircraft. After the fall of Singapore, when the Japanese controlled an area which ranged from Japan to Honolulu, to New Guinea and to the eastern coast of India, Malaya was out of range of available aircraft. Submarines could have been used to land agents, but there was no point in using them for that purpose until two years later. The destruction of a few Japanese trucks could hardly justify risking such a valuable commodity as a submarine.

Only in the later stages of the war, when it seemed that the Allies might make a landing in Malaya, did the establishment of SOE agents seem cost-effective. Even then there were doubts, some entertained by SOE itself. To make an effective fighting force meant involving the Chinese communists, and there was no knowing what the members of the Malayan Communist Party (an illegal organization in pre-war Malaya) would do when it had been well supplied and armed. It might direct all its energies to defeating the Japanese and rebuilding a rejuvenated democracy in Malaya and Singapore, but then again it might not. In the event it was decided that the risk must be taken. Three years after the liberation of Malaya, the Malayan People's Anti-Japanese Army rose from its quiescent state to become the Malayan People's Anti-British Army. It did not consist of Malayan people, of course, but of Chinese who had never been assimilated and become Malayan citizens. The ensuing war, which the MPABA fought very skilfully using tactics learnt from SOE, and weapons unaccountably lost from supply drops or presented by the defeated Japanese, lasted ten years.

However, in spite of official discouragement there were SOE agents in Malaya before the Japanese overran it; and it had established a training school. Colonel J. M. G. Gavin (not to be confused with General J. M. Gavin of US 82nd Airborne) and Captain F. Spencer Chapman were already in position. Spencer Chapman gave an account of his experiences in his book *The Jungle is Neutral*, but in view of the hardships he suffered it might have been more appropriately entitled 'The Jungle is Hostile'.

In the following years there were five small raids on the Andaman Islands, partly to see what use the Japanese were making of these and partly to prepare the way for a successful Allied landing later. These were conducted by Dutch submarines from Colombo.

In May 1943 SOE agents were landed on the west coast of Malaya with the mission of contacting the Chinese communist guerrillas, and creating a joint organization in central Malaya. They found a strong movement, based on remote jungle camps, which was led by an intelligent, dedicated communist named Chin Peng. The MPAJA seemed to be doing little except survive, but it was determined and reliable; the local Malay and Tamil villagers were not trusted for it was thought, on the basis of experience, that they would betray guerrillas to the Japanese for the sake of the rewards offered. There were, of course, trustworthy Malays, but they were unlikely to be found in the remote kampongs (villages) which neither knew, nor cared, what the war was about. Gradually it was established that the Chinese would act under SOE instruction, and confine their efforts for the present to the sabotage of shipping. In addition, a complex intelligence operation was built up, so that every move of the Japanese was monitored. But it was by no means all success. Communication with India and Ceylon was difficult, and the Japanese, now aware of the presence of guerrillas, made occasional sorties to eliminate them. Moves were then made to involve the Malays in the resistance movement, for it would be important for them to have taken part when a post-war government was established. These steps were not very popular with the Chinese communists, who wished to appear as the only effective resistance force to the Japanese.

One small party of Malays which landed in Malaya in late 1944 was betrayed and captured. Instead of beheading them the Japanese decided to use them as double agents. The leader of the party, Captain Ibrahim, managed to persuade the Japanese that he was collaborating, although in fact he had sent off a message saying he was a captive and operating under Japanese orders. It was important, if Ibrahim and his fellows were to survive, that the Japanese should believe that they were deceiving the British headquarters link. (The head of that link was Peter Fleming, the distinguished writer.) The Japanese were anxious that another party should be invited in immediately, but when this failed to arrive Ibrahim had the difficult task of explaining that SOE never did things quickly and that to try to hurry them would arouse suspicion. Fleming's men realized that some action was needed to reassure the Japanese, so they arranged a supply drop. When the containers eventually arrived, all the essentials were missing. The war came to an end before the 'mistake' could be rectified. Ibrahim received a Japanese decoration for his loyal services, and thus shared 'Garbo's' distinction in Europe of being decorated by both sides.

By mid 1945 an extensive network of resistance had been created in Malaya. Force 136 was powerfully established in Johore just north of Singapore, and was prepared to embark on a campaign of sabotage and behind-the-lines activity when the expected British invasion code-named 'Zipper' took place. This had originally been planned for November 1945 but, in view of the good progress made in other parts of the theatre, it was decided to advance it by three months. It is generally thought that the efforts of Force 136 would have enabled the invasion to take place without much difficulty, but that view was not shared by those who went over the intended invasion area subsequently. The war came to an end before the real 'Zipper' could take place but, in order to see what military lessons might be learnt, a mock 'Zipper' was staged subsequently. Needless to say, there were no Japanese troops to make it more realistic. It was then clear to those concerned, including SOE, that had 'Zipper' taken place with the Japanese opposing it would have been a very bloody business indeed. Every road and bridge had been mined and the Japanese had defensive positions in which they could, and undoubtedly would, have fought with the tenacity displayed on Iwo Jima and Okinawa. Although SOE undoubtedly had a strong position in Malaya (there were nearly a hundred British officers and some 5,000 guerrillas), the assumption that SOE teams would have been as successful in Malaya as they had been in Burma may be over-optimistic. When the Japanese in Burma were harried in the final stages of their time there, they had been under enormous pressure for a long period. By contrast, the Japanese in Malaya were fresh troops.

Sumatra, which is the most northerly island of the NEI, and about the size of Britain, produced little but frustration for SOE. The inhabitants, although not well treated by the Japanese, believed that in the future they would do better than in the past; Japanese propaganda had claimed that their war was for a 'Co-Prosperity Sphere in Asia'. The Japanese were at least fellow Asians; the Dutch, although heavily intermarried with the local population, were still regarded as outsiders. However, the Dutch in Ceylon were anxious to mount commando raids; the few which did take place proved abortive. Ironically, when the war was over there was plenty of resistance in Java and Sumatra, but it was directed against the Dutch and Europeans. Order was eventually restored by using Japanese troops under British command to help in policing.

Thailand (until 1939, known as Siam) was in an anomalous position for several reasons. The first was that it was nobody's colony. The reason for this lay less in the sturdy independence of the Thais – although there was plenty of that – than in the fact that Thailand did not appear to possess the natural wealth which tempted European powers into neighbouring territory.

In late 1941 the Japanese put pressure on Thailand to allow their troops to move through that country towards northern Malaya. The ruler of Thailand at that time, a dictator named Pibul Songramm, at the instigation of the Japanese declared war on both Britain and America. Britain promptly declared war in return, but America contemptuously – or perhaps diplomatically – refused to do so. Thai politics were extremely complex, and political leaders displayed astonishing resilience. While Pibul was in favour, his great rival Pridi was secretly running the Free Thai Association. Force 136 realized that this Free Thai Association would make a valuable ally, but had some difficulty in contacting it initially. In 1944 Pibul's regime was overturned and Pridi became head of state. This somewhat surprising turn of events occurred because Pridi, instead of wasting arms, ammunition and effort on guerrilla activities, had prudently stored the munitions he had been sent by SOE and was able to convince Pibul that his turn was over. All that was necessary was to demonstrate potential strength; there was no need to use it. However, Pridi was well aware that maintaining his position largely depended on not upsetting the Japanese. He therefore continued to maintain his close links with Force 136 but did nothing to weaken his own political position. Pridi was clearly a man of exceptional quality; he needed to be.

Thailand was in an interesting but delicate position. To the north-west was Burma, to the south was Malaya and to the east was Indo-China. Control of Thailand was therefore vital to the Japanese war effort in the area. By using prisoner-of-war and Asian labour, the Japanese had built a railway from Bangkok to Moulmein. The cost in lives had been roughly a death to every sleeper, but there were still several thousand surviving Allied prisoners-of-war, kept there partly because they could do maintenance work on the railway and partly because there was nowhere else more suitable. By a policy of near starvation combined with overwork, the POW population had been made too enfeebled with disease to offer any help to a resistance force, but they were a useful form of hostage for the Japanese who, if they could not take reprisals on anyone else, could always massacre a few prisoners. In all the territories they still controlled the Japanese had plans for getting rid of their prisoners if danger threatened, but the end of the war came so quickly that they did not carry them out; had they faced a long fight to the finish the story would doubtless have been very different.

However, before the Japanese laid down their arms (or gave them to guerrillas likely to cause future trouble to the Allies) SOE was by no means sure that, atomic bombs or not, the Japanese in Malaya, Thailand, China and the NEI would surrender peacefully. VJ-Day was 15 August 1945, but even in September some SOE parties could see little sign that the Japanese in remote areas regarded the war as over. When eventually they did, SOE and MI9 were once again busy trying to trace all the isolated groups of POWs, arrange for doctors and supplies, and marshal the Japanese back to their homeland – disarmed. SOE therefore found life busier when the war was over than it had been when fighting was still continuing. Their radio links were hard pressed. Volunteers from released prisoners helped. Capt G. H. Haddow (Royal Signals) ran the Bangkok link for two months.

General MacArthur would not allow the OSS to operate in the area under his command, partly due to hostility to special forces and OSS in particular, and partly because he did not wish anyone but himself to have a direct link to Washington. However, he did not object to SOE operating from Australia, where it was known as SOA.

SOA was responsible for an exceptionally heroic and effective operation in 1943. Maj. Ivan Lyon had been a regular soldier in Malaya before Singapore fell in 1942 and, unlike many of his contemporaries, thought there was a very real chance of the Japanese making a successful attack on the peninsula. Singapore had a flourishing sailing club and Lyon combined this hobby with some military exploration among the numerous islands in the area. He realized that there were many places where small ships could be concealed and threaten enemy shipping. On the fall of Singapore, Lyon made his way to Australia – no mean feat, for the distance is some 2,000 miles – and linked up with SOA. There he began careful preparations for what must have been one of the most arduous and daring ventures in the history of SOE. Eventually, with three Australian companions, he set off in a fishing boat, threaded his way past islands and shipping lanes patrolled by the Japanese and slipped quietly into Singapore Harbour.

There they attached limpet mines to Japanese ships and sank some 40,000 tons. They then found their way back to Australia where no one believed they could have accomplished such a feat. They were quietly triumphant when intercepted Japanese signals were decoded and reported the loss of the ships which Lyon and his friends had sunk. The event put the Japanese into a state of alarm, for it was assumed that a new type of Allied submarine must have been at work: the thought of lonely saboteurs never crossed their minds.

In September 1944 Lyon decided to try again on a bigger scale. The party numbered twenty-three and this time avoided the tedious surface journey from Australia by being transported from Fremantle by submarine. They took with them fifteen submersible canoes of the type known as 'Sleeping Beauties' (SBs). SBs were single-seaters which could travel up to forty miles at four and a half knots on the surface, and at three and a half knots below it. Their advantages were obvious but they also had the disadvantage of having a tendency to plunge up and down in the water. The plan was to capture a junk and tie up on Merapas island, near Singapore. This was accomplished and the submarine returned to Australia with the intention of collecting them later. In the event it had engine trouble and another submarine was detailed for the task in its place. After some delay the second submarine reached Merapas, but found no trace of the party. The story was a sad one. The junk had reached Singapore but when at anchor had aroused the suspicion of a Malay police launch, which challenged it. Under the impression that the launch was Japanese, Lyon promptly gave the order to open fire, killed all the crew of the police launch, scuttled the junk, and set off in the SBs to reach Merapas without being observed. The Japanese quickly realized what was afoot and spared no effort to catch them. Although they reached Merapas, it was only after a series of running battles with the Japanese in which they sustained casualties. They tried to get clear of the area but the ten survivors were eventually captured. They were kept in captivity for nearly six months, then beheaded on 7 July 1945. The war ended five weeks later.

However, the expedition was not entirely in vain. In spite of their desperate situation, before leaving Singapore after the encounter with the police launch they had succeeded in putting an explosive charge on the side of a Japanese cruiser. And they had done enough to show that if more of such expeditions were to be mounted in the future some would undoubtedly get through, with devasting results.

An entirely different type of SOE operation was the manipulation of currency and trade. This grew from the realization that Japan now had far more rubber than it could use and that producers with stocks piling up might be glad to sell some of it. This would be useful to the Allies and was just the sort of situation in which Chinese would be perfect intermediaries. Obviously, the Japanese would wish to prevent this valuable strategic material reaching their enemies, so the matter would need to be handled with the utmost delicacy. A London rubber broker named Walter Fletcher, who was keen to assist the Allied war effort, was put in charge. Fletcher was the son of a naturalized Austrian (Paul Fleischel). He subsequently became an MP and was knighted, but his reputation was for commercial acumen rather than benign chivalry. Cruickshank quotes one SOE member as saying, 'He was not the sort of man to whom you would trust the private means of a widow or an orphan.'

Initially, the plan was treated with some scepticism. Fletcher discussed it in Washington but the US government would only put up the equivalent of £25,000 as its contribution to the scheme. The British Treasury added £100,000, but these sums were trifling in relation to the possible benefits. Admittedly, Fletcher's sudden changes of plan did little to inspire confidence. The first one was to collect the rubber in Borneo and then ship it quietly from there; his American counterpart, Major L. W. Elliot, had already taken steps to organize its onward transmission. However, this plan seemed too obvious and was abandoned in favour of others, no less convincing.

Rubber, decided Fletcher after a while, was too bulky and too cheap to be worth handling on its own. He then raised the possibility of dealing with quinine and tungsten as well. Here they faced difficulties involved in collecting them from under the noses of the Japanese. The operation was switched to China, which already had a useful traffic in goods smuggled from Japanese controlled territories. To everyone's surprise, the normally suspicious Chinese accepted Fletcher's improbable ideas partly perhaps because they enjoy a gamble and partly because Fletcher had a very compelling personality. However, the British Ministry of Production, which was financing Fletcher, was less easily impressed and said that enough was enough; the Fletcher enterprise which had produced no rubber, tungsten, tin, quinine or anything except expansive promises, must now cease.

Fletcher was not deterred. He countered with the suggestion that the Chinese would fall over themselves to sell the Allies smuggled goods if they were paid in diamonds. Diamonds would be best, but he did not draw the line at other precious stones. Just to show what could be done in the way of playing the 'hard currency' market, Fletcher sold the Chinese a number of rupees at over twice the current rate of exchange for the Chinese dollar. This did not even involve precious stones, but it opened the eyes of the British government to the possibilities of using the black market in money. Fletcher proved he could acquire Chinese dollars at approximately a quarter of the price Britain had to pay for them officially. As Britain needed a considerable number of Chinese dollars to finance its diplomats, businessmen and soldiers, this was an enormous advantage.

Unbelievably, Fletcher was now running a monetary black market on a scale never hitherto approached, and running it with the full approval and cooperation of the British government. The Chinese government would obviously disapprove strongly if it learnt that its carefully arranged exchange values were being outflanked by a black market operator, so Fletcher had to be given the cover of running a trade mission. With considerable prescience, he organized a syndicate involving leading Chinese businessmen, banks and government officials, of which his own company was a member. One-fifteenth of the profits went to the Chinese secret service, a heavy-handed organization run by a much disliked general named Tai Li: this had the advantage of enabling Fletcher to operate with the approval rather than the hostility of this organization.

And so it went on. Soon the Chinese syndicate was a vast trading organization as well as a black market in currency. Meanwhile the Americans, with the backing of the all-powerful dollar, were able to make arrangements satisfactory to themselves. Eventually, when the war came to an end and with it the China Syndicate, Fletcher had saved the Allies £77 million in financing necessary trade with China.

Another one-man enterprise, though nothing to do with SOE or OSS, was that of Wendell Fertig, an American mining engineer. Fertig had been on Mindanao when the American forces surrendered in the Philippines in May 1942. Although an ordinary map shows less than a dozen islands, this group actually includes several thousand. Of the larger ones, Luzon is the most northerly and Mindanao the most southerly. When Fertig was informed that a surrender had been arranged, and that in due course he would be interned in a prison camp, he did not take kindly to the news. Instead he collected a few like-minded men and set off for the parts of Mindanao into which it seemed unlikely that the Japanese would wish to follow them. Their journey proved even worse than they had anticipated. They encountered the hazards known all too well to travellers in the jungle: they were often lost; they were bitten by leeches and by insects; their clothes rotted; scratches festered and soon became deep ulcers; fevers exhausted them. Nevertheless, they struggled through to a safe area, and then made contact with other groups which had decided to become guerrilla fighters rather than accept the surrender. Mindanao was large enough to make this possible. However, there were other, less well-intentioned, forces on the island. These were nothing more than bandits who had taken advantage of the breakdown of law and order to prey on the long-suffering villagers.

In the early months after the Japanese victory in their country the Filipinos saw little point in trying to resist the inevitable. They had seen conquerors before and knew that if you waited long enough their rule became tolerable or was superseded by another. However, Japanese conquest was so tyrannical that large numbers of Filipinos were soon happy to engage in any means of fighting back. Thus Fertig received many recruits. When MacArthur's headquarters appreciated the potential strength of Fertig's army, it began to supply them with arms, ammunition and other stores. Sometimes – as might be expected – these were totally unnecessary and unsuitable. However, at long last, his 35,000-strong force was able to inflict considerable damage on the Japanese, a fact to which the Japanese responded by making increasingly systematic attempts to eliminate him. Fortunately the American relief forces arrived before that happened, although there were harrowing moments when it was thought that they were going to by-pass the Philippines altogether in their island-hopping path of conquest to Japan. But when MacArthur had left the Philippines in 1942 he had given a pledge: 'I will return.' Honouring this promise was more important than short-term military requirements.

Clearly, Fertig's courageous fight had little influence on the outcome of the war, but deserves a place here for its unique quality. It was not an attempt to organize guerrilla forces and saboteurs from the outside with the backing of a powerful, even if distant, state military machine; it was an attempt by a determined man to fight back in impossible circumstances. Unfortunately, much of the goodwill which Fertig's spirited action had created for the Americans in the Philippines was dispersed by the behaviour of the troops used as occupying forces. John Keats, who wrote an account of Fertig's private war in the

Philippines, said that, 'it was during the extirpation of the Japanese, and in the months following the victory that the war was lost in the Philippines'. He described how the Americans upset local values by overpaying the Filipinos, by black-marketeering, by treating all their women as potential prostitutes, and by despising them as 'Flips'. Fortunately it seemed a temporary phase, for when Fertig returned years later and revisited the places where he had stayed and fought he was given an almost incredible welcome. Thousands lined the roads on which he travelled. The good memories remained: the bad ones seemed merely a distant nightmare.

Although Fertig's resistance group was the largest operating in the Philippines, it was not the only one. Another American on Mindanao was Maj. William Dyess. With nine other Americans he escaped from a prison camp and joined a band of guerrillas. The guerrillas had collected a number of other Americans and were very happy to receive Dyess, who was an experienced infantry soldier.

Another successful guerrilla leader was an American sergeant who was not even an infantry soldier but a draughtsman. This was Sergeant G. R. Moore. When the Philippines fell he got away by boat, but was captured. He escaped again and joined a force of Filipino guerrillas which was causing the Japanese considerable trouble. Moore soon demonstrated such powers of aggressive leadership that he became its leader. However, the Japanese captured him in one of their anti-guerrilla sweeps. After a very unpleasant period of incarceration, during which he was beaten regularly to make him betray his comrades, he managed to escape again. He survived the war.

A remarkable one-man escape story is that of the Englishman, Private Jim Wright, who was left behind in the Malayan jungle after being wounded in the foot. Without food, water or bandages for his foot, he began a nightmare journey to what he hoped would be Singapore. After several days he was picked up by Chinese guerrillas, with whom he stayed for the rest of the war. Twenty-five other British and Australian soldiers were also collected up, but only Wright and one other survived the three and a half years in the jungle. Wright was an excellent marksman and used to instruct the guerrillas, who were almost invariably poor shots. His story is told in a book entitled *A Fearful Freedom*.

9: *Oriental Tangles*

One of the most disturbing aspects of World War II is the extent of the jealousy and intrigue between and within the warring states. Thus America was pledged to prevent the return of colonial empires, France was equally determined to regain its status, and Russia was prepared to go to any lengths to expand Soviet communism. Britain's chief preoccupation was not to lose markets and influence as a result of the war. Secret forces had their individual policies too, and jealousy and intrigue were not unknown in their rivalries. The difference between different branches in Europe is not a happy story, but compared with the situation in China it presents a picture of unruffled harmony.

The main obstacle to the creation of an effective resistance movement in Indo-China came from the political views of those *outside* the country. Nobody knew how to assess the feelings of the French in Indo-China who were nominally under Vichy control. Were they as anti-British (and probably anti-American too) as their fellows in French North Africa? Would they actively assist the Japanese, or would they help a Free French resistance movement? Just when it seemed that there were grounds for supposing that a Free French resistance movement might work, Roosevelt threw an enormous stone into the murky waters of the Indo-Chinese pond by issuing a statement to the representatives of Britain, Russia, China and Turkey, among others, that the French should never again be allowed to control Indo-China. He gave as the basis for his viewpoint the fact that during the last hundred years the French had done nothing for the country.

This remarkable statement was clearly based on emotion and ignorance, and with an eye to home political opinion. Nothing could be done to make Roosevelt change his mind and Churchill was unwilling to risk offending him over a relatively unimportant matter. However, a strong force of Free French was anxious to enter the country in 1944 and work with Force 136. Churchill therefore agreed to the SOE proposal that the French should be allowed to send a force to back up any local resistance. Thus America would not be involved.

However, when the nature of the Free French force was disclosed, and it turned out to be 1,200 men from North Africa, the British Foreign Office objected strenuously. Its protests were then dismissed peremptorily by the Free French as merely an attempt to butter up Roosevelt. In spite of these and many other difficulties, contacts were made with the indigenous resistance groups; agents were sent in and arms dropped. The plan was to build up a strong force, so that when the Japanese were attacked from outside, the resistance would be of great value. In 1944 there seemed no other possible end to the war against Japan than a long grinding campaign of attrition. So far, MacArthur had turned the tide in the Pacific and was progressing towards Japan by way of Guadalcanal, the Solomons, Saipan, the Philippines and other strategic islands. In Burma the 14th Army was about to launch a massive offensive to dispossess the Japanese, and in Malaya Force 136 was making preparations for the part it would play when that country was invaded. Submarine warfare was taking a damaging toll of Japanese shipping. Indo-China's turn for liberation would probably come immediately after Malaya's, perhaps in late 1945.

The Japanese were not unaware of the plans which were being made for their ultimate defeat and, not surprisingly, wished to frustrate them as quickly as possible wherever they occurred. They decided to make an example of Indo-China, and in March 1945 they struck. They did not, however, seek out and destroy the resistance groups themselves but instead demanded complete control of the French army which, acting on Vichy orders, had done nothing to help or hinder them. When the French objected, their fate was dramatic. Unaware of the ruthlessness of the Japanese, officers were decoyed to social functions and killed; soldiers who resisted the Japanese entering their barracks were caught and beheaded. The Japanese excuse was that the French army harboured most of the resistance groups.

A few of the French officers and men were warned in time and tried to fight a rearguard action on the way to finding sanctuary in China. They were desperately short of ammunition and appealed to the US government for supplies. At first Roosevelt refused, then after an appeal by Churchill relented. It was all too little and too late. Had the large Free French force been allowed in earlier, a much more effective resistance to this treacherous blow from the Japanese could have been mounted. As it was, of the 10,000 who tried to reach China, only 5,000 succeeded. Nor were the casualties limited to the army. Women and children, refugees from a Japanese army which seemed to have gone mad, were seized and beheaded. The Indo-Chinese people had been caught up in a war which they did not understand, between foreign powers which were completely remote from them in every sense; all they wished to do was to cultivate their rice fields and live an undisturbed life in the poverty to which they were accustomed and inured.

Some of the blame seems to lie with the French. Much earlier, when the Japanese had abandoned any attempt at pretending to be friendly, the French in Indo-China were more concerned with internal jealousies than a common resistance. Free French supporters detested the Vichyites; both feared and distrusted the communist-inspired resistance group run by Ho Chi Minh and Nguyen Giap, although this was a regular source of valuable intelligence. Later, Ho Chi Minh would be the architect of the communist state of Vietnam and General Giap would inflict on the French a crushing and humiliating defeat at Dien Bien Phu.

Although official American policy was not to help the French recover their former power in Indo-China, there was considerable sympathy for the French army among members of the OSS in China. When the remnants of the Indo-China resistance groups reached China, the OSS was quick to help them. However, the OSS realized that any worthwhile resistance to the Japanese would now have to come from the Viet Minh, who were being ably led by Giap. They therefore gave the Viet Minh as much help as they could. Nevertheless, they soon realized that if the French were allowed to return to Indo-China their path would be far from smooth: the Viet Minh had very definite ideas about the future of the country. However, when this somewhat ominous forecast was given to the French government, it was received with scorn.

One of the achievements of the OSS team, which they might have been less pleased about later, was to save the life of Ho Chi Minh. When the OSS doctor saw the communist leader he decided that the man was probably dying from malaria and dysentery, as well as other debilitating diseases. Ho Chi Minh was then treated with modern drugs and soon recovered. In gratitude he offered the OSS 'jungle aphrodisiacs' and the company of pretty young Vietnamese girls from

Hanoi. Sadly for the OSS their military briefings had issued strict orders against taking fraternization to this degree.

The end of the war came as an even bigger surprise in Indo-China than it did everywhere else. However, the Viet Minh had prepared for such an event and, before the Allies could take control, hoisted the Viet Minh flag on all the most prominent sites in Hanoi. They also requested complete independence from colonial rule, which they said had been promised by the United Nations. They threatened, if the request were refused, to keep on fighting until they got things their way. As the world, and particularly the United States, learnt later, they were as good as their word.

China was even more complicated than its neighbour Indo-China. As early as 1941, before the Allies were at war with Japan, there had been suggestions that SOE teams led by Danes should enter China and set up a training school for Chinese guerrillas. (It was thought that open British participation in this area would be unpopular with the Chinese, and diplomatically unwise.) The resulting force would be called the Chinese Commando Group. However, the 'school' did not open till March 1942, and soon found itself in difficulties. The Chinese army resented the independent newcomer and demanded that it should be incorporated into its own forces. That would mean changing its name and also handing over all its valuable stores. Not surprisingly, the British ambassador to China reported that that would be impossible; and the Commando Group came to an end.

The Americans were in a different, but not necessarily easier, position. They enjoyed – as they thought – a special relationship with China, a relationship which had been built up on trade, on their avowed dislike of all forms of colonialism, and the fact that at no time in their history had they tried to wring concessions from China. In fact, in the 1890s, they had managed to obtain the agreement of other powers to the Open Door policy for China. The 'Open Door' meant that everyone would be able to trade freely, while Chinese territorial and political independence would be preserved. The Chinese had eyed the Open Door policy with scepticism, as America had bought the Philippines from Spain in 1898 and annexed the Hawaiian islands at the same time. But in 1941 the US felt benevolently disposed towards them and hoped that these feelings were reciprocated. So far they were; after 1948 it was a very different story.

The OSS planned to operate in China as 'Detachment 101'. 101

was commanded by Maj. Carl Eiffler, an impressive and experienced warrior who also had the advantage of being liked by Stilwell. However, Stilwell intensively disliked irregular forces and initially wanted nothing to do with Detachment 101, friendship with Eiffler notwithstanding. An even more hostile attitude to 101 was shown by the Chinese government. To complete the picture, Stilwell was also at loggerheads with Gen. Claire Chennault, who was General Chiang Kai-shek's air adviser. Chennault commanded a very small air force of American volunteers who were known as the 'Flying Tigers'. He was always happy to explain to anyone who cared to listen that he could finish off the China war with the Flying Tigers alone, provided he was adequately supplied and supported.

A more promising line seemed to be the friendship which was developing between the naval captain Milton 'Mary' Miles and General Tai Li. Miles seemed to have had a fairly broad brief when he was sent to China in 1942 to collect intelligence and to make life unpleasant for the Japanese. Tai Li was head of the Secret Police and Chinese intelligence: this enabled him to wield enormous power which he did without hesitation or scruple. One of his instruments was the Green Gang, which sometimes practised thuggery for Tai Li, and at others operated purely for its own profit.

Tai Li, who was well known for his loathing of all foreigners, surprised Miles by suggesting a joint Chinese–American plan for the training of guerrillas and spies. Reluctantly and not without misgivings, Washington agreed. It was hoped that this might induce Stilwell to soften his attitude towards guerrillas, but the hope proved vain. Nor did it do anything for SOE. Tai Li loathed the British with the intensity of one who had been arrested by them in Hong Kong and accused of being pro-German. Another factor which scarcely led to friendly relations was the British belief that the Chinese were no longer interested in fighting the Japanese and that, quite unofficially, they had come to terms on a live-and-let-live basis. However, Stilwell was in no position to let such a state of affairs exist on the Burma front, where he was now under considerable pressure. When Eiffler offered the services of Det. 101, Stilwell had to forget his dislike of irregular troops and agree to their participation. They went into action as the Kachin Rangers (see p.69) and performed so well that Stilwell, for once, could find nothing to criticize. However, he did find plenty to criticize in the fact that without warning Captain Miles was appointed Chief of OSS for the Far East. Stilwell thought little of Tai Li and the

Chinese intelligence service in general. In his view Chinese intelligence was either inaccurate or wholly imaginary. But as long as MacArthur continued to refuse to allow the OSS to operate within his command area the OSS needed a base reasonably close to Japan. The most convenient area was undoubtedly China, cooperative, reliable, secure, or not. In consequence, in 1943 the Sino-American Cooperative Organization (SACO) was created. Tai Li was the director, in addition to his duties as head of the Chinese secret police and espionage organization; Miles was deputy director although still chief of OSS and head of Navy Group China. The Chinese would supply the men; the US would supply the munitions.

Stilwell despised SACO from the start, as did many other people, but he probably had more reason than most, for he had caught one of Tai Li's agents going through his papers; the man had been planted on him as a servant.

With this promising start SACO followed a predictable course. Nothing tangible was accomplished. Miles was replaced at the end of 1943 by an experiened American army colonel. Disenchantment with Chiang Kai-shek's entourage grew. Then came the news that Mao Tse-tung's communists, who were firmly established in Yenan, might, if adequately supplied, turn their attentions to harassing the Japanese. Contact was made with them, for it was thought they might prevent a threatened Japanese drive into central China. However, Washington felt that the only way to stop such an offensive when it came would be by a joint effort from Chiang Kai-shek's troops and the communists of Mao Tse-tung – bitterly though they hated each other.

On this occasion Washington had read the situation correctly. Both Chiang Kai-shek and Mao Tse-tung realized that if the Japanese advanced further into China their own future would be at risk. It therefore seemed better to ally with a hated rival, who could be destroyed later, than risk immediate defeat by a ruthless enemy such as the Japanese. But Chiang Kai-shek moved too slowly for Washington's liking, and was given a sharp reminder that immediate action was now essential. Chiang, quick to take offence, looked around for a scapegoat. He convinced himself that Washington's abrupt order must have been the result of Stilwell's prodding, and promptly demanded that 'Vinegar Joe' should be recalled. This was manifestly unjust but these were desperate times and to placate Chiang, Roosevelt reluctantly agreed.

Further trouble occurred in summer 1944 when an 'independent force' of marauding Chinese soldiers sallied out of China and plundered and destroyed a number of Burmese villages. The Kachin (OSS) promptly followed the invaders back into China and taught them a lesson. Unfortunately it then transpired that the marauders really belonged to Chiang Kai-shek, and not to a local warlord as had been thought. Furthermore, Tai Li was found to be involved: doubtless he had included suitable targets for loot. Tempers cooled when an 'impartial' investigation found that everyone was equally to blame, and therefore blameless.

And so it went on. Japanese spies were said to be operating at high levels in Chiang's government, probably with the connivance of Tai Li. American officials and soldiers were appalled at the misuse or waste of material sent to Chiang's army, which remained badly clothed, badly equipped and, still worse, badly armed and ill-trained. OSS was at loggerheads with SACO, and regarded Tai Li with hatred and contempt. (Tai Li was eventually killed in an air crash in 1946; it was widely believed that the crash was not entirely accidental.) But Tai Li, as we saw earlier, was a vital link in the black-market currency deals. 'Old China hands' were, of course, in no way surprised or dismayed at the web of intrigue, double-dealing, and deception practised in a country fighting for its life; newly-arrived members of OSS found these matters somewhat disheartening.

But gradually, under the leadership of Gen. Albert Wedermeyer, the dogged persistence of the OSS made some headway. It was far short of what they had hoped, and it was mainly in organization rather than in active service. Most of their plans were frustrated by Chiang's government. When Jedburgh teams and a military commanders' network were despatched in 1945, with a view to helping the communists, they were never allowed past Chiang's headquarters.

In view of the size of China, its warring factions, and the fact that it had been fighting a losing war with the Japanese for over ten years, it is not surprising that SOE and OSS could accomplish so little. But in assessing the value of their efforts it should not be forgotten that the real test of them never came. If there had been no atomic bombs and the war had continued through 1945 and 1946, as was expected, the OSS teams in China would have found plenty to do. The Japanese would have tried to withdraw their armies to defend the homeland (there were nearly 2 million Japanese soldiers in China) and preventing them from getting there would have given OSS and SOE all the scope they needed. Not even Chiang Kai-shek could have prevented that.

* * *

In following the troubled story of the OSS in China I have omitted the role of SOE. The latter's policy was to interfere with the facilities which the Japanese were using to great advantage: these were the ships and repair facilities at Hong Kong, the industry of Shanghai and the arsenal at Canton. There were other targets of almost equal importance.

Sabotage at Hong Kong was to take a somewhat unusual form. Instead of blowing up material objects, SOE planned to decoy away the skilled Chinese labourers who were essential to the Japanese use of the dockyards. All that was needed for this was for them to be persuaded to travel sixty miles to a place called Waichow, where they would be clear of the Japanese. All expenses would be paid by the British government, which would then take them to Eritrea, employ them in ship repairing, pay them handsomely and repatriate them at the end of the war.

Contact with the potential recruits was to be made by the British Army Aid Group (BAAG). BAAG was an organization created by Colonel L. T. Ride when he and some of his companions had escaped from Hong Kong in 1942 and made their way to Free China. 'Free China' meant a part of that country that had not been occupied by the Japanese but was under the jurisdiction of Chiang Kai-shek's government. In fairness it should be said that Chiang regarded Mao Tse-tung's communists as an even greater menace than the Japanese; there were also two breakaway régimes, one at Nanking, the other at Peking, both of which had reached an accommodation with Japan. Chiang was also aware of the feeling, widespread among the Chinese and which he probably shared, that Russia was a bigger and closer threat than Japan; therefore the presence of Japanese armies in China would probably be an advantage in the long run, for they would deter the Russians from making adventurous forays – or worse.

Ride had been commander of the Hong Kong Field Ambulance when the Japanese invaded the colony. He was also Professor of Physiology at Hong Kong University. This had come after an interesting career, which in the early years had included service as a private in the Australian army in France in World War I. Escape from Hong Kong was possible, though by no means easy or safe: from the other areas the Japanese had overrun it was virtually impossible. As soon as he reached safety, Ride set about creating an organization which would enable others to escape from the colony. He did not know at the time that there was already in existence an organization named MI9 which operated on a world-wide basis to enable prisoners, wrecked sailors, shot-down airmen or soldiers separated from their units to regain their homelands. MI9 was not in China officially, for China itself was not an official Allied war zone, though Hong Kong of course was.

Prisoners, or others, who wished to escape from Hong Kong needed instructions and help. If they were caught by the Japanese, their fate would be unpleasant to say the least. Once clear of the colony they would find themselves in a tract of land controlled by Chinese communists who might not be particularly friendly. Ride organized a system of trustworthy guides. Chinese could move in and out of Hong Kong without difficulty if they looked like peasants or labourers. Over the next two years Ride built up an establishment of 248. With these he organized a medical service which dealt with some 30,000 patients a year. It functioned where no medical service of any kind had ever been seen before.

With the welfare organization went a highly efficient intelligence service. It was disciplined and completely honest. It supplied valuable information to the Chinese about their Japanese enemies. It even ran a weather reporting service which was of great value to airmen in China. Weather reports have considerable military value: for that reason no weather report was broadcast from the BBC in Great Britain between 1939 and 1945.

Unfortunately, the ubiquitous Tai Li had his eye on Ride's activities and did not like what he saw. He suspected, with no reason to do so, that Ride was hand-in-glove with the communists. Whenever he could, Tai Li impeded BAAG; one way of doing this was to ensure that BAAG never received the radios which were sent to it.

The SOE plan to encourage dockyard labourers to leave the colony and take employment in Eritrea failed. Very few tried to take advantage of the offer. In contrast BAAG was able to entice away many dockyard artificers, and thus make it necessary for experienced Japanese to be withdrawn from Japanese ports where they were also badly needed. Without the Japanese replacements the Hong Kong dockyards would not have been able to function.

Perhaps the most valuable effect of Ride's work was on the attitude of the Chinese to the British. Having seen the British defeated so rapidly at Hong Kong, the Chinese, who had resented the presence of all foreigners on their territory, not least the British, were both pleased and contemptuous. Although they personally disliked the Japanese, whom they referred to as 'yellow monkeys', there was no denying that they were Asian, and for an Asian to dispose of a European power swiftly and thoroughly was heart-warming. But now Ride had shown that the British were not finished, that the British had more to offer than anyone else had ever offered before, and that they were as good as their word. The Chinese respected that. A Chinese businessman may not be an easy person to pin down, but when he gives his word that a deal will be completed, or money be paid at a certain time, the promise is kept. Ride could be trusted; he was also brave and if he was prepared to risk his life in military operations against the Japanese, so would they.

But, according to Professor Michael Foot, Ride worked under more difficulties than were provided by the enemy or the terrain. SOE gave him what help it could; MI9 seemed to regard BAAG as a rival organization; OSS appeared cooperative but tried to tap Ride's intelligence before it reached him, and when Ride had at last got his hands on some radio and telephone equipment, the British army (British Troops China) decreed that its equipment could be operated only by members of the Royal Signals. In the background, but operating very efficiently from it, was Tai Li, who lost no opportunity to represent Ride as being in collusion with the communists and therefore a danger to the government of Chiang Kai-shek. And just when Ride's escape route was working at maximum efficiency, the American equivalent of MI9 which was called MIS-X set up a rescue service for airmen called AGAS (Air Ground Rescue Service). In the event, BAAG and AGAS worked very well together, but that was due to the good sense of the executives and no credit to the planners on their remote and lofty pedestals.

As the armies closed in round Japan, Ride found his work becoming more difficult rather than easier. Too many agencies were now involved. And Wedermeyer, who already disapproved of Ride's ability to work with the communists, had now been made overall theatre commander. Wedermeyer, of course, did not merely disapprove of Ride's tactics in the field; he held a not unreasonable belief that Ride wished to be one of the first arrivals in Hong Kong when that port was liberated. Not surprisingly that was Ride's intention, although he did not broadcast it. Wedermeyer, however, did not need confirmation of his deep-seated convictions and gave priority to the planning of an operation for the capture of Hong Kong Canton district (Canton lies up river from Hong Kong) by a joint Chinese–American force. It was an interesting clash of moral opinions. Ride, an Australian, firmly believed that the British should resume control of Hong Kong, if only to discharge their responsibility to those who had remained loyal to Britain through the long years of Japanese occupation. Wedermeyer, on the other hand, preferred to listen to Chinese voices which told him that the colony would be much better off under Chinese–American supervision.

For that reason Wedermeyer opposed an SOE plan to send a major, a sergeant, and fourteen Chinese to Hong Kong in December 1944. The party had an extended brief in terms of sabotage and intelligence but to arrive unobtrusively in Hong Kong it needed a submarine which had to be sent from Australia. Wedermeyer said this would be a waste of resources and vetoed it.

In the event the British were the first arrivals in Hong Kong because the Royal Navy made sure they were. And the fact that the work of brave and resourceful men on the ground was often frustrated by political prejudice and inter-departmental jealousies makes Ride's astonishing success with BAAG all the more creditable.

10: *Other Interested Parties*

It would have been reasonable to suppose that when the war was coming to an end in Europe, with Allied armies closing in on Berlin, the time for Special Forces was past. It was not so, and not merely because Japan was still far from being defeated and might continue for years before she was. The Allied High Command was well aware that the European war had been won in the nick of time, that the Germans might have one more weapon up their sleeves (perhaps a V3?) and that if that were so the war might end in an appalling holocaust. There were also rumours to be investigated. Hitler was thought to have an impregnable stronghold at Berchtesgarten, from which, as it was defended by fanatical Nazis, it would be extremely difficult to dislodge him. And while Hitler was alive and surrounded by fighting troops, however beleagured, there would be no possibility of organizing a peaceful Germany. Stories were told of gold being sunk in deep lakes ready for future retrieval; it was known that bulky stores had been hidden in mines. If these were Nazi loot (as they turned out to be) they could be recovered at leisure: however, if they were parts of some new, diabolical weapon system, they must be recovered without delay. In November 1984 Austrian soldiers discovered an experimental underwater rocket launching platform which had been concealed in a lake by the Nazis in 1945. During the war neither gas nor chemicals had been used, though both sides were known to possess stocks. It was thought that Hitler had refrained from using gas because he believed that the Allies had much greater resources in that field, but if he felt he was in the final stages of some Wagnerian twilight of the gods who was to say what he might not do?

The need for highly mobile, secret forces to deal with these possibilities had been appreciated long before the war closed in on Germany. During the Italian campaign a formation known as 'S Force' had been created by the Allies to seize special intelligence targets. This had had considerable success in Naples and Rome, where enemy operational, scientific, and technical intelligence had all been acquired. In France this function was carried out by 'T Force' ('T', in this instance, stood for nothing more esoteric than 'target').

In July 1944 Supreme Headquarters Allied Expeditionary Force (SHAEF) had recommended that special groups should be created from members of the Royal Engineers, Royal Signals and the Intelligence Corps, whose normal duties included deception and camouflage. It was thought that these occupations would make them less likely to be misled than other troops might have been.

Regrettably, these groups were not at first a great success and this was attributed to the fact that they were given too little information on the whereabouts of specific targets in France. The fact that fighting was still taking place in some of the areas they were expected to investigate added to their difficulties. Manpower was now very short and when the T Force reported few results there was considerable pressure for their members to be allowed to return to their parent units where they were badly needed.

But T Force was too valuable a concept to be dispersed. SHAEF emphasized that it was of the greatest importance to identify and secure factories (where munitions were being made), documents and fuel stores, any of which might be bypassed, destroyed or subsequently looted by civilians. One unit assigned to T Force work was 30 Assault Unit, Royal Navy (which was later given the less belligerent title of 30 Advanced Unit). 30 Assault was in fact a naval Commando which had been specially selected for technical assignments.

In practice, 30 AU was strong enough to capture key targets when there was still enemy resistance. It then handed over to the specialists (who were, of course, also fighting troops) for further investigation and general duties. It was reported that some of the targets made such desirable billets that there was some reluctance to leave them.

Information on targets for T Force to investigate came from two main sources. One was the Combined Intelligence Sub Committee, which drew up what was known as the Black List. The other was the Inter-Services Topographical Unit (ISTU). The latter, which was based in Oxford, had a vast store of information on targets but, being remote from the scene and out of touch with local military progress, had no idea what size units would be needed for the capture of defended points. It was therefore necessary to earmark certain units for specific military duties. Examples were the 5th Battalion of the

King's Liverpool Regiment, the Royal Berkshire Regiment, the 1st Oxfordshire and Buckinghamshire Light Infantry, Pioneer Corps men (with anti-aircraft and smoke-screen experience) and Royal Engineers (for bomb disposal, anti-booby trap work and safe-breaking). Selected NCOs in the Royal Engineers were sent on special burglary courses in Britain, and burglars' equipment was always carried by T Force. It was probably the first time that housebreaking tools had been used in the cause of law and order and given trade pay, but these were exceptional circumstances.

Once a target had been acquired, it was handed over to Consolidated Advanced Field Teams (CAFTS) for assessment. Experience showed that these always needed a military unit on standby; important targets were liable to be counter-attacked by do-or-die enemy units, looters, refugees and even Allied troops on the look-out for souvenirs.

Krupps and the Meppen Proving Ground were targets of the utmost importance as these would contain the most recent German experiments in weaponry.

In mid-March 1945, Section 6 of T Force was given the assignment of discovering any material relating to chemical warfare in Germany. Although the CISC knew the Germans *might* have made some progress in the field of nuclear warfare, the whole subject was so top secret that ordinary teams would not be able to deal with it; another, even more specialized, unit would have to be brought in. Section 6 was therefore shown a diagram of a cyclotron (defined by the dictionary as 'Apparatus for acceleration of charged atomic particles revolving in a magnetic field') and told that if they found one they must not touch it but guard it carefully.

This particular unit was accompanied by a battalion from the Buffs. It included a number of civilians who had been taken from their reserved occupations, such as senior scientists, and put in uniform with a rank approximately equal to their civilian station. There can seldom have been so many senior ranks in one unit: the lowest rank was captain, and colonels and brigadiers abounded. The uniform was necessary because if the Germans had captured the unit in a counter-attack they would undoubtedly have shot the civilians as spies.

Section 6 had been told there was a suspected chemical warfare establishment in Germany at Münsterlager. Here the section found some laboratories and storehouses which looked as if they had been vacated rather hurriedly; there were open notebooks lying around.

Many of the laboratory workers had fled to the adjoining forest, but they returned within a few days when they realized they were not going to be shot on sight. The team met a very charming and helpful German who said he was the chief forester. He spoke good English and told them he had been a U-boat commander in World War I, but had subsequently taken up forestry. He could not tell them where the commandant of the establishment was, for that officer had disappeared.

Fortunately for Section 6, but less so for the chief forester, the commandant had been caught by forward troops. Under interrogation he had disclosed that the 'chief forester' was in fact the chief Nazi organizer for the area and was busy organizing sabotage. He was soon in a prisoner of war camp.

The laboratories disclosed nothing of interest, but one American in the party, Captain Kraus, investigated a barn within the perimeter of the establishment. The concrete floor seemed unusually clean and he noticed a trap door. He found that under it was a stairway leading to an underground chamber full of furnaces, condensers and tubing. The scientists found it to be a pilot plant for the production of 'Tabun', a colourless, odourless and tasteless nerve gas, against which Allied army respirators were no protection at all. Also in the laboratory were cabinets full of slides which the medical officer identified as showing the effects of this, and other chemical warfare gases, on human organs. It looked as if we were winning the war not a moment too soon. A company of the Buffs was left on guard against attempts at sabotage. No one among the Allies had suspected that the Germans had manufactured this deadly gas.

The Canadian major who had led Section 6 when it made this important discovery had a special satisfaction in the fact. Thirty years earlier, on 22 April 1915, the Germans had used gas against the Canadians at St Julien Wood. The effect of the surprise, and the casualties, made it seem likely they would break through to Calais. But the Canadians held and, against all expectations, counter-attacked. Their action saved Calais. It seemed appropriate that Canadians, who had suffered so much from gas in World War I, should track down this even more lethal form of it in World War II.

Towards the end of the war in Germany there was considerable anxiety about the prospects for Allied prisoners of war, many of whom had been herded back by the retreating Germans. There seemed a possibility that their captors might try to use them as hostages and to bargain with them. A more unpleasant possibility was that bands of fanatical SS men might burst into the camps and shoot down the unarmed men in sadistic revenge for Germany's defeat. In order to obtain an up-to-date picture at Altengrabow, where some 146,000 Allied prisoners were said to be incarcerated, it was decided to launch 'Operation Violet'. Even if the Germans had no evil intentions towards the prisoners, it was important for the Allies to know where they were so as not to bomb or shell them by mistake.

To obtain the necessary information six teams were to be parachuted into the area. Two would be British, two American and two French. Leading one of the two British teams was Maj. Philip Worrall whom we last encountered volunteering for an undefined parachuting assignment after his lengthy sojourn with Italian troops in Greece. The unit was called the Special Allied Airborne Reconnaissance Force (SAARF).

Altengrabow is twenty miles east of Magdeburg and at that time was fifteen miles behind the German front line. Finding the camps without being discovered themselves was clearly going to be a considerable task. There were many German troops in the area and all the civilians they saw were armed. Transmissions had to be brief and at irregular intervals to avoid interception. They learnt that lewisite gas shells in an artillery ammunition dump were in danger of being blown up by fanatics. They discovered that Russians, French, Belgians, Poles, Serbs and Indians were in the camps, but few British, as far as they could find out. Some of the local civilians had apparently gone mad and were shooting foreign workers and each other. Twenty-four hours after their arrival, Worrall's team were surrounded by large German forces and taken prisoner themselves.

This was by no means the end of the matter. For the next three days Worrall, as the senior officer, argued with the German camp commandant at Altengrabow that the war was virtually over and his best course was to surrender and hand the camp over to Worrall.

The German did not fall in with this argument but he allowed Worrall to use his transmitter to try to make contact with SHAEF. This enabled Worrall to give full information about the camp, which was very short of food and which had eight cases of typhus and no anti-typhus vaccine.

The German commandant soon decided that dealing with Worrall required more authority than he himself possessed and he took him to the local divisional commander. The latter reluctantly allowed

Worrall to set up an Allied Control Commission within the camp. However, events were now moving very quickly and on 1 May 1945 the camp commandant gave an order that all the British (700) and Americans (1,300) were to march east. Worrall promptly declared this was impossible and ordered a 'sit-down strike'.

This unexpected development unnerved the Germans, who were already worried and perplexed. Their first reaction was to threaten to shoot Worrall, whom they considered, quite rightly, was the cause of many of their difficulties. Worrall, however, displayed such confidence, that instead of shooting him the Germans decided to let him contact the US 83rd Division.

This was by no means the end of Worrall's problems. It would be some time before the Americans arrived and even when they did it was unlikely that a combat division, still facing determined, even desperate, German troops, would be able to do much for the 15,000 troops still in that particular camp. The essential need was the preservation of order. As long as the German guards remained on the camp, there was no danger that it would be invaded by armed civilians or the Volkssturm. The Volkssturm (the people's attack) was a form of Home Guard, made up of Germans aged from sixteen to sixty, and was liable to be exceptionally vicious.

The American divisional commander, knowing that the Russians would reach the camp before they did, then took a calculated risk. He suspected that if the Russians acquired custody of several thousand British and American troops, there might be considerable delay before these were repatriated to their own countries. Although the area in front of him was crowded with German tanks which might well open fire, the US commander sent seventy trucks and thirty ambulances, loaded with rations, to the camp. They filled up with British, American, Dutch and Belgian prisoners and departed. Soon they were back, with more rations, and collected more prisoners. SAARF allocated places to the remaining prisoners, some of whom had come into the camp recently. They included French, Italians and Poles. Then the Russians arrived. Worrall described the subsequent events as follows:

'Just before lunch on 4th May yet another huge convoy of American trucks arrived and we allocated places to the remainder of the French, 700 Italians, and 1,000 Poles. But before they could leave, we heard shouting and firing.

'At about 1400 the Russian army arrived and this caused consternation. They suspended all further evacuation. Eventually they allowed the trucks to go, taking only the French. I pleaded for the Italians, remembering my eighteen months with their soldiers in the Greek mountains. The Russian colonel was adamant. I also told him that a lot of the ill-fated Poles wanted to go west. This made him furious. We could do no more and he certainly didn't thank us for what we had done for the Russian prisoners.'

Subsequently Worrall was taken to meet the Russian divisional commander. 'The General was in a small room, made even smaller by a huge ceramic stove taking up one corner. The only light was from a sputtering candle. Behind a table sat a Russian general. Not having seen one before I was mesmerized by the scene, particularly I remember by what he had pinned on his chest: a strip of tin on which it seemed a dozen or so medals had been painted. The warm room felt comfortable and homely and far less threatening than the one in which the black-macintoshed stick-twirling Gestapo men had interrogated me after my capture.

'With a smile and scarcely a movement of his hand the general motioned us to sit down [Worrall was accompanied by another British officer and an interpreter] and quickly said "Who are you and what are you doing here?"

'"General, we have come on the orders of General Eisenhower, the Supreme Allied Commander, to help the prisoners in this Stalag. We understand there is a Russian liaison team at his HQ and they know all about our mission."

'"Major, I have never heard of this Eisenhower, and if I had it would not make any difference, as I, alone, am in command here. My orders are to evacuate all prisoners eastwards to Odessa on the Black Sea. But in your case I am prepared to listen to you before I decide your final destination."

'"General, much as we would like to leave, I'm afraid this is not possible. We must have time to look for five missing Frenchmen from our mission. And we have a lot of our kit buried in a barn."

'"Major, I will take my decision tonight." . . .

'All through the night a stream of Germans came to ask for security but we had to turn them away. However, we did take pity on a couple of girls who offered their services in return for a lift to the West. They told us they were Allied intelligence agents, adding that they had been raped by the Russians. But of course they had no papers to prove anything. But we took them on to do the washing up, and cook our breakfast. I expect they felt surprised that other services were not demanded of them.

'At 0730 the next morning, 5th May, we knew our fate, for another Russian Colonel arrived and told us we were to leave in two hours. He said the General had decided we would be taken in Russian transport to the Americans on the Elbe. We asked permission to take the two girls and a Red Cross truck driven by a Frenchman, but all our requests were politely refused.

'At 0930 the Colonel came back with two battered old trucks. We asked to go to the HQ of the 83rd American Division at Zerbat but for some reason best known to himself he told us we were going to Magdeburg.'

The ride to Magdeburg for the thirteen members of the SAARF mission was a unique experience.

'We passed miles and miles of horse-drawn wagons and one man dog-carts [two-wheeled carts]. On the wagons were hung chickens, pots and pans and even the proverbial kitchen stove. The Russians lived entirely off the country and took the girls along with them. Everything they came upon belonged to them. Scrawled on walls were arrows and a few words; they said "Such and such a battalion or company to be in a certain village by a certain time." No red-capped military policeman in jeeps at every crossroads for them. One was left with the uneasy impression that the Russian soldiers we passed were like a stream of ants which could be routed anywhere, through France to Spain and on to Gibraltar and Timbuctoo.

'But the idea that the Russian armies had not evolved since the Napoleonic wars, or that they had left their armour in Stalingrad, Berlin or Prague, was dispelled when we neared Magdeburg. There we saw dozens of huge tracked guns, their barrels pointing at the Americans on the other side of the river.'

From Magdeburg they were transported to the American HQ at Calbe, twenty miles south of Magdeburg.

'We spent that night in an American barracks. SOE–OSS operational staff were not easily disciplined and, anyhow, who was I to order them around. Somehow our numbers dwindled as individuals found good reasons to fall out and visit friendly units.'

And then home. 'Again the spotlight fell on "lucky" Worrall as they now called me for of course everyone had read the press reports. Amongst a very few, I was one of the last "oddities" of the war in Europe. For who had heard of anybody dropping outside Berlin and lifting from under the very noses of the Russians nearly 20,000 prisoners. And most extraordinary from my point of view I must have been one of the very few to have been a prisoner of war for less than a week.'

But Worrall's duties in Germany were not yet over. During June 1945 he was a member of the T Force team which scoured Europe for missing agents, military records, evidence of atrocities, and any signs that subversive activity by the Nazi underground was still continuing.

The end of the war in Europe did not, of course, mean the end of the war as a whole. Out in the Far East the relentless battle against Japan was continuing and looked like doing so to a very bloody and protracted finish. At least another year's fighting was envisaged, and even that was an optimistic forecast. All the special units were examined and assessed against what they might be able to achieve in the very different, vast, expanse of Asia.

As we know, that part of World War II ended on 15 August 1945. As the armies of the west were demobilized, the special forces were often first to go. Commandos, SAS, SOE, SBS: there was clearly no need for them in the peaceful future. Several years later their dissolution seemed premature; old names began to reappear and, apart from SOE, are with us today.

The purpose of this book has been to trace the development of special forces, to show how they were complementary to each other, and to give some assessment of their contribution to final victory. In 1939 'Special Forces' did not exist, and any member of the services who had predicted them would have been considered to be over-imaginative and unstable. The need for intelligence was accepted, but the services were not usually impressed by reports which did not accord with their own opinions. This was not a characteristic of British forces only.

It was also said that the British underestimated the effect of aircraft on surface ships because when air/naval manoeuvres were held, the umpires were all comfortably entertained by the navy and did not wish to displease their generous hosts by decisions which might seem ungrateful and unwelcome. This *may* have caused the *Prince of Wales* and *Repulse* to take unjustifiable risks in 1941.

After the blitzkrieg attacks on Norway, Denmark, Belgium, Holland and France in 1940 the services sharply revised their previous ideas of the probable development of the war. Churchill ordered secret forces to 'set Europe ablaze'. Initially this instruction was carried out by the

Commandos and SOE. A further step forward came with the creation of the SAS and SBS in the Middle East but, even before that, there had been further shocks for Britain in the Far East when Japan burst unannounced into the war. America learnt all too well at Pearl Harbor what can be achieved by secret, surprise attack.

From 1942 secret forces expanded and often worked in close liaison with more orthodox arms. Relationships were not always harmonious, as we saw, but the good far outweighed the bad. To the very end the outcome of the war was in the balance, and this made combined operations vital.

It has sometimes been alleged that results did not justify the trouble and expense of operations by secret forces. Yet time and again during World War II we have examples of the vital role they played. Instances are the denial of heavy water to Germany, which prevented that country making an atomic bomb; the specialized airborne attacks by the German airborne units which won them the Ems Emael fortress in 1940 and Crete in 1942; the effect of the SAS on the balance of air power in the Western Desert in 1942; the Commandos in Norway and on D-Day; SOE in France and the Balkans.

From the days of the Trojan horse, small bands of brave, resourceful men have made victory possible when larger armies were faltering. We hope the world will never see another great war but if ever it does it will probably be decided not by large formations but by numerous small groups.

Glossary

Wartime code-names and abbreviations were chosen to deceive the enemy. As the war progressed, some duplication was inevitable. Even today, confusing duplication persists. Thus 'PR' stands for Public Relations as well as Photographic Reconnaissance. In wartime, small, short-lived enterprises were often given local code-names, but the same code-name, once it was no longer in use, could be allocated to an activity in a different area. The list given here is not complete. A full listing would run into hundreds, perhaps thousands.

Some harmless-sounding names often concealed more military functions. Thus 'Van Group' was not a collection of transport, but an advance strike force.

A.14	Branch of Air Intelligence responsible for the Y Service
Abwehr	German Secret Intelligence Branch of the Reichswehr
AGAS	Air Ground Air Service (used in China)
BAAG	British Army Aid Group. Group for helping prisoners and others to escape from Hong Kong 1942–7
B Division	Branch of MI5 dealing with counter-espionage
BCRA	Bureau Central de Renseignements et d'Action. Free French Intelligence and Sabotage Service
BRAL	Bureau de Recherches et d'Action à Londres. London department of General de Gaulle's Secret Service
CAFTS	Consolidated Advanced Field Teams (for target assessment)
CIA	Central Intelligence Agency. US Secret Service

D Section	Section of MI6 concerned with sabotage. Preceded SOE
DZ	Dropping Zone (for parachutists)
EAM	Greek National Liberation Front
EDES	Greek National Republican Army
ELAS	Greek liberation army
Enigma	German coding machine
F1	French Force of the Interior (para-military resistance)
FBI	Federal Bureau of Investigation. Roughly equivalent to MI5
GCCS	Government Code and Cipher School, Bletchley Park
Gestapo	German secret police
ISTU	Inter Services Topographical Unit/Department
HDU	Home Defence Units
LRDG	Long Range Desert Group
LRPG	Long Range Penetration Group
M18	Military Intelligence working with Americans. Also radio security service
MGB	Motor Gunboat
MI5	Secret Security Service which dealt with enemy spying and subversion
MI6	Secret Service. Espionage, etc., overseas. Also known as SIS
MI9	Unit for Escape and Evasion
MIR	Military Intelligence Research
MIS-X	Escape and Evasion department
MTB	Motor Torpedo Boat
NID9	Naval Intelligence Department
NKVD	Russian Secret Service (forerunner of KGB)
OCSI	Office for Co-ordination of Strategic Information
OSS	Office of Strategic Services. US Intelligence Service, forerunner of CIA
PAIFORCE	Persia and Iraq Force

PID	Political Intelligence Department
PPA	Popski's Private Army
SAARF	Special Allied Airborne Reconnaissance Force
SACO	Sino-American Cooperative Organization
SAS	Special Air Service
SBS	Special Boat Section/Special Boat Squadron
SD	Sicherheitsdienst. Intelligence Branch of SS
SEAC	South-East Asia Command
Section D	Branch of Secret Intelligence Service which later developed into SOE. Concerned with sabotage
SHAEF	Supreme Headquarters Allied Expeditionary Force
SIS	See MI6 (above)
SLU	Special Liaison Unit (for distribution of Ultra information)
SO1	Special Operation 1. Organisation for Black Propaganda
SO2	Special Operations. Name given to that part of SOE which undertook operational work
SOE	Special Operations Executive
Ultra	Code word for intercepts from Enigma

Units

Regiment	Title of Army unit which might consist of one or many battalions
Battalion	Unit of approximately 750 men
Squadron	In Navy, detachment of warships
	In RAF, 10–18 machines
	In Army, approximately 120 men, equivalent of company or artillery battery
Troop	Unit of approximately 30 men. Equivalent to platoon
Brigade	Three or more battalions, plus supporting troops. Approx. 3,000
Division	Group of army units. Approximately 15,000 men

Select Bibliography

Louis Allen, *Burma: The Longest War,* Dent, 1984
C. Babington-Smith, *Evidence in Camera,* Chatto & Windus, 1958
J.G. Beevor, *SOE,* Bodley Head, 1981
Andrew Boyle, *The Climate of Treachery,* Hutchinson, 1979
A. Cave Brown, *Bodyguard of Lies,* Harper & Row, 1975
Peter Calvocoressi, *Top Secret Ultra,* Pantheon, 1981
Winston Churchill, *The Second World War,* Vols I-VI, Houghton Mifflin, 1948-53
Aileen Clayton, *The Enemy Is Listening,* Ballantine, 1982
E.H. Cookridge, *They Came from the Sky,* Heinemann, 1963
Inside SOE, Arthur Barker, 1966
Charles Cruickshank, *Deception in World War II,* OUP, 1979
SOE in the Far East, Oxford, 1983
Richard Deacon, *A History of the Russian Secret Service,* Muller, 1971
A History of the Chinese Secret Service, Taplinger, 1974
A History of the British Secret Service, Academy Chicago
Kempei Tai: The Japanese Secret Service, Beaufort Books
D. Dodds-Parker, *Set Europe Ablaze,* Springwood, 1983
J. Durnford-Slater, *Commando,* Kimber, 1953
Bazna Elyese, *I Was Cicero,* André Deutsch, 1962
F.D. Fane and Don Moore, *The Naked Warriors,* Allen Wingate, 1957
Xan Fielding, *Hide and Seek,* Secker & Warburg, 1954
Constantine Fitzgibbon, *Secret Intelligence in the 20th Century,* Stein and Day, 1976
C. Foley, *Commando Extraordinary,* Longman, 1954
M.R.D. Foot, *SOE in France,* University Publications of America, 1984
Resistance, McGraw-Hill, 1977
SOE: The Special Operations Executive 1940-46, BBC, 1984
M.R.D. Foot and J.M. Langley, *Escape and Evasion 1939-1945,* Bodley Head, 1979
R. Foxall, *The Guinea Pigs,* Robert Hale, 1983

Jósef Garlinski, *The Enigma War,* Scribner, 1980
P. Gregory, *British Airborne Troops*, Macdonald & Jane, 1974
R. A. Haldane, *The Hidden War*, Robert Hale, 1978
Robert Hammond, *A Fearful Freedom*, Leo Cooper/Secker, 1984
A. C. Hampshire, *Undercover Sailors,* Kimber, 1981
The Beachhead Commandos, Kimber, 1983
T. Harrison, *Living through the Blitz,* Penguin, 1978
F. H. Hinsley, *British Intelligence in the Second World War*, Vols. I–III, *Cambridge University Press, 1979, 1981, 1984*
David Howarth, *We Die Alone*, Collins, 1955
Patrick Howarth, *Special Operations*, Routledge & Kegan Paul, 1955
Undercover, Routledge & Kegan Paul, 1980
Ellic Howe, *The Black Game,* Michael Joseph, 1982
H. Montgomery Hyde, *Secret Intelligence Agent*, Constable, 1982
Allison Ind, *A History of Modern Espionage*, Hodder & Stoughton, 1965
R. Rhodes James, *Chindit*, John Murray, 1980
Rhodri Jeffreys-Jones, *American Espionage*, Free Press, 1977
P. Johns, *Within Two Cloaks,* Kimber, 1979
R. V. Jones, *Most Secret War*, Hamish Hamilton, 1978
John Keats, *They Fought Alone*, Secker & Warburg, 1963
Graeme Kent, *Espionage*, Batsford, 1974
Sherman Kent, *Strategic Intelligence for American Foreign Policy,* Princeton University Press, 1947
David Lampe, *The Savage Canary: The Story of Danish Resistance*, Cassell, 1957
Evelyn Le Chêne, *Watch for Me by Moonlight*, Eyre Methuen, 1973
Ronald Lewin, *Ultra Goes to War,* McGraw-Hill, 1978
The American Magic, Farrar, Straus & Giroux, 1982
Fitzroy Maclean, *Eastern Approaches,* Atheneum, 1984
Max Manus, *Underwater Saboteur*, Kimber, 1953
Jasper Maskelyn, *Magic Top Secret*, Stanley Paul, 1949
Sir John Masterman, *The Double-Cross System in the War of 1939–45*, Yale University Press, 1972
Ronald McKie, *The Heroes*, Angus & Robertson, 1960
M. Leslie Melville, *The Story of the Lovat Scouts 1900–1980*, St Andrews Press, 1981
A. Merglen (tr. K. Morgan), *Surprise Warfare*, Allen & Unwin, 1968
G. Millar, *The Bruneval Raid*, Bodley Head, 1974
Ewen Montagu, *The Man Who Never Was*, Evans, 1966
Beyond Top Secret U, Peter Davies, 1977

W. Stanley Moss, *Ill Met by Moonlight*, Harrap, 1950
A War of Shadows, Boardman, 1952
Malcolm Muggeridge, *Chronicles of Wasted Time,* Morrow, 1982
David Mure, *Practise to Deceive*, Kimber, 1977
Master of Deception, Kimber, 1980
Airey Neave, *Saturday at MI9*, Hodder & Stoughton, 1969
G. G. Norton, *The Red Devils*, Leo Cooper, 1971
J. Overton-Fuller, *The German Penetration of SOE*, Kimber, 1975
Lauran Paine, *German Military Intelligence in World War II: The Abwehr,* Stein and Day, 1984
Gerald Pawle, *The Secret War 1939–45*, Harrap, 1956
V. Peniakoff, *Popski's Private Army,* dist. by Academy Chicago, 1975
Chapman Pincher, *Inside Story*, Sidgwick & Jackson, 1978
Their Trade Is Treachery, Sidgwick & Jackson, 1981
Edwin Ride, *British Army Aid Group Hong Kong Resistance 1942–1945*, OUP, 1981
Harry Rositzke, *The KGB*, Doubleday, 1981
Francis Russell, *The Secret War*, Time-Life Books, 1981
H. St G. Saunders, *The Green Beret*, Michael Joseph, 1949
David Smiley, *Albanian Assignment*, Chatto, 1984
Bradley Smith, *The Shadow Warriors, Basic Books, 1983*
Myron J. Smith Jr., *The Secret Wars,* Clio Press, 1984
Richard Harris Smith, *OSS,* University of California Press, 1972
David Stafford, Britain and European Resistance 1940-1945, University of Toronto Press, 1980
Roy M. Stanley II, USAF, *World War II Photo Intelligence,* Scribner, 1981
Maj-Gen. Sir K. Strong, *Intelligence at the Top,* Doubleday, 1969
B. Sweet-Escott, *Baker Street Irregular*, Eyre Methuen, 1965
M. Tugwell, *Airborne to Battle*, Kimber, 1971
Philip Warner, *The Special Air Service*, Kimber, 1971
The D Day Landings, Kimber, 1980
Invasion Road, Cassell, 1980
Phantom, Kimber, 1982
The Special Boat Squadron, Sphere, 1983
Gordon Welchman, *The Hut 6 Story,* McGraw-Hill, 1982
Nigel West, *MI5: British Security Service Operations 1909-1945,* Stein and Day, 1982
Denis Wheatly, *The Deception Planners*, Hutchinson, 1980
Burke Wilkinson, *By Sea and by Stealth*, Peter Davies, 1949

J. H. Williams, *Elephant Bill*, Hart-Davis, 1950
Sir Ronald Wingate, *Not in the Limelight*, Hutchinson, 1979
F.W. Winterbotham, *The Ultra Secret,* Harper & Row, 1974
Peter Young, *Storm from the Sea*, Kimber, 1955
Commando, Ballantine, 1972

Index

Names and ranks (when given) are those which applied at the time. Subsequently the latter may have changed because they were temporary or acting, or because the holder received further promotion.